ENCYCLOPEDIA OF U.S. MARINES

Alan Axelrod

☑Checkmark Books®
An imprint of Infobase Publishing

Encyclopedia of the U.S. Marines

Copyright © 2006 by Alan Axelrod

Checkmark Books
An imprint of Infobase Publishing
132 West 31st Street
New York NY 10001

Library of Congress Cataloging-in-Publication Data

Axelrod, Alan, 1952–
Encyclopedia of the U.S. Marines / Alan Axelrod.
p. cm.
Includes index.
ISBN 0-8160-4714-6 (pb: alk. paper)
1. United States. Marine Corps—Encyclopedias—Juvenile Literature.
2. United States. Marine Corps—Biography—Juvenile Literature.
I. Title.

VE23.A1394 2006
359.9'6097303—dc22   2005027686

Checkmark Books are available at special discounts when purchased in bulk quantities for businesses, associations, institutions, or sales promotions. Please call our Special Sales Department in New York at (212) 967-8800 or (800) 322-8755.

You can find Facts On File on the World Wide Web at http://www.factsonfile.com

Text design by Joan M. Toro
Text design adapted by Erika K. Arroyo
Cover design by Dorothy Preston

Printed in the United States of America

VB FOF 10 9 8 7 6 5 4 3 2 1

This book is printed on acid-free paper.

Contents

LIST OF ENTRIES: UNITED STATES MARINES

v

UNITED STATES MARINES ENTRIES A–Z

1

U.S. MARINES ABBREVIATIONS AND ACRONYMS

180

BIBLIOGRAPHY

183

INDEX

191

List of Entries

UNITED STATES MARINE CORPS

Act of July 11, 1798
Act of June 30, 1834
advance guard
advance party
African Americans in the USMC
aiguillette
aircraft, fixed-wing
aircraft, rotary-wing
air defense artillery
air-launched weapons
American Revolution
amphibious assault
amphibious operation
amphibious vehicles
amphibious warfare ships
antiarmor weapons
assault craft
Barbary pirates
Barnett, George
bases, camps, and other installa-
    tions
basic training
Basilone, John
beachhead
Belleau Wood
bellhop
Biddle, William P.
Bladensburg, Battle of
Boomer, Walter E.
Bougainville, Battle of
Boxer Rebellion
Boyington, Gregory "Pappy"

brig
burp
Burrows, William Ward
Butler, Smedley D.
camp
Carlson, Evans F.
Cates, Clifton B.
Chapman, Leonard F., Jr.
Chapultepec, Battle of
Château-Thierry
chicken plate
chief of naval operations
Choiseul Raid
Chosin Reservoir, Battle of
Close Quarters Battle/Direct
    Action Program
color sergeant of the U.S.
    Marine Corps
Combat Service Support
    Schools
combined arms team
commandant of the Marine
    Corps
communications equipment
company clerk
Continental Marines
corpsman
Cuban Rebellion
Cushman, Robert E., Jr.
Daly, Daniel
decorations and medals
Devereux, James P. S.

Dominican Republic
double trouble
drill instructor
Elliott, George F.
embarked marines
emblem, USMC
Eniwetok Atoll, Battle of
expeditionary force
fire base
fire support base
Fleet Marine Force
forward observer
Fuller, Ben H.
Functions Paper, The
Gale, Anthony
Geiger, Roy S.
Gilbert Islands, USMC assaults
    on
Glenn, John H., Jr.
Gray, Alfred M., Jr.
Greene, Wallace M., Jr.
Grenada invasion
grunt
Guadalcanal
Guam
Guantánamo Bay
gung-ho
Gungi Marine
gyrene
Hagaru-ri, breakout from
Haiti
Han River Forts, Battle of the

Harpers Ferry
Harris, John
hash marks
hasty defense
Headquarters Marine Corps
Henderson, Archibald
Heywood, Charles
higher
history, overview of USMC
hit the deck!
Holcomb, Thomas
Horse Marines
Hue, action in and around
Inchon
indirect fire systems
inspector-instructor
Iran Hostage Crisis
Iwo Jima
Iwo Jima Memorial
jarhead
Jones, James L.
Kelley, Paul X.
Khe Sanh
Korean War
Krulak, Charles C.
Krulak, Victor H.
Kwajalein, Battle of
landing craft
Landing Operations Doctrine
leatherneck
Lebanon
Lejeune, John A.
Makin, Battle of
Mameluke Sword
Mariana Islands Campaign
Marine Aircraft Group 36
Marine Air Ground Task Force
   Training Command
Marine Aviation Weapons and
   Tactics Squadron One
Marine Barracks
Marine Corps Combat
   Development Command
Marine Corps Combat
   Identification Program

Marine Corps Intelligence
Marine Corps Reserve
Marine Corps Schools
Marine Corps Supply
Marine Forces
Marine Helicopter Squadron
   One
Marine Hymn
Marine One
Maritime Prepositioning
   Squadrons
Marshall Islands Campaign
mascot
Mayaguez incident
McCawley, Charles G.
Midway, Battle of
Mundy, Carl E., Jr.
Navajo code talkers
naval relations
Neville, Wendell C.
New Britain, Battle of
New Georgia, Battle of
new man rule
new meat
New Orleans, Battle of
Nicaragua
Nicholas, Samuel
nuclear-biological-chemical
   equipment
O'Bannon, Presley
Okinawa
Operation Starlight
organization, administrative and
   by major commands
organization by units
Panama
Pate, Randolph McCall
Peleliu
Pendleton, Joseph H.
Penobscot Bay Fiasco
Persian Gulf War
personal and miscellaneous
   equipment
Personnel Administration
   School

Philippine Insurrection
poolees
promotion system
pugil stick
Puller, Lewis B. "Chesty"
Pusan, Defense of
quad body
ranks and grades
recruit
recruiter
Roi-Namur, Battle of
Russell, John H.
Saint-Mihiel
Saipan
Samar, USMC action in
Santo Domingo
School of Infantry
Second Seminole War
secretary of the navy
Semper Fidelis
Sergeant Rock
Shepherd, Lemuel C.
Shoup, David M.
skinhead
Smith, Oliver P.
sniper
sniper team
Soldiers of the Sea
Solomon Islands Campaign
Somalia
Sousa, John Philip
Spanish-American War
Streeter, Ruth Cheney
Supply School
Suribachi
Tactical Petroleum Laboratory,
   Medium
Tarawa
"Tell It to the Marines!"
Tinian
tracked vehicles
Training and Education
   Command
triple threat
unconventional warfare

uniforms
unmanned aerial vehicle
unmanned ground vehicle
urban warfare
U.S.-French Quasi-War
U.S. Marine Band
U.S. Marine Corps Air-Ground
  Task Force Expeditionary
  Training Center
U.S. Marine Corps Code
U.S. Marine Corps Color Guard
U.S. Marine Corps Combat
  Development Command
U.S. Marine Corps
  Development Center

U.S. Marine Corps Mountain
  Warfare Training Center
U.S. Marine Corps Reconnais-
  sance Battalions
U.S. Marine Corps Research
  Center
U.S. Marine Corps Security Force
U.S. Marine Corps Security
  Guard Battalion
U.S. Marine Corps Women's
  Reserve
U.S. Marine Drum and Bugle
  Corps
U.S.-Mexican War
Vandegrift, Alexander

Veracruz
Vietnam War
Wake Island
War of 1812
weapons, individual and crew-
  served
Wharton, Franklin
wheeled vehicles
Wilson, Louis H., Jr.
World War I
World War II
Zeilin, Jacob

A-3 Falcon See AIRCRAFT, FIXED-WING.

A-4 Skyhawk See AIRCRAFT, FIXED-WING.

A-6 Intruder See AIRCRAFT, FIXED-WING.

A-12 Avenger See AIRCRAFT, FIXED-WING.

A-25/SB2C Helldiver See AIRCRAFT, FIXED-WING.

AAVC-7A1 Assault Amphibian Vehicle Command Model 7A1 See AMPHIBIOUS VEHICLES.

AAVP-7 See AMPHIBIOUS VEHICLES.

AAVR-7A1 Assault Amphibian Vehicle Recovery Model 7A1 See AMPHIBIOUS VEHICLES.

Act of July 11, 1798
The Act of July 11, 1798, was the first U.S. law organizing a "Corps of Marines" from the U.S. Navy's marines. It is titled "An Act for Establishing a Marine Corps" and provided for the three-year enlistment of 32 marines as ship guards. A major was to be chosen as COMMANDANT OF THE MARINE CORPS to administer the USMC. Thirty-two captains and lieutenants were authorized (no distinction was made between first lieutenants and second lieutenants). In addition, 48 sergeants and corporals were authorized, along with 720 privates, 32 fifers, and 32 drummers. While serving ashore, the marines would follow the Articles of War, the same regulations that governed the U.S. Army. Embarked at sea, however, the marines were to be governed by navy regulations. The 1798 legislation did not give the Marine Corps an organization or mission independent of the U.S. Navy. It did, however, provide that the president of the United States might use the USMC as he saw fit.

Act of June 30, 1834
The ACT OF JULY 11, 1798, established the USMC as a separate armed service and roughly put marines under the Articles of War when they served ashore but under navy regulations when they served aboard ships at sea. This left the USMC's role in the defense establishment of the United States rather nebulous. Commandant ARCHIBALD HENDERSON complained that the USMC was effectively isolated, with the army on one side and the navy on the other—and neither

friendly to the corps. Henderson and others agitated for a clearer definition and legal establishment of the USMC as a matter of the survival of the Corps. Congress responded with the Act of June 30, 1834, which specifically provided that "the Marine Corps . . . shall at all times be subject to the laws and regulations established for the government of the Navy, except when detached for service with the Army by order of the President." Not only did this make the USMC's position and governance clearer, it formalized its relationship to the U.S. Navy. For the next 113 years, until the National Security Act of 1947, the USMC was governed by the 1834 law. Only twice during this period did the president see fit to detach the USMC for service with the army: during the U.S.-MEXICAN WAR and during WORLD WAR I. In WORLD WAR II, the USMC functioned closely in coordination with the navy. By the time of the KOREAN WAR, its role had been definitively redefined, along with the roles of the other services, by the National Defense Act.

AD-1 through AD-7 Skyraider   See AIR-
CRAFT, FIXED-WING.

Advanced Field Artillery Tactical Data System   See INDIRECT FIRE SYSTEMS.

advance guard
A security element that operates ahead of the main body of a moving force. The advance guard operates within the indirect-fire-support range of the main body and is responsible for finding the enemy; for locating gaps, flanks, and other weaknesses in the enemy formation; for determining the enemy's intentions; for preventing the main force from running into an ambush or surprise attack; and for providing cover for the main body, if necessary. The advance guard may also engage and destroy enemy reconnaissance elements, repair roads and bridges, clear obstacles, conduct general reconnaissance, and secure key terrain features, such as high-ground positions.

advance party
A relatively small group of troops or specialists sent ahead of a larger unit to prepare a new site of operations.

African Americans in the USMC
Prior to WORLD WAR II, the USMC accepted no black enlistments. Pursuant to directives from President Franklin D. Roosevelt, however, the COMMANDANT OF THE MARINE CORPS appointed a commission to study how black marines could best be used. However, it was not until after the Japanese attack on Pearl Harbor, December 7, 1941, that actual enlistments were accepted, and a segregated training facility, Camp Johnson, was established outside Marine Corps Base Camp Lejeune. The first recruits arrived at Camp Johnson in August 1942 to make up the 51st Defense Battalion. Initially, DRILL INSTRUCTORS were white, but they were replaced by black instructors as soon as they were available.

African-American marines of the Third Ammunition Battalion ride captured bicycles on Saipan, June 1944. (*National Archives and Records Administration*)

The 51st Defense Battalion was brought to a strength of 1,400 and sent to the Pacific, first in the Ellice Islands and then in the Marshalls. They remained posted there throughout the war. A second black unit, the 52nd Defense Battalion, was established in December 1943 and dispatched to Roi-Namur and then to the Marianas. The black marines were used almost exclusively as stewards and laborers, not as combat troops. In all, 19,000 African Americans served in the USMC. Most had been drafted. No black marine was commissioned an officer during the war. In November 1945, a black second lieutenant was commissioned in the MARINE CORPS RESERVE, and in May 1948, a black man was given a commission in the regular force.

Despite President Harry S. Truman's 1948 Executive Order 9981, calling for an immediate end to segregation in all of the armed forces, the USMC remained segregated, with a 10 percent cap on black enlistments, until the secretary of the navy ordered complete integration of the USN and USMC in mid-1949. Since that time, blacks have been fully integrated as members of the USMC.

AGM-45 Shrike   See AIR-LAUNCHED WEAPONS.

AGM-65E Maverick Missile   See AIR-LAUNCHED WEAPONS.

AGM-114 Hellfire   See AIR-LAUNCHED WEAPONS.

AGM-122 Sidearm   See AIR-LAUNCHED WEAPONS.

AGM-123 Skipper II   See AIR-LAUNCHED WEAPONS.

AH-1J SeaCobra   See AIRCRAFT, ROTARY-WING.

aiguillette
Braided and looped cord that serves as a badge of office for officers who perform specialized staff duty for senior officers or for senior government officials. Presidential USMC aides wear gold aiguillettes, while USMC aides to other officials wear aiguillettes braided in red and gold.

AIM-7 Sparrow   See AIR-LAUNCHED WEAPONS.

AIM-9 Sidewinder Missile   See AIR-LAUNCHED WEAPONS.

aircraft, fixed-wing
The following fixed-wing aircraft are either currently included in the USMC inventory or are of historical importance in the service.

A-3 Falcon
A Curtiss observation biplane first flown in 1924, the A-3 version was designed for the army and USMC as an attack aircraft. Top speed was 147 miles per hour, and armament consisted of two .30-caliber machine guns firing through the propeller, with two more mounted under the wings. Twin Lewis guns were operated by an observer in the rear cockpit. The aircraft could also carry a modest antipersonnel bomb load.

A-4 Skyhawk
A single-engine daylight attack aircraft designed for the navy and the marines, the A-4 was developed in the 1950s and first delivered in 1962. The principal missions of USMC A-4s are to attack and destroy surface targets in support of landing forces and to escort helicopters. With a wingspan of 26 feet 6 inches, and a length of just over 40 feet, the A-4 can make 586 knots with a 4,000-pound bomb load and has a range of 2,000 miles.

Originally produced by McDonnell Douglas, the A-4 remains in use despite its age. Currently, USMC Reserve squadrons use the A-4M and a

An A-4 Skyhawk deploys ordnance over Vietnam. *(U.S. Marine Corps)*

craft had a top speed of 563 knots and a ceiling of 40,600 feet. The Intruder was capable of carrying a wide variety of ordnance, including: 10 2.75-inch Rocket Pods; 10 5-inch Zuni Rocket Pods; 28 Mk-20 Rockeyes; Mk-77 Napalm; 28 Mk-81 250-pound bombs; 28 Mk-82 Snakeyes; 13 Mk-83 1,000-pound bombs; five Mk-84 2,000-pound bombs; 20 Mk-117 750-pound bombs; GBU-10E Laser Guided Bomb; GBU-12D Laser Guided Bomb; GBU-16B Laser Guided Bomb; AGM-123A Skipper II; AGM-45 Shrike; AGM-62 Walleye; and AIM-9 Sidewinder.

A-12 Avenger

This aircraft was planned to replace the navy and USMC A-6 Intruder. It was conceived by McDonnell Douglas/General Dynamics as a subsonic, carrier-based attack aircraft with the most advanced stealth characteristics and was officially designated as an Advanced Technology Aircraft (ATA). The USMC was planning to purchase 238 Avengers, the navy 620, and the air force perhaps 400. Planned to cost $100 million each, the A-12 soon proved more expensive; on January 7, 1991, Secretary of Defense Richard Cheney canceled the program—the largest contract termination in the history of the Department of Defense.

A-25/SB2C Helldiver

The Curtiss Helldiver was first flown in June 1942 and was sent to the Pacific in November 1943. It was intended to replace the venerable Dauntless bomber (A-24) and was larger and capable of carrying more bombs than its predecessor. In the USMC, the Helldiver never completely replaced the Dauntless, although some bombing squadrons used it.

AD-1 through AD-7 Skyraider

The last single-engine, propeller-driven attack bomber built for the U.S. military, the Douglas Skyraider was first flown in March 1945, but did not see service until after WORLD WAR II. Although the aircraft came into being on the verge of the jet era, the Skyraider served in the navy and USMC for 15 years and was flown in attack missions during

training version, the TA-4F. Upon its introduction, the navy-version A-4 was the only nuclear-capable strike aircraft available for use in large numbers from aircraft carriers.

A-6 Intruder

Built by Grumman and introduced in 1979, the A-6 Intruder was a two-seat, subsonic, all-weather, carrier-based attack aircraft used by the navy and the USMC. It was designed as a deep-penetration aircraft, capable of night or daylight operation, and it was equipped with repeatedly upgraded avionics and highly advanced weapons-release systems, as well as a single, integrated track and search radar. The A-6E was equipped with a target recognition/attack multi-sensor (TRAM), as well as a chin turret containing a forward-looking infrared (FLIR) system and a laser designator and receiver. In its prime, the Intruder was one of the best all-weather precision bombers in the world. The aircraft was withdrawn from service in 1997.

The Intruder was almost 55 feet long, with a 53-foot wingspan. Crewed by two and powered by a pair of Pratt and Whitney J52-P8B engines, the air-

both the KOREAN WAR and the early part of the VIETNAM WAR.

Although it was designed to carry a single 1,000-pound bomb, its Korean missions often saw it loaded with some five tons of ordnance, an incredible load for this single-engine aircraft. Service ceiling was 25,000 feet and top speed 365 miles per hour. By the end of the Korean War, the USMC had 11 AD squadrons.

AV-8B Harrier II

The Harrier II is a vertical/short takeoff and landing (VSTOL) aircraft of British design used by the USMC for light attack and close air support. Using vectored thrust, the Harrier II jet can take off and land vertically, making it ideal for takeoff and landing from amphibious vessels as well as from unimproved ground landing areas.

The AV-8B replaced the original Harrier in 1984 and is crewed by a single pilot. The aircraft is a little over 46 feet long, with a wingspan of 30 feet 4 inches. Its single Rolls Royce F402-RR-408 jet engine delivers 23,800 pounds of thrust, which gives the aircraft a top speed of 661 miles per hour. Ferry range is 2,840 miles; its combat range is 165 miles with a full bomb load. Armament includes a GAU-12 five-barrel 25-mm cannon with 300 rounds. Six wing pylons on each wing can accommodate a total of nearly 8,000 pounds of bombs or other ordnance, including B-61 nuclear bombs, ADM-65 Maverick missiles, and AIM-9 Sidewinder missiles.

Boeing PW-9

A post–WORLD WAR I single-seat, all-metal pursuit plane first produced in 1926 by Boeing, the PW-9 was built mainly for the U.S. Navy and U.S. Army Air Corps, but was also flown briefly by the USMC. It was one of the last of the biplane fighters, with a top speed of 163 miles per hour and a ceiling of 20,000 feet.

C-12 Huron

This twin turbo-prop airplane is used by the USMC, as well as the army, air force, and navy, as a transport and utility aircraft. It is sometimes used to support attaché and military assistance advisory missions. The Huron is crewed by a pilot and copilot and carries up to eight passengers. Its length is almost 44 feet, its wingspan 54 feet 6 inches, and it is powered by two Pratt and Whitney PT6A-41 turboprops. Maximum speed is 333 miles per hour, ceiling is 35,000 feet, and range is 2,140 miles.

Dauntless Bombers

The Dauntless A-24 dive bomber, also built in a scout bomber version, was designed by Douglas Aircraft for the USN and USMC in the 1930s and served in the Pacific during World War II until it was replaced by the SB2 dive bomber from Curtiss in mid-1943.

The Dauntless was powered by a Wright engine and could achieve 255 miles per hour. Armament consisted of two .50-caliber guns firing through the prop and twin-mounted .50s operated by the radio operator/observer in the rear cockpit. Rigged for dive bombing, the Dauntless carried a single 1,000-pound bomb under the fuselage and two 100-pound bombs on wing racks. The USMC used the Dauntless at GUADALCANAL and in every USMC close air support–mission through the Philippines campaign.

EA-6B Prowler

The USMC flies the EA-6B Prowler primarily to provide airborne Command and Control (C^2) support to FLEET MARINE FORCES, including electronic attack (EA), tactical electronic support (ES), electronic protection (EP), and high-speed anti-radiation missile (HARM) defense. The aircraft collects tactical electronic order-of-battle data, which is immediately and in real time disseminated to field commanders. The data can also be recorded and processed for analysis after missions. Additionally, the aircraft provides a platform for active radar jamming support for assault aircraft as well as ground units. Using HARM missiles, the Prowler acts against enemy air defenses.

USMC Prowlers operate from land bases or from aircraft carriers. As of late 2003, the USMC inventory included 20 Prowlers in four active squadrons. General characteristics of the aircraft include:

Manufacturer: Grumman Aircraft Corporation
Power plant: two Pratt and Whitney J52-P408 turbofan engines
Thrust: 11,200 lb per engine
Length: 59 ft
Height: 15 ft
Wing span: 53 ft
Speed, maximum: Mach .99
Ceiling: 40,000 ft
Maximum takeoff weight: 61,500 lb
Range: Unrefueled—977.5 mi; Refueled—unlimited
Armament: ALQ-99 Tactical Jamming System (TJS); High Speed Anti-Radiation Missile (HARM)
Sensors: ALQ-99 On-board System (OBS)
Crew: four

F2A Buffalo

This single-seat, single-engine fighter was built by Brewster Aeronautical and ordered by the navy and USMC in 1938 as a carrier-based fighter. In early combat with Japanese Zeros, the Buffalo was outclassed. Although speedy at 337 miles per hour, its slow rate of climb and limited maneuverability were lethal handicaps. The aircraft was considered obsolete well before the end of the first year of World War II Pacific combat.

F2H Banshee

This single-seat jet fighter was built by McDonnell Douglas and flown in prototype in 1947, then delivered to the navy and USMC in the early 1950s. The F2H-2, flown by the USMC, was powered by two Westinghouse engines, which propelled the jet to 600 miles per hour and a ceiling of 50,000 feet. Action radius was 600 miles. By 1953, the Banshee was obsolete.

F2T Black Widow

A twin-engine, twin-boom night fighter built by North American Aviation Company for the U.S. Army Air Forces, the aircraft was also used by USMC squadrons in the Pacific late in World War II. Radar equipped, the aircraft carried a pilot, gunner, and radar operator and was formidably armed with four 20-mm cannon and four .50-caliber machine guns.

F4-B Phantom II

The McDonnell Douglas Phantom II was adopted by the air force, navy, and USMC in 1960 and was produced through 1979. With a top speed of more than Mach 2, the Phantom II had an operating radius of 900 miles and could carry heavy weapon loads of eight tons, including Sparrow III and Sidewinder missiles. In 1966, the USMC took delivery of the F4-J modification, designed for ground attack. It was this version the USMC used extensively in the Vietnam War.

F4D Skyray

This Douglas jet was built for the U.S. Navy and intended primarily for carrier operations, but was also adopted by the USMC as a fighter and fighter-bomber. The first production model was flown in 1954 and was delivered to the USN and USMC four years later.

As its name suggests, the Skyray was a delta-wing design. Its Pratt and Whitney J57-P-813 turbojet engine with afterburner was capable of Mach 1.06, and it could carry ordnance loads of 2,000-pound bombs, Sidewinder (AIM-9C/D) missiles, and rocket pods with up to 19 rockets per pod. The aircraft was produced through December 1958.

F4F Wildcat

This single-seat Grumman fighter was introduced as a carrier aircraft in 1940 and went into service (version F4F-3) with the USMC in 1941. It was the principal USMC fighter from the beginning of World War II until 1943. Top speed was 315 miles per hour, with a service ceiling of 34,000 feet and a range of 925 miles. The plane was armed with six .50-caliber wing guns and could carry two 250-pound bombs on wing racks. The Wildcat was indispensable in many USMC Pacific operations, especially the defense of WAKE ISLAND and the GUADALCANAL campaign.

F4U Corsair

Built by Chance Vought, this single-engine, gull-wing, carrier-based fighter was used extensively by the navy and USMC during World War II. The first models were flown in June 1942, and production continued through the end of the war, until 1947.

The Corsair was an extraordinary fighter, capable of speeds in excess of 450 miles per hour and with a ceiling of 20,000 feet. The Corsair outmatched the Japanese Zero and other fighters, although USN aviators found it difficult to operate from carriers. USMC pilots, who flew from island bases, had no operating problems, and by the middle of 1943, the F4U was the standard USMC fighter. It also served as a bomber for close air support.

F6F Hellcat

The Hellcat was a navy and USMC single-seat fighter designed early in 1942, deliberately incorporating certain features of the Japanese Zero, which at the time was outperforming all U.S. aircraft. Designed and produced quickly, the Hellcat was first flown in August 1942 and was sent to the Pacific, first seeing action at Marcus Island in September 1943. The USN widely adopted the Hellcat, while the USMC used it along with the older F4U Corsair.

The Hellcat had a top speed of 375 miles per hour, a ceiling of 36,000 feet, and a range of 1,050 miles without drop tanks. Armament consisted of six .50-caliber wing guns, and it could carry a pair of 1,000-pound bombs. The Grumman Aircraft Corporation produced more than 10,000 Hellcats before production stopped in December 1945.

F8 Crusader

The Vought Crusader was first flown in 1955. The USMC flew the F8D version, introduced in 1960 and powered by a Pratt and Whitney turbojet that drove it to Mach 2. Operating radius was 600 miles. In 1967, the USMC upgraded the D version to the H version.

The F8D and F8H were equipped with state-of-the-art radar systems and armed with four 20-mm cannon and four Sidewinder missiles, fired from the side of the fuselage. The aircraft flew extensively during the Vietnam War.

F8C-5 Helldiver

This Curtiss two-seat biplane was put into U.S. Navy service in 1922 and first delivered to the USMC in the 1930s. Top speed was 140 miles per hour with a service ceiling of 18,000 feet. Built as a fighter, the aircraft was completely obsolete at the outbreak of World War II.

F9F-8 Cougar

The Cougar was a swept-wing version of the straight-wing F9F-1, the first jet aircraft produced by Grumman. Equipped with a J48 Pratt and Whitney engine, the F9F-8 had a top speed of 712 miles per hour and a service ceiling of 42,000 feet, with a range of 1,100 miles. Armament consisted of four nose-mounted, 20-mm cannon and wing racks for bombs, rockets, or Sidewinder missiles. The F9F-8 entered service with the USMC during the late 1950s and continued in service until the end of the 1960s.

F9F Panther

The Grumman Panther was a single-seat jet fighter first flown in 1946 and delivered to the USMC (as the F9F-2 series) in 1948. The F9F-5 version was adopted after 1950 and served as the first-line USMC fighter until the mid-1950s, when it was replaced by the FJ-1 Fury. The F9F-5 had a maximum speed of 625 miles per hour and a service ceiling above 50,000 feet. Armed with four 20-mm cannon, it was also equipped with wing racks for bombs, rockets, or napalm.

F/A-18A/C/CN Hornet

The USMC F/A-18A/C/CN Hornet is tasked with intercepting and destroying enemy aircraft in concert with ground or airborne fighter control and under all-weather conditions. In addition, the Hornet provides close air support in day or night conditions. Another mission is day and night deep air support, consisting of radar search and attack, interdiction, and strikes against enemy installations. Secondarily, the Hornet provides armed escort of friendly aircraft. USMC Hornets may be deployed from aircraft carriers, advanced land bases, and expeditionary airfields. The USMC F/A-18A/C/CN strike fighter was designed to replace the F4-B Phantom II.

As of 2004, the USMC had 168 of the aircraft deployed in 10 active and four reserve squadrons. The service first used them in Operation Desert Storm (PERSIAN GULF WAR). USMC Hornet squadrons flew more than 4,600 sorties without combat loss.

General characteristics of the aircraft include:

Manufacturer: Boeing-McDonnell Douglas
Propulsion: two General Electric F404-GE-400 afterburning, low-bypass turbofan engines
Thrust: 16,000 lb per engine
Length: 56 ft
Wing span: 37.5 ft
Cruise speed: high subsonic to supersonic
Ferry range: over 2,300 mi
Range, fighter mission: 460 mi
Range, attack mission: 661.25 mi
Armament: nine external wing stations, comprising two wingtip stations for an assortment of air-to-air and air-to-ground weapons, including AIM-7 Sparrows, AIM-9 Sidewinders, AMRAAMs, AGM-84 Harpoons, and AGM-65 Maverick missiles; two inboard wing stations for external fuel tanks or air-to-ground stations; two nacelle fuselage stations for either Sparrows or AN/AAS-38 Forward Looking Infrared Radar (FLIR) pods; and a center station for fuel tank or air-to-ground weapons. Air-to-ground weapons include GBU-10 and -12 laser-guided bombs, Mk-80 series general purpose bombs, and CBU-59 cluster bombs. An M61 six-barrel 20-mm gun is mounted in the nose and has a Boeing-McDonnell Douglas director gunsight.
Crew: one

F/A-18D Hornet

The mission of the USMC F/A-18D Hornet is to attack and destroy surface targets, day or night, under all weather conditions; to conduct multi-sensor imagery reconnaissance; to provide supporting arms coordination; and to intercept and destroy enemy aircraft under all weather conditions. The aircraft conducts day and night deep air support, in all weather. This includes armed reconnaissance, radar search and attack, interdiction, and strikes against enemy installations. Additionally, the F/A-18D conducts multi-sensor imagery reconnaissance, including prestrike and poststrike target damage assessment and visual reconnaissance. By day or night, the F/A-18D provides supporting arms coordination, including forward air control, tactical air coordination, and artillery/naval gunfire spotting. In concert with ground and airborne fighter direction, the F/A-18D intercepts and destroys enemy aircraft. Secondarily, the aircraft can provide battlefield illumination and target illumination and conduct armed escort of friendly aircraft. USMC F/A-18Ds operate from aircraft carriers, advanced bases, and expeditionary airfields.

As of 2004, the USMC maintained 72 aircraft in six active squadrons. The USMC first deployed these aircraft in combat during Operation Desert Storm (Persian Gulf War) in 1991. They were used to provide target location and identification, threat updates, and the overall battlefield situation. A single F/A-18D controlled as many as 20 strike fighters in a 30-minute period.

General characteristics of the F/A-18D include:

Manufacturer: Boeing-McDonnell Douglas
Propulsion: two General Electric F404-GE-400 afterburning, low-bypass turbofan engines
Thrust: 16,000 lb per engine
Length: 56 ft
Wing span: 37.5 ft
Cruise speed: high subsonic to supersonic
Ferry range: over 2,300 mi
Combat radius, fighter mission: 460 mi
Combat radius, attack mission: 661.25 mi
Armament: nine external wing stations, comprising two wingtip stations for AIM-9 Sidewinder air-to-air missiles; two outboard wing stations for an assortment of air-to-air and air-to-ground weapons, including AIM-

7 Sparrows, AIM-9 Sidewinders, AMRAAMs, AGM-84 Harpoons, and AGM-65 Maverick missiles; two inboard wing stations for external fuel tanks or air-to-ground stations; two nacelle fuselage stations for Sparrows or AN/AAS-38 Forward Looking Infrared Radar (FLIR) pods; and a center station for fuel tank or air-to-ground weapons such as GBU-10 and -12 laser-guided bombs, Mk-80 series general purpose bombs, and CBU-59 cluster bombs. An M61 six-barrel 20-mm gun is mounted in the nose and has a Boeing-McDonnell Douglas director gunsight.

Crew: Two

FJ1-FJ4 Fury

This series of North American aircraft were carrier-oriented versions of the F-86 Saberjet flown by the USAF in the Korean War. Five USMC squadrons flew the FJ2 during the Korean War, and the fighter remained the principal USMC jet fighter until it was replaced by the F8U Crusader late in the 1950s.

The FJ2 Fury had a top speed of 650 miles per hour and a service ceiling of 45,000 feet. Its range was 1,000 miles.

KC-130 Hercules

The four-engine Hercules cargo aircraft was designed by Lockheed in 1952 and has been modified for various cargo and transport functions and even as a gunship for close air support. The USMC uses a version modified as an in-flight tanker,

A USMC KC-130 Hercules   *(U.S. Marine Corps)*

including versions capable of refueling fixed-wing aircraft and helicopters. The version built to refuel helicopters, HC-130P, can also be used to retrieve parachute-borne payloads. All USMC Hercules are also capable of use for tactical transport.

The KC-130 is powered by four Allison T56-A-16 engines to a top speed of 362.25 miles per hour and a service ceiling of 30,000 feet. The aircraft is 97 feet 9 inches long, with a 41-foot cargo compartment. Wing span is 132 feet 7 inches and maximum takeoff weight is 175,000 pounds. Tanker capacity is 10,183 to 13,280 gallons, depending on configuration. As a tanker, the Hercules's range is 1,000 nautical miles; as a cargo carrier, it is 2,875 miles.

Mitchell PBJ

During World War II, the USMC flew this medium bomber (designated by the USAAF as the B-25) in its seven USMC bomber squadrons. Built by North American Aviation Company, the Mitchell was crewed by five and could carry 3,000 pounds of bombs in the bomb bay and another 2,400 pounds on wing racks. Top speed was 300 miles per hour with a service ceiling of 24,000 feet. Modified as the PBJ-15, the Mitchell employed radar to guide night rocket attacks against Japanese positions in the Marianas.

OE-1 Bird Dog

A single-engine Cessna introduced during the 1950s primarily as a reconnaissance and surveillance aircraft. OE-1 is the USMC and navy designation; the air force and army, which use the plane primarily as a liaison aircraft, designate it O-1.

Length is 25 feet 9 inches, with a wingspan of 36 feet and a gross weight of 2,399 pounds. Its powerplant is a single Continental O-470 piston engine making 213 horsepower and driving the aircraft to a maximum speed of 150 miles per hour. Range is 530 miles and ceiling 20,300 feet.

OV-10 Bronco

This twin-turboprop armed reconnaissance aircraft was used by the USMC in counterinsurgency operations; until 1993, it was also used for light

Until it was replaced in 1993, the Bronco was a USMC workhorse. *(U.S. Marine Corps)*

attack, helicopter escort, forward air control, and general reconnaissance. The aircraft entered production in 1967 and saw extensive service in the Vietnam War.

Crewed by two, the OV-10 can carry 3,200 pounds of cargo, five paratroopers, or two litter patients and attendants. The USMC has modified some OV-10s as Night Observations Surveillance (NOS) aircraft.

The Bronco is 44 feet long, with a wingspan of 40 feet. It is powered by twin Garrett T-76-G-420 turboprop engines and can reach a top speed of 288 miles per hour. Its combat radius is 228 miles. Armament typically consists of two sponsons mounted on the fuselage, each of which houses four 7.62-mm machine guns. Additionally the sponsons are racked for two 600-pound bombs each, or for rocket pods or auxiliary fuel tanks. Other armament configurations are also possible.

In 1993, the USMC replaced the OV-10 with the F/A-18D Hornet for forward air control, light attack, close-support, and tactical air control missions.

PBY-5A Catalina

The USMC adopted this twin-engine Consolidated Aircraft design as an amphibious plane prior to World War II. Whereas the U.S. Navy used it mainly for long-range reconnaissance during the war, the USMC used the Catalina for logistics and for long-range VIP transport. The Catalina was slow, but it had a range of 2,500 miles.

R4D Skytrain

Better known by its U.S. Army designation, C-47, and its civilian passenger transport designation, DC-3, the USMC R4D was used in the Pacific theater for airborne supply and transport. All Skytrains were powered by two Pratt and Whitney R-1830 engines and had a cruising speed of 230 miles per hour and a service ceiling of 10,000 feet. The first DC-3 aircraft were produced in 1935. A surprisingly large number are still in service in civilian applications.

T-34C Turbo Mentor

Primary trainer used by the USMC and USN and nicknamed the Tormentor. The aircraft is a two-seat turboprop Beechcraft, based on a 1934 design updated in 1973.

Student and instructor sit in tandem. The plane is 28 feet 8 inches long and has a wingspan of 33 feet 4 inches. The aircraft is powered by a 715-horsepower Pratt and Whitney PT6A-25 turboprop, offset to the right and down from the centerline to give the aircraft a jetlike feel in preparation for the student's step up to a jet trainer. Maximum speed is 240 miles per hour, range is 345 miles, and ceiling is about 30,000 feet. Up to 1,200 pounds of weapons can be carried, typically for armament training.

T-44 Pegasus

A twin-engine light-transport aircraft modified from the Beechcraft King Air C90 for use in the advanced training of USMC, navy, and Coast Guard multiengine pilots. The plane can accommodate two crew and up to eight passengers. It is 35 feet 6 inches long, with a wingspan of 50 feet 3 inches, and is powered by two Pratt and Whitney PT6A-34B turboprops, each producing 750 horsepower. Cruising speed is 256 miles per hour, range is 1,474 miles, and ceiling is 28,100 feet.

T-45A Goshawk

A tandem-seat McDonnell Douglas jet trainer used by USMC and U.S. Navy pilots. Procurement of this carrier-capable aircraft began in 1988. Length is 39 feet 2 inches, wingspan 30 feet 8 inches, powerplant is a Rolls-Royce F-405-RR-400. The aircraft has a top speed of 620 miles per hour, a range of 950 miles, and a service ceiling of 50,000 feet.

TA-4J Skyhawk

An advanced jet trainer used by the USMC and U.S. Navy until it was replaced by the T-45 Goshawk beginning in 1988.

aircraft, rotary-wing

The following rotary-wing aircraft are either currently included in the USMC inventory or are of historical importance in the service.

AH-1J SeaCobra

This Bell Helicopter design is a version of the AH-1 Cobra series that was specifically designed for the USMC. The AH-1J has a twin turboshaft powered by an 1,800-horsepower PW T400-CP-400 engine and carries a night-vision system. Armament includes a three-barrel 20-mm cannon in a chin turret. An attack helicopter, the AH-1J can launch Hellfire, TOW, and Sidewinder missiles. Top speed is 141 miles per hour, ceiling is 12,000 feet, range 315 miles, endurance three hours. The helicopter is crewed by a pilot and copilot, who also serves as gunner, seated in tandem behind the pilot.

Bell introduced the Model 209 Huey Cobra in 1965. A single-engine AH-1G Huey Cobra was acquired for the U.S. Army, and the two-engine AH-1J SeaCobra for the USMC. Deliveries to both services began in 1969. In 1977, the USMC began taking delivery of the AH-1T Improved Cobra, and, in 1986, the AH-lW Super Cobra.

CH-37

Sometimes referred to by its army designation, Mojave, the CH-37 was a Sikorsky-built helicopter introduced in 1955 and powered by two 2,100-horsepower engines mounted in outboard nacelles affixed to wing stubs. The CH-37 could cruise at 130 miles per hour over a range of 145 miles, carrying 20 marines or 24 litter patients in addition to a two-person crew. Configured to carry cargo, the helicopter had the advantage of loading and unloading through a clamshell door in the nose or through a rear door.

CH-46 Sea Knight

Since 1964, the Sea Knight has been the primary assault helicopter of the USMC. As of 2005, the MV-22 Osprey tilt-rotor aircraft is slated to replace the Sea Knight.

The Sea Knight is a tandem-rotor, medium-lift helicopter, which can carry 10,000 pounds of cargo, 17 troops, or 15 litter patients. The craft is equipped with a rear ramp to expedite loading and unloading. The Sea Knight is amphibious and can land on land or water.

The Sea Knight is 46 feet 8 inches long, with a rotor diameter of 51 feet. It is powered by two GE T58-GE-16 turboshaft engines, can reach 166 miles per hour, and has an assault range of 173 miles (ferry range is 650 miles). The ship's operating ceiling is 14,000 feet. The Sea Knight ordinarily carries no weapons, although two .50-caliber machine guns can be readily fitted. The USMC inventory includes about six Sea Knights specially modified for VIP transport service; these are based at Andrews Air Force Base, outside of Washington, D.C.

View of a USMC CH-46D Sea Knight   (*U.S. Marine Corps*)

CH-53D Sea Stallion

This all-weather, heavy-lift assault helicopter can carry 55 troops with equipment (or 24 litter patients, with four attendants) or 18,500 pounds of cargo, including heavy equipment and vehicles. The helicopter entered USMC service in 1966 and has been continuously upgraded since.

Sea Stallion is used in assault as well as in mine-countermeasure roles, and two Sea Stallions have been specially modified for VIP transport with MARINE HELICOPTER SQUADRON ONE (HMX-1). Crew consists of a pilot, copilot, and crewman; the RH-53D mine countermeasures configuration has seven crew members. The helicopter is 67 feet long, with a rotor diameter of 72 feet 3 inches, and is powered by two GE T64-GE-412/413 turboshafts, which can drive the Sea Stallion to 196 miles per hour and a maximum ceiling of 21,000 feet. Ordinarily, the Sea Stallion is unarmed, but it can be fitted with two 0.5-inch machine guns. Also see CH-53E Super Stallion.

CH-53E Super Stallion

The largest helicopter in U.S. service, the CH-53E is flown by the U.S. Navy and USMC and is used in assault and heavy lift operation. Similar in appearance to the CH-53D Sea Stallion, the Super Stallion has three engines (General Electric T64-GE-416) instead of two, is longer, and sports a seven-blade rotor instead of the conventional six-blade rotor. The additional power gives the Super Stallion almost twice the lifting capacity of the Sea Stallion—16 tons—and can lift more than 90 percent of the heavy equipment used by a USMC division.

The Super Stallion is crewed by a pilot, copilot, and crew chief and can carry 55 fully equipped troops. Its length is 73 feet 4 inches, and rotor diameter is 79 feet. Top speed is 195 miles per hour, with an 18,500-foot service ceiling. Like the Sea Stallion, the Super Stallion is normally unarmed, but can be fitted with 0.5-inch machine guns. Additionally, it can be equipped with Stinger missiles and AIM-9L Sidewinders.

HH-1H Iroquois

This light-lift helicopter is crewed by a pilot and, optionally, a flight engineer. The USMC uses the Iroquois principally for rescue and utility purposes. Forty-two feet long, the HH-1H has a rotor

A USMC HH-1H Iroquois light-lift helicopter *(U.S. Marine Corps)*

diameter of 48 feet 4 inches, weighs 9,500 pounds, can carry 2,400 pounds of cargo, and is equipped with a single Lycoming turboshaft engine, which propels the ship to 133 miles per hour. Its range is 345 miles, with a ceiling of 15,000 feet. The helicopter is unarmed.

HRP Rescuer ("Flying Banana")

This large, twin-rotor Piasecki-built helicopter was introduced at the end of WORLD WAR II, in March 1945, and flew with the navy and USMC as late as 1962. Dubbed by sailors and marines the "Flying Banana" because of its elongated shape and up-turned aft portion, the HRP was produced in two versions, a fabric-skin HRP-1 and an all-metal HRP-2. The navy used the HRP mainly for rescue, while the USMC conducted extensive experimentation with an airborne assault role.

Length was 54 feet, rotor span 41 feet, top speed 104 miles per hour. The helicopter's twin rotors were driven by a single Pratt and Whitney 600-horsepower engine.

RH-53D

The mine-countermeasures version of the CH-53 Sea Stallion. The RH-53D is currently used by Marine Air Reserve units.

Tactical Bulk Fuel Delivery System, CH-53E (TBFDS, CH-53E)

The Tactical Bulk Fuel Delivery System, CH-53E supports the USMC's over-the-horizon concept—that is, the tactical ability to operate as an expeditionary force at great range. TBFDS, CH-53E is a three-tank, air-transportable fuel-delivery, forward area refueling, range-extension system consisting of four subsystems: three 800-gallon fuel tanks, a restraint system, an electrical fuel control panel, and a Forward Area Refueling Equipment (FARE) system. The system is ballistically self-sealing and crashworthy.

As configured together, the system allows the CH-53E Super Stallion helicopter to transport and dispense aviation fuel to aircraft or tactical ground vehicles at forward landing zones or Forward Area Refueling Points (FARP). The system's three internal

fuel tanks can be rapidly installed and removed from the CH-53E's cargo area to transform any Super Stallion into a tanker. The installation procedure can be carried out by a crew of four in under an hour. Removal takes less than 40 minutes. This quick conversion allows for rapid mission changes, freeing up the helicopter for other missions as required. Also, the system is designed to permit one, two, or three tanks to be installed, as the need may be. The installed internal tanks may be refilled while on the ground or in flight. They can accept fuel through the helicopter's single-point pressure refueling adapter, the in-flight refueling probe, or via the tank manifold or filler opening in the top of each tank. The system is equipped with internal pumps, which can be used to transfer fuel to the helicopter's tanks, thereby extending its range, or dispensed to other aircraft or vehicles using the Forward Area Refueling Equipment (FARE). The FARE subsystem is two-point capable, with a combined flow rate of 120 gallons per minute, and 200 feet separation from the host aircraft to the aircraft or vehicles being refueled.

General characteristics of the Tactical Bulk Fuel Delivery System, CH-53E (TBFDS, CH-53E) include:

Contractor: Serv-Air, Inc., Lexington, Kentucky (prime), Robertson Aviation, Inc. (subcontractor)
Capacity: 2,400 gallons in three 800-gallon tanks
Tank length: 62 in
Tank width: 58 in
Tank height: 64 in
Weight, empty: 600 lb per tank
Weight, full (JP-5/8 fuel): 6,100 lb per tank
Operating area: Cargo area of the helicopter
Aircraft: CH-53E Super Stallion
Ballistic tolerances: Self-sealing and crash resistant
Crashworthiness: 10 G forward; 7.5 G aft; 3 G vertical; 3 G lateral

UH-34/VH-34 Seahorse

The Sikorsky UH-34 helicopter was introduced in 1954 and was a large utility helicopter capable of transporting 18 troops or carrying eight stretchers. The VH-34 version was modified for VIP transport and could carry 12 passengers. Both aircraft have a top speed just under 100 miles per hour and a service ceiling of 9,500 miles. Range was short, at only 250 miles. The USMC made extensive use of the utility version of the helicopter in the VIET-NAM WAR and used the VH-34 to transport senior officials.

V-22 Osprey

This medium-lift, high-speed, rotary-wing V/STOL aircraft was designed and built by Bell-Boeing to replace the USMC's principal assault helicopters, the CH-46E Sea Knight and CH-53A/D Sea Stallion. Two 6,150-shaft-horsepower turboshaft engines drive two three-bladed proprotors, each 38 feet in diameter and mounted as tiltrotors, which can be angled forward to drive the aircraft as a conventional fixed-wing airplane or angled vertically, to fly it as a helicopter. Thus the Osprey combines the vertical flight capabilities of a helicopter with the speed and range of a turboprop airplane. The development program began in 1986, and the first operational test period took place during 1994. Unfortunately, the Osprey was plagued by accidents, some fatal, which have called into question the viability of the aircraft as built and perhaps even the design. USMC command placed such a high priority on the aircraft that some testing procedures were called into question; however, in 2004, the Osprey finally entered active service with the USMC.

The Osprey functions primarily in the amphibious assault transport of marines, equipment, and supplies from assault ships and land bases. The Osprey is 57 feet 4 inches long, with a wingspan of 84 feet 7 inches. Range is 200 nautical miles, carrying 18 to 24 assault-equipped marines. Cruise airspeed is 240 knots.

VH-3D Sea King

Marine Helicopter Squadron One uses the VH-3D and the VH-60N Seahawk for presidential transport and for other VIP transport. Built by Sikorsky, the VH-3D began service in 1962 and has been continuously updated. Crewed by three, the VH-3D is 72 feet 9 inches long, with a rotor diameter of 62 feet. It is powered by two General Electric T58-GE-400B turboshafts and can reach 160 miles per hour. Service ceiling is 14,700 feet.

VH-60A Black Hawk

This is the USMC version of the U.S. Army's UH-60 Black Hawk helicopter. The VH-60A is flown by the Executive Flight Detachment of Helicopter Squadron One, which is assigned to transport VIPs. The VH-60A is used for routine VIP transport as well as for emergency evacuation of government officials.

The VH-60A is crewed by two pilots and a crew chief and can carry up to 14 passengers. Fuselage length is 50 feet, height 16 feet 10 inches, and the diameter of the four-bladed rotor is 53 feet 8 inches. Two General Electric T700-GE-700/701C turboshafts power the aircraft, which can cruise at 145 miles per hour and with a range of 500 miles using auxiliary tanks. Ceiling is 19,000 feet.

VH-60N Seahawk

With the VH-3D Sea King, the VH-60N is used by Marine Helicopter Squadron One for presidential transport and for other VIP transport. Top speed is 184 miles per hour, and range is 320 miles. The aircraft seats 10 passengers in addition to a pilot, co-pilot, crew chief, and a communication system operator. The VH-60N can be folded in less than two hours for loading and storage onto a USAF C-5A/B, C-17, C-130, or C-141.

The VH-60N is a single main rotor, twin-engine helicopter produced by Sikorsky Aircraft Division of United Technologies.

air defense artillery

The following air defense artillery weapons are currently included in the marine inventory:

Avenger

The Avenger is an air-defense system used by both the USMC and the army. Typically mounted on a vehicle, the Avenger system employs a variety of sensors (including infrared, laser, and optical) to guide the fire of Stinger missiles or .50-caliber machine guns against low-flying, high-speed, fixed-wing aircraft and helicopters.

FIM-92A Stinger

This shoulder-launched antiaircraft rocket is designed to be fired by a single marine and provides passive infrared and ultraviolet "fire and forget" homing on low-flying aircraft. The FIM-92A is a 5-foot-long missile, capable of Mach 2, and loaded with a high-explosive warhead. Its range is in excess of three miles and it is designed to hit targets as low as 33 feet and as high as 15,750 feet. The FIM-92A is in service with the USMC, USA, USAF, and USN.

HAWK

This is an acronym for the MIM-23B "Homing All the Way Killer" medium-range surface-to-air missile system. HAWK systems provide medium-altitude air defense coverage for ground forces. The system was first introduced in 1960. Its homing system is semiactive, and has a two-stage solid-fuel motor capable of attaining Mach 2.5. The missile, 16.5 feet long and 15 inches in diameter, has a range of 24 miles and carries a 120-pound proximity-fuse warhead.

HAWK is fired by a specialized platoon, equipped with an acquisition and tracking radar as well as an optical tracking system. The typical platoon carries four launchers, each with three missiles.

Stinger Weapons System: RMP and Basic

Stinger Weapons Systems are close-in, surface-to-air weapons for the defense of forward combat areas, vital areas, and other installations against low-altitude air attacks. The Stinger is man-portable and shoulder-fired. It launches a guided missile, which enables an individual marine to engage low-altitude jet, propeller-driven, and helicopter aircraft.

The system was developed by the United States Army Missile Command as a follow-up to the Redeye Weapon System. The Stinger is a "fire-and-for-get" weapon, which uses a passive infrared seeker and proportional navigation system. Fired in the general direction of the target, its heat-seeking IR sensor homes in on the heat source, typically the aircraft's engine. The latest Stingers incorporate all-aspect engagement capability and IFF (Identification-Friend-or-Foe), as well as improved range, maneuverability, and significant countermeasures immunity.

The Stinger missile is packaged within a disposable launch tube. It is delivered as a certified round, requiring no field testing or direct support maintenance. A gripstock, separable and reusable, is attached to the round prior to use.

In addition to the shoulder-fired configuration, Stingers may be installed on the Pedestal-Mounted Stinger Air Defense Vehicle and the LAV-AD, the Light Armored Vehicle, Air Defense Variant. As of the end of 2003, the USMC had 13,431 Stinger missiles in its inventory.

General characteristics of the Stinger Weapons Systems include:

Manufacturer: General Dynamics/Raytheon Corporation
Propulsion: dual-thrust solid fuel rocket motor
Length: 5 ft
Width: 5.5 in
Weight: 12.5 lb
Weight fully armed: 34.5 lb
Maximum system span: 3.6 in
Range: 1 to 8 km
Fuzing: penetration, impact, self-destruct
Ceiling: 10,000 ft
Speed: supersonic
Crew: two enlisted marines
Guidance system: fire-and-forget passive infrared seeker
Warheads: high explosive
Rate of fire: one missile every three to seven sec

The Stinger was introduced to the USMC inventory in 1982. In 1989 the USMC began fielding an improved Stinger, equipped with a reprogrammable microprocessor (RPM), a modular enhancement that allows the Stinger to engage and destroy more sophisticated air threats.

air-launched weapons

USMC aviators use the following air-launched weapons systems.

AGM-45 Shrike

The AGM-45 Shrike is an air-to-surface antiradiation missile, which homes in on hostile antiaircraft radar. It was developed by the navy's Naval Weapons Center at China Lake in 1963 and is still used by the USMC, USN, and USAF as well as by the air force of Israel.

General characteristics of the AGM-45 Shrike include:

Propulsion: solid-fuel rocket
Length: 10 ft
Weight: 390 lb
Diameter: 8 in
Warhead: conventional
Span: 3 ft
Guidance: passive radar homing
Platforms: A-4 Skyhawk, A-6 Intruder

AGM-65E Maverick Missile

The AGM-65E Maverick is an air-to-surface missile designed expressly for use against tanks. The AGM-65E version has been especially adapted as the USMC laser Maverick weapon for use from USMC aircraft. The USMC also uses Maverick versions with electro-optical or infrared guidance.

General characteristics of the AGM-65E Maverick missile include:

Propulsion: solid-fuel rocket
Length: 8 ft, 6 in
Weight: 630 lb
Span: 2 ft, 4 in
Diameter: 12 in
Guidance: laser (AGM-65E version only)
Warhead: conventional, with 300-lb blast/penetration
Platforms: F/A-18A/C/CN Hornet, F/A-18D Hornet, and AV-8B Harrier II

AGM-114 Hellfire

This air-to-ground missile system provides heavy antiarmor capability for attack helicopters. The first three generations of Hellfire missiles use a laser seeker, while the latest, fourth-generation missile, Longbow Hellfire, uses a radar frequency seeker. The first-generation missiles constitute the main armament of the U.S. Army's AH-64 Apache and USMC's AH-1W Super Cobra helicopters. The missiles were introduced in 1982 by Martin Marietta and Rockwell International.

An AGM-114B Hellfire missile roars off the rails of a U.S. Navy SH-60 Seahawk helicopter toward a laser designated surface target during training off the coast of San Clemente Island, California, on August 25, 1999. *(Department of Defense)*

The AGM-114K Hellfire II missile incorporates dual warheads for defeating reactive armor, electro-optical countermeasures hardening, semiactive laser seeker, and a programmable autopilot for trajectory shaping. The planned Longbow Hellfire missile will provide an adverse-weather, fire-and-forget, heavy antiarmor capability for attack helicopters.

The Hellfire missile is 5 feet 4 inches long, weighs 99 pounds, and is propelled by a Thiokol TX657 solid-propellant rocket motor. Its range is more than three miles.

AGM-122 Sidearm

The AGM-122 is a small, supersonic anti-radiation missile carried on the army AH-64A/D Apache and USMC AH-1W SuperCobra attack helicopters for self-defense against antiaircraft guns and SAM radars. The AGM-122 uses an AIM-9C Sidewinder guidance section modified to detect and track ground-based enemy radar, to home in on that radar, and to attack it.

The Sidearm retains the Sidewinder's original Mk-17 motor and WDU-17 warhead, but substitutes a DSU-15 active fuse and a modification of control electronics to provide a dive attack on the target radar.

AGM-123 Skipper II

Developed by the USN, the AGM-123 Skipper II is a short-range precision attack missile, consisting of a Paveway II laser guidance system and a small booster rocket attached to a Mk-83 bomb. Built by Emerson Electric, it was introduced in 1985 and, as used by the USMC, was launched from the A-6 Intruder.

The Skipper II's wingspan is 5.25 feet, its length 14.1 feet, and its maximum range 15.5 miles.

AIM-7 Sparrow

The AIM-7 Sparrow is a radar-guided, air-to-air missile with a high-explosive warhead, which is deployed on airforce, navy, and USMC aircraft. Manufactured by Raytheon Systems, the missile was introduced in 1976. It is powered by a Hercules Mk-58 solid-propellant rocket motor, weighs about 500 pounds, and carries an annular blast fragmentation warhead.

AIM-9 Sidewinder Missile

The AIM-9 Sidewinder is a short-range, heat-seeking air-to-air missile, which uses an infrared seeker to find its target. The AIM-9 incorporates an enhanced warhead and an enhanced guidance system, which permits all-angle attacks. The most widely used air-to-air missile in the West, the USMC is one of many military users.

General characteristics of the AIM-9 Sidewinder missile include:

Primary function: Close-range, air-to-air missile
Length: 9 ft, 6 in
Weight: 186 lb
Span: 2 ft
Diameter: 5 in
Propulsion: Solid-fuel rocket
Guidance: Infrared homing
Warhead: Conventional
Speed: Mach 2.5
Platforms: F/A-18A/C/CN Hornet, F/A-18D Hornet, and AV-8B Harrier II, and AH-1J Seacobra.

Air-to-Ground Missile Systems (AGMS)

See AIR-LAUNCHED WEAPONS.

American Revolution

The USMC was created as the CONTINENTAL MARINES during the American Revolution, on November 10, 1775, when the Second Continental Congress authorized two marine battalions for service aboard ships of the newly formed U.S. Navy. Under its de facto commandant, Captain SAMUEL NICHOLAS, the marines saw some action during the war, beginning with a landing on New Providence Island in the Bahamas on March 3, 1776. Two hundred thirty-four marines under Captain Nicholas took Britain's Fort Montague there and captured powder and arms. Three companies of Continental

Marines accompanied General George Washington in the triumphant assault against Trenton (December 26, 1776) and the follow-up action against Princeton.

The last significant marine action of the war was an assault on Fort St. George on Penobscot Bay, Maine, on July 28, 1779. The landing and advance proceeded briskly until a quarrel between the overall commander and the commander of militia brought the operation to a standstill. During the delay, a British frigate arrived, prompting the commanders to scrub the assault altogether.

Both the USN and the USMC were disbanded, even before the conclusion of the 1783 Treaty of Paris, which formally ended the war.

amphibious assault

A USMC specialty, an amphibious assault is an offensive operation in which troops and equipment are landed on an enemy shore by LANDING CRAFT, AMPHIBIOUS VEHICLES, helicopter, or some combination of these.

See also AMPHIBIOUS OPERATION; AMPHIBIOUS WARFARE SHIPS.

amphibious operation

An attack launched against an enemy shore from the sea by forces embarked on ships. The AMPHIBIOUS ASSAULT is the culmination of the operation, which begins with planning and proceeds through embarkation, rehearsal, and movement. Marines specialize in amphibious operations.

See also AMPHIBIOUS VEHICLES; AMPHIBIOUS WARFARE SHIPS; and LANDING CRAFT.

amphibious vehicles

Amphibious vehicles are wheeled or tracked vehicles that can operate in the water or on land. They transport troops and equipment from ship to shore during the AMPHIBIOUS ASSAULT phase of an AMPHIBIOUS OPERATION. The AAVP7 vehicle, described below, is the primary USMC amphibious vehicle.

AAVC-7A1 Assault Amphibian Vehicle Command Model 7A1

The AAVC-7A1 is an assault amphibious fully tracked landing vehicle that serves USMC mobile task force commanders as a communication center in water operations from ship to shore and to inland objectives after arriving ashore. The vehicle's communication center system consists of five radio operator stations, three staff stations, and two master stations. The command comm system contains equipment to provide external, secure radio transmission between each AAVC-7A1 vehicle fielded and other vehicles and radios. The vehicle was prototyped in 1979, and the first production vehicle entered USMC service in 1983.

General characteristics of the AAVC-7A1 Assault Amphibian Vehicle Command Model 7A1 include:

Manufacturer: FMC Corporation
Weight, unloaded: 46,314 lb
Weight, combat equipped: 50,758 lb
Fuel capacity: 171 gal
Cruising range, land at 25 mph: 300 mi
Cruising range, water at 2,600 rpm: 7 hr
Cruising speed, land: 20 to 30 mph
Cruising speed, water: 6 mph
Maximum speed forward, land: 45 mph
Maximum speed forward, water: 8.2 mph
Maximum speed reverse, land: 12 mph
Maximum speed reverse, water: 4.5 mph
Engine: Cummins Model VT400, 4-cycle, 8-cylinder, water-cooled, turbocharged
Fuel Type: multifuel
Cargo compartment length: 13.5 ft
Cargo compartment width: 6.0 ft
Cargo compartment height: 5.5 ft
Cargo compartment volume: 445.5 c ft
Total vehicle capacity: 21 combat-equipped marines
Armament: 7.62 machine gun
Crew: three

AAVR-7A1 Assault Amphibian Vehicle Recovery Model 7A1

The AAVR-7A1 is a fully tracked armored assault amphibious vehicle designed to recover in the field

An amphibious assault vehicle belonging to Delta Company, 2nd Amphibious Assault Battalion, speeds toward the enemy during an assault by marines of Kilo Company at Camp Lejeune, North Carolina.   *(Department of Defense)*

and under combat conditions vehicles of similar or smaller size. In addition to recovery, the AAVR-7A1 serves as a platform for the performance of field repairs and support. It carries a full set of basic maintenance equipment for this mission. The vehicle was prototyped in 1979, and it was first fielded by the USMC in 1983.

General characteristics of the AAVR-7A1 Assault Amphibian Vehicle Recovery Model 7A1 include:

Manufacturer: FMC Corporation
Weight, unloaded: 50,113 lb
Weight, combat equipped: 52,123 lb
Vehicle load capacity: 21 combat-equipped marines or 10,000 lb of cargo
Fuel capacity: 171 gal
Cruising range, land at 25 mph: 300 mi
Cruising range, water at 2,600 rpm: 7 hr
Cruising speed, land: 20 to 30 mph
Cruising speed, water: 6 mph
Maximum speed forward, land: 45 mph
Maximum speed forward, water: 8.2 mph
Maximum speed reverse, land: 12 mph

Maximum speed reverse, water: 4.5 mph
Engine: Cummins Model VT400, 4-cycle, 8-cylinder, water-cooled, turbocharged
Fuel type: multifuel
Generator: 120 VAC Output
Air compressor: 145 PSIG to 175 PSIG
Welder: Miller Maxtron 300
Hydraulic crane: 6,000-lb capacity
Crane winch: 23,000-lb breaking strength
Winch length: 85 ft
Armament: M60D machine gun
Crew: five

AAVP-7

The USMC uses this amphibious assault vehicle to transport troops and equipment from assault ships to areas beyond the shore. The vehicle is fully tracked and can carry 21 troops and three crew. Highly versatile, it is capable of operating in rough seas and in surf up to 10 feet high. On land, top speed is 40 miles per hour; on water, 8.4 miles per hour. Land range is 300 miles at 25 miles per hour; water range is 55 miles, near its top 8-mile-per-hour speed. Regular armament includes a .50-caliber machine gun and a 40-mm grenade launcher.

The vehicle has been refurbished repeatedly to extend its useful life, most recently in 1999, as the AAVP-7A1, using engines and parts adapted from the U.S. Army's M-2 Bradley Fighting Vehicle. AAVP variants include a command vehicle (AAVC-7) and a repair and recovery vehicle (AAVR-7).

DUKW

Pronounced "duck," this 2.5-ton, six-wheel-drive amphibious vehicle was put into service with the USMC and U.S. Army in 1942. Built on a truck chassis, the DUKW could carry 25 fully equipped troops. Clumsy and slow, DUKWs were little used by the USMC in the Pacific during WORLD WAR II, although a USMC DUKW company saw action at IWO JIMA. Most DUKWs were used by the army in the European theater.

LAV-25

An eight-wheeled light assault vehicle, also used as a personnel carrier. Crewed by three—commander, driver, and gunner—the LAV-25 carries six combat-ready marines. The vehicle is equipped with gun ports, enabling marines to fire from within the cargo hold of the vehicle. A periscope is placed above each port. The LAV-25 is relatively lightly armored, able to withstand 7.62-mm armor-piercing rounds, and it is equipped with an M-242 Bushmaster 25-mm turret-mounted chain gun.

The LAV-25 has been developed in six major variations: a command and control vehicle, an antitank vehicle (carrying twin TOW II missiles), a mortar vehicle (equipped with an 81 mm mortar), a recovery vehicle, an air-defense vehicle (equipped with Stinger missile launchers and a 25 mm GAU-12 Gatling gun), and the standard LAV (armed with the 25-mm chain gun).

The vehicle is 21 feet long and 7 feet 2 inches wide. Its empty weight is 19,050 pounds, and its power plant is a turbocharged diesel, capable of driving the LAV up to 60 miles per hour. Its range is 485 miles. Like most USMC assault vehicles, the LAV-25 is amphibious. Top speed in water is 6 miles per hour.

LAV-C2 Light Armored Vehicle– Command and Control

The USMC's Light Armored Vehicle–Command and Control (LAV-C2) is used primarily as a mobile command station to provide field commanders with all necessary resources to control and coordinate light armored units in all assigned roles. The vehicle operates on all terrains and in all weather conditions and also has night-operation capabilities. It can be transported by air, using the KC-130 Hercules or other fixed-wing cargo aircraft, as well as the CH-53E Super Stallion helicopter. In its combat-loaded status, the LAV-C2 carries 200 ready rounds and 800 stowed rounds of 7.62-mm ammunition. Additionally, there are eight ready rounds and eight stowed rounds of smoke grenades. The vehicle can be made fully amphibious within three minutes.

General characteristics of the Light Armored Vehicle–Command and Control (LAV-C2) include:

Length: 253.5 in
Height: 110.0 in
Width: 98.4 in
Weight: 24,840 lb
Combat weight: 27,060 lb
Range: 410 mi
Speed: 62 mph
Swim speed: 6 mph
Crew: seven, consisting of driver, vehicle commander, two radio operators, two staff members, and battalion commander
Armament: M240E1 7.62-mm machine gun
Communication equipment: two SINCGARS AN/VRC 92 radios; one VHF/UHF AN/VRC-83(V)2 radio; one UHF position location reporting system; one HF AN/GRC-213 radio; one VHF AN/PRC-68 radio (stowed)

LAV-L Light Armored Vehicle–Logistics

The USMC's Light Armored Vehicle–Logistics (LAV-L) primarily functions to supply ammunition, rations, and POL (petroleum, oil and lubricant) as required to sustain operations of first-line armored vehicles. The vehicle operates on all terrains and in all weather conditions and has night capabilities. It can be transported by air, using the KC-130 Hercules or other fixed-wing cargo aircraft, as well as the CH-53E Super Stallion helicopter. In a combat-loaded condition, the LAV-L carries 200 ready rounds and 800 stowed rounds of 7.62-mm ammunition. Additionally, there are eight ready rounds and eight stowed rounds of smoke grenades. The vehicle can be made fully amphibious within three minutes.

General characteristics of the Light Armored Vehicle–Logistics (LAV-L) include:

Length: 254.6 in
Height: 109.0 in
Width: 98.4 in
Weight: 22,960 lb
Combat weight: 28,200 lb
Range: 410 mi
Speed: 62 mph
Swim speed: 6 mph
Crew: three, consisting of driver, vehicle commander, and crewmember
Armament: M240E1 7.62-mm machine gun
Payload: 5,240 lb

LAV-M Light Armored Vehicle–Mortar

The USMC employs the Light Armored Vehicle–Mortar (LAV-M) to provide indirect fire support to light infantry and reconnaissance forces and to provide high-explosive area fire, covering smoke, and illumination for first-line units. An all-terrain, all-weather vehicle with night capabilities, the LAV-M can be transported by air, using the KC-130 Hercules or other fixed-wing cargo aircraft, as well as the CH-53E Super Stallion helicopter. In its combat-loaded configuration, the LAV-M holds five ready and 94 stowed 81-mm bombs as well as 200 ready rounds and 800 stowed rounds of 7.62-mm ammunition. Additionally, there are eight ready rounds and eight stowed rounds of smoke grenades. Stowed within the vehicle is the base plate and bipod for a ground-mounted mortar. The vehicle can be made fully amphibious within three minutes.

General characteristics of the Light Armored Vehicle–Mortar (LAV-M) include:

Length: 252.6 in
Height: 110.0 in, reducible to 98 in
Width: 98.4 in
Weight: 22,750 lb
Combat weight: 26,700 lb
Range: 410 mi
Speed: 62 mph
Swim speed: 6 mph
Crew: driver, mortar crew, and commander
Armament: M252 81-mm mortar, M240E1 7.62-mm machine gun

LAV-R Light Armored Vehicle–Recovery

The USMC's Light Armored Vehicle–Recovery (LAV-R) provides the tactical mobility to reach and recover or support disabled vehicles. Like the USMC's other LAVs, the LAV-R is an all-terrain, all-weather vehicle with night capabilities and can be airlifted aboard the KC-130 Hercules or other fixed-wing cargo aircraft, as well as the CH-53E Super Stallion helicopter. Combat loaded, the vehicle holds 200 ready rounds and 800 stowed rounds of 7.62-mm ammunition. Additionally, there are eight ready rounds and eight stowed rounds of smoke grenades. The vehicle can be made fully amphibious within three minutes.

General characteristics of the Light Armored Vehicle–Recovery (LAV-R) include:

Length, crane forward: 21.3 ft
Length, crane aft: 24.16 ft
Height, crane forward: 8.83 ft
Height, crane aft: 9.08 ft
Width: 109.0 in
Weight: 26,220 lb
Combat weight: 28,320 lb
Range: 410 mi
Speed: 62 mph
Swim speed: 6 mph
Crew: Three, consisting of driver, vehicle commander, and rigger
Armament: M240E1 7.62-mm machine gun
On-board equipment: one boom crane rated at 9,000 lb (4,086 kgs); flood lights; one

winch rated at 30,000 lb; 230-volt three-phase or 120-volt single-phase power; 10-kilowatt hydraulic-driven output; and one welder.

LVT and LVT(A) Landing Vehicle, Tracked

The LVT was developed for the USMC in 1940 and was intended to be launched from ships, sail through surf and negotiate coral reefs, then move forward on tank tracks once landed. The LVT-1 was replaced in 1942–43 by the Water Buffalo (LVT-2), which was more powerful than the LVT-1 and had a suspension system that provided far greater traction and maneuverability. The LVT-2 was also larger. A total of 1,225 LVT-1s were built, and more than 3,000 of the LVT-2 and LVT(A)-2 models were produced. They were extremely valuable for landing troops inland, rather than exposing troops on foot to fire on a beachhead. The only drawback these vehicles suffered from was the lack of an off-loading ramp. Marines clambered over the sides—an action that rendered them vulnerable to fire.

amphibious warfare ships

Familiarly called "amphibs" or "gators," these are vessels expressly designed to transport troops from bases to landing beaches in AMPHIBIOUS OPERATIONS. The ships are operated by U.S. Navy personnel and include the following types:

LST (Landing Ship, Tank). This vessel runs right up to the beach and is equipped with a bow ramp, which is lowered so that land vehicles can drive off. A stern ramp may be used to launch AMPHIBIOUS VEHICLES.

LSD (Landing Ship, Dock). These vessels incorporate a well dock, which can be flooded to float landing craft and amphibious vehicles out through a stern gate.

LPD (Amphibious Transport Dock). Like the LSD, these incorporate a well dock, which can be flooded to float landing craft and amphibious vehicles out through a stern

gate; in addition, they have a flight deck for helicopter operations.

LKA (Amphibious Cargo Ship). These vessels are for off-loading cargo necessary to the AMPHIBIOUS ASSAULT.

LPH (Amphibious Assault Ship). These carry helicopters and can land 2,000 marines and equipment (battalion strength).

LHA (General-Purpose Assault Ship). These are larger versions of the LPD.

LHD (Multipurpose Assault Ship). These vessels operate air-cushion vehicles as well as helicopters.

LCC (Amphibious Command Ship). Used as a seaborne command post during the amphibious assault.

See also LANDING CRAFT.

AN/PAQ-3 Modular Universal Laser Equipment (MULE)   See WEAPONS, INDIVIDUAL AND CREW-SERVED.

AN/PAQ-4A/4C Infrared Aiming Light

See WEAPONS, INDIVIDUAL AND CREW-SERVED.

AN/PSN-11 Precision Lightweight GPS Receiver (PLGR)   See PERSONAL AND MISCELLANEOUS EQUIPMENT.

AN/PSS-12 Metallic Mine Detector   See PERSONAL AND MISCELLANEOUS EQUIPMENT.

AN/PVS-4 Individual Weapon Night Sight

See WEAPONS, INDIVIDUAL AND CREW-SERVED.

AN/PVS-5 Night Vision Goggles (NVG)

See WEAPONS, INDIVIDUAL AND CREW-SERVED.

AN/PVS-7B Night Vision Goggle (NVG)

See WEAPONS, INDIVIDUAL AND CREW-SERVED.

antiarmor weapons

The following antiarmor weapons are currently included in the marine inventory:

AT-4 Light Antiarmor Weapon

The AT-4 is a shoulder-fired light antiarmor weapon designed to be effective against main battle tanks. Manufactured by FFV Ordnance of Sweden and Alliant Techsystems of the United States, the weapon measures 40 inches in length and weighs 14.75 pounds. Its bore diameter is 84 mm, and it has an effective range of 984.3 feet. At this range, the AT-4 is capable of firing a projectile that penetrates 400 mm of rolled homogenous armor. Time of flight is under one second, and muzzle velocity is 950 feet per second. The ammunition for the weapon is a rocket with a shaped-charge warhead.

Dragon Weapon System

The Dragon antiarmor weapon system has as its primary mission engagement and destruction of armor and light armored vehicles. Secondarily, the Dragon Weapon System is effective against such hard targets as bunkers and field fortifications. This man-portable weapon system makes it possible for a single marine to defeat armored vehicles, fortified bunkers, concrete gun emplacements, and other hard targets. The launcher consists of a smoothbore fiberglass tube, breech/gas generator, tracker and support, bipod, battery, sling, and forward and aft shock absorbers. Additionally, a day or night sight—not integral to the system—is required. Essentially, the system consists of the launcher, the tracker, and the missile, which is installed in the launcher during final factory

A marine sets up a Dragon antiarmor weapon as his spotter/loader watches for movement during an assault by marines of Kilo Company at Camp Lejeune, North Carolina.   *(Department of Defense)*

assembly and is received by the USMC ready to fire. The launch tube functions as a storage and carrying case for the missile as well as its launcher.

The predecessor of the modern USMC Dragon was a Dragon weapon developed for the army and first deployed in 1970. It required 11.2 seconds flight-to-target time. The weapon was improved in a USMC program in 1985 and designated Dragon II, using a retrofit of warheads to the first-generation Dragon missiles already in the USMC inventory.

General characteristics of the Dragon Weapon System include:

Manufacturer: McDonnell Douglas Aerospace and Missile Systems and Raytheon
Length, launcher: 45.4 in
Length, missile: 33.3 in
Weight: 33.9 lb (Day Tracker version); 48.7 lb (Night Tracker version)
Maximum effective range: 3,281 ft
Time of flight: 11.2 sec
Armor penetration: will defeat T-55, T-62, or T-72 tanks

Javelin

Javelin is a portable antitank weapon manufactured by a Raytheon/Lockheed Martin joint venture. It can be shoulder-fired or installed on tracked, wheeled, or amphibious vehicles. Development began as a replacement for the M-47 Dragon II, and the weapon entered full-rate production in 1994; it was first deployed in 1996.

The Javelin system consists of a Command Launch Unit (CLU) and the round. The CLU incorporates a passive target acquisition and fire control unit with an integrated day sight and a thermal-imaging sight. The round is a Javelin missile and the ATK (Alliant Techsystems) Launch Tube Assembly. The range of the missile is 8,200 feet, and the weapon is "fire-and-forget"; it locks on to its target prior to launch and has automatic self-guidance. The missile has a tandem warhead fitted with two shaped charges, one (the "precursor") to initiate explosive-reactive armor, and

another (the "main") to penetrate base armor. The Javelin is propelled by a two-stage solid-fuel motor.

In contrast to conventional wire-guided, fiber-optic cable-guided, or laser beam-riding missiles, Javelin is autonomously guided, allowing the gunner to reposition or reload immediately after launch. This makes the gunner far less vulnerable to retaliatory fire.

M-3A1 Antitank Gun

This 37-mm gun was developed in the 1930s to replace World War I–era artillery. A towed weapon, it fired a 1.6-pound shell 500 yards. By the time the United States entered World War II, German tanks were sufficiently well armored to render the weapon obsolete. In the Pacific and against the Japanese, however, the USMC still found the gun highly effective, because Japanese tanks were much less well armored. Marines also used the guns against pillboxes and against banzai charges by infantry troops.

M-47 Dragon II

A disposable antitank weapon used by the USMC as well as the army. The Dragon II can be fired by a single marine, although a crew of two is ideal. The Dragon II weighs 32.6 pounds and has a range of 195 to 3,000 feet. It is equipped with a tracker system capable of tracking targets moving at 30 miles per hour. The fiberglass launch tube is discarded after firing, but the tracking system is retained and refitted to another tube and rocket.

During the 1990s, the M-47 was in the process of being replaced by the Javelin.

M-151 TOW

A long-range, tube-launched, optically tracked, wire-guided antitank missile, TOW is used by the USMC and army. TOW launchers may be fitted to helicopters and to armored vehicles. Infantry units may be equipped with tripod-mounted portable TOWs.

The TOW system consists of a launch tube, missile guidance set, optical sight, traversing unit, and missile. Weighing 280 pounds, the TOW system is operated by a three-person crew.

TOW has a reliability factor of 95 percent over a maximum range of 2.3 miles. Its 6-inch-diameter missile is subsonic (625 mph) and is guided by signals transmitted along wires that deploy as the missile travels toward its target. The latest iteration of the TOW is the TOW II, which includes a 21-inch probe that detonates the target's reactive armor, allowing the main warhead to penetrate and destroy the enemy vehicle.

Saboted Light Armor Penetrator (SLAP) Ammunition

The USMC developed .50-caliber SLAP ammunition during the mid- to late 1980s. It first saw combat service in 1990–91 during Operation Desert Storm (PERSIAN GULF WAR). The structure of this armor-penetrating ammunition is unique. A reduced-caliber, heavy metal (tungsten), .30-inch-diameter penetrator is wrapped in a plastic, .50-inch-diameter *sabot* (shoe). This renders the saboted ammunition much lighter than the normal ball .50-caliber ammunition, so that velocity is significantly and safely increased in an unmodified M2-HB Browning machine gun. The result is a very fast round with a very flat trajectory that significantly increases hit probability.

Maximum velocity of SLAP ammunition is 3,985 feet per second. Effective range is 4,921.5 feet against 3/4-inch-high hard armor.

Tube-Launched, Optically Tracked, Wire-Guided (TOW) Missile Weapon System

The Tube-Launched, Optically Tracked, Wire-Guided (TOW) Missile Weapon System is a vehicle- or tripod-mounted guided-missile weapon system widely used by the USMC. Its primary mission is to destroy enemy armored vehicles, especially tanks. Secondarily, the TOW system is used to destroy other point targets, including non-armored vehicles and crew-served weapons and launchers.

First fielded in 1970, the TOW was and is primarily used in antitank warfare. It is a wire-guided line-of-sight weapon, which will operate in all weather conditions. The TOW 2 launcher,

the most recent launcher upgrade, is compatible with all TOW missiles and consists of a reusable launcher, a missile guidance set, and a sight system. Although the system can be mounted on a tripod, it is sufficiently heavy that it is more usually mounted on the High Mobility Multipurpose Wheeled Vehicle (HMMWV) (M-998 Truck) or on a Landing Vehicle, Tracked (LVT and LVT[A]).

The earliest TOW missiles were 5 inches in diameter and had a range of 9,850 feet. The Improved TOW (ITOW), delivered in 1982, also has a 5-inch diameter warhead, but incorporates an extended probe for greater standoff and penetration and an enhanced flight motor, which increased the missile's range to 12,300 feet. The TOW 2 series of improvements includes TOW 2 Hardware, TOW 2 Missile, TOW 2A Missile, and TOW 2B Missile. The TOW 2 Hardware improvements include a thermal beacon guidance system, which enables the gunner to more easily track a target at night, and many improvements to the missile guidance system. Warhead diameter was also increased to 6 inches. The extended probe introduced with ITOW is also included in the TOW 2A. The TOW 2B introduces new fly-over, shoot-down technology.

General characteristics of the Tube-Launched, Optically Tracked, Wire-Guided (TOW) Missile Weapon System include:

Manufacturer: Hughes (missiles); Hughes and Kollsman (night sights); Electro Design Manufacturing (launchers)
Diameter, TOW 2A Missile: 5.87 in
Length, TOW 2A Missile: 50.40 in
Diameter, TOW 2B Missile: 5.8 in
Length, TOW 2B Missile: 48.0 in
Maximum effective range: 2.33 mi
Time of flight to maximum effective range, 2A: 20 sec; **2B,** 21 sec
Weight, launcher w/TOW 2 mods: 204.6 lb
Weight, missile guidance set: 52.8 lb
Weight, TOW 2 Missile: 47.4 lb
Weight, TOW 2A Missile: 49.9 lb
Weight, TOW 2B Missile: 49.8 lb

A tube-launched, optically tracked, wire-guided (TOW) missile hurtles out of its launcher mounted on a U.S. Marine Corps Humvee at the Marine Corps Air Ground Combat Center, Twentynine Pines, California. *(Department of Defense)*

AN/TPQ-36 Firefinder Radar   See INDIRECT FIRE SYSTEMS.

AN/TTC-42 (V) Automatic Telephone Central Office   See COMMUNICATIONS EQUIPMENT.

AN/TVS-5 Crew-Served Weapon Night Sight   See WEAPONS, INDIVIDUAL AND CREW-SERVED.

AN/USQ-70 Position Azimuth Determining System   See INDIRECT FIRE SYSTEMS.

assault craft
General term for LANDING CRAFT.
    See also AMPHIBIOUS WARFARE SHIPS.

AT-4 Light Antiarmor Weapon   See ANTIARMOR WEAPONS.

AV-8B Harrier II   See AIRCRAFT, FIXED-WING.

Avenger   See AIR DEFENSE ARTILLERY.

B

Barbary pirates

For a long time, the Muslim rulers of the so-called Barbary States—Morocco, Algiers, Tripoli, and Tunis—sanctioned piracy against the vessels of Christian nations plying the Mediterranean near the coast of North Africa. The so-called Barbary Pirates demanded tribute—protection money—in return for allowing shipping to be conducted unmolested. In its early years, the United States, a struggling young republic in no position to wage war against the Barbary Pirates, concluded tribute treaties. However, in May 1801, a new bey assumed the Tripolitan throne, demanded a more exorbitant tribute, then declared war on the United States in an effort to get it. In 1803, during the course of the war, the bey's navy captured the USN frigate *Philadelphia*. Lieutenant Stephen Decatur, USN, led a daring raid, which included marines, to set fire to the *Philadelphia* while it was in harbor, thereby depriving the bey of his prize.

In 1804, while the U.S. Navy blockaded the harbor of Tripoli, a mixed force of Egyptians, European troops, and eight U.S. Marines under the command of Lieutenant PRESLEY O'BANNON incited a revolt against the bey. O'Bannon and his marine detachment led the force 600 miles across the Libyan desert and attacked and took Derna on April 27, 1805, defeating superior forces. Shortly afterward, the bey concluded a favorable peace treaty with the United States—and presented O'Bannon with a jeweled MAMELUKE SWORD, which became the model for that worn by USMC officers on ceremonial occasions. O'Bannon's victory was also the source of the reference to the "shores of Tripoli" in the MARINE HYMN.

Barnett, George (1859–1930) *Marine Corps commandant*

Barnett was the 12th COMMANDANT OF THE MARINE CORPS. He graduated from the U.S. Naval Academy in 1881, served as a midshipman in the USN, and was commissioned a second lieutenant in the USMC in 1883. He served at sea during the SPANISH-AMERICAN WAR and in PANAMA, the Philippines, and Cuba. Barrett briefly commanded the MARINE BARRACKS in Washington, D.C., then served on legation duty in China before returning to Cuba during 1911–13. Barnett succeeded General WILLIAM P. BIDDLE as USMC commandant on February 25, 1914. A conflict with Secretary of the Navy Josephus Daniels prompted his resignation in 1920, and his last assignment was as commander of the newly created Department of the Pacific.

bases, camps, and other installations

The principal USMC installations include the Marine Barracks in Washington, D.C., seven air stations, five major bases (three of which are also known by their earlier designation as "camps"), two logistics bases, and two recruit depots.

Marine Barracks

"Marine Barracks" has two meanings as used in the USMC. It denotes a special guard unit assigned to ensure the internal security of major U.S. Navy shore stations, including the protection of USN nuclear weapons. It is also the name of the ceremonial and special security unit assigned to Washington, D.C., and located at 8th and I Streets (often nicknamed "8th and Eye"). Established in 1801, the MARINE BARRACKS is the oldest USMC post. Since 1806, it has included the residence of the COMMANDANT OF THE MARINE CORPS and is considered the "spiritual home" of the USMC.

The site of the Marine Barracks was selected with the personal approval of President Thomas Jefferson because it lay near the Navy Yard and was also within easy marching distance of the Capitol. The only remaining building that dates from the earliest days of the Marine Barracks is the 1806 Commandant's House at the north end of the Barracks quadrangle. The rest of the present Marine Barracks was built between 1900 and 1907.

Originally, the Marine Barracks was the principal site for training new USMC officers and recruits. Until 1901, it was also the location of HEADQUARTERS MARINE CORPS. From the beginning, the Marine Barracks has also been home of the U.S. MARINE BAND. Today, marines based at the Barracks undergo light infantry training, participate in ceremonies, and perform presidential support duty. The barracks is also home of the Marine Corps Institute, a training center responsible for all USMC nonresident military education programs.

Further reading: Marine Barracks web site: www.mbw.usmc.mil.

Marine Corps Air Station Beaufort

Located in Beaufort, South Carolina, the air station is the home of the USMC's Atlantic Coast fixed-wing, fighter-attack aircraft assets, Marine Air Group 31, which consists of seven USMC F/A-18 squadrons. Two U.S. Navy F/A-18 squadrons are also based at "Fightertown." The base is home to some 3,400 marines.

Further reading: MCAS Beaufort web site: www.beaufort.usmc.mil.

Marine Corps Air Station Cherry Point

Construction of the 8,000-acre Marine Corps airfield at Cherry Point, located in Craven County, North Carolina, between New Bern and Morehead City, began in summer 1941 and the site was commissioned as Cunningham Field during WORLD WAR II, on May 20, 1942, in honor of the first USMC aviator, Lieutenant Colonel Alfred A. Cunningham. The facility was redesignated Marine Corps Air Station, Cherry Point.

During World War II, Cherry Point was a training center as well as a base for anti-submarine operations. During the KOREAN WAR, it trained not only aviators and air crewmen but also maintenance and support personnel. During the VIETNAM WAR, Cherry Point deployed three A-6 Intruder squadrons to the Far East in addition to carrying out training functions. Cherry Point contributed to Operation Desert Storm during the PERSIAN GULF WAR, supporting the deployment of three AV-8B Harrier squadrons, two A-6E Intruder squadrons, one KC-130 Hercules squadron, one EA-6B Prowler squadron, and provided headquarters detachments from Marine Air Group 14, Marine Air Group 32, and the 2nd Marine Aircraft Wing. Cherry Point marines and sailors participated in operations in Afghanistan following the terrorist attacks of September 11, 2001, on the United States.

Further reading: MCAS Cherry Point web site: www.cherrypoint.usmc.mil.

Marine Corps Air Station Futenma

Located in Futenma, Okinawa, Japan, MCAS Futenma is home to MARINE AIRCRAFT GROUP 36 and Marine Air Control Group 18.

Further reading: MCAS Futenma web site: www.futenma.usmc.mil.

Marine Corps Air Station Iwakuni

MCAS Iwakuni is located on the main island of Honshu, Japan, about 25 miles south of Hiroshima.

It was originally a Japanese naval air facility, built in 1940, and, after World War II, was used by the British Royal Air Force, the Royal Australian Air Force, the U.S. Air Force, and the U.S. Navy. It was reassigned to the USMC in 1958 and is home to Marine Aircraft Group 12, Marine Wing Support Squadron 171, Combat Service Support Detachment 36, and the Japanese Maritime Self-Defense Force. The base deploys F-18 Hornets, AV-8 Harriers, EA-6 Prowlers, and the CH-53D Sea Stallion.

Further reading: MCAS Iwakuni web site: www.iwakuni.usmc.mil.

Marine Corps Air Station Miramar

MCAS Miramar is home to the 3rd Marine Aircraft Wing and houses some 11,000 personnel. Located in San Diego, California, Miramar started military life as an army base, Camp Kearny, in 1917, during WORLD WAR I. The U.S. Navy took it over in 1932, as a base for dirigible operations, and during World War II, both the USN and USMC occupied Miramar. After the war, the base was redesignated Marine Corps Air Station Miramar, but in 1947 the marines moved to El Toro, near Los Angeles. Miramar was redesignated a Naval Auxiliary Air Station, but was revived during the VIETNAM WAR as the USN's "Top Gun" school and "Fightertown, USA." In 1993, Naval Air Station Miramar was redesignated as Marine Corps Air Station Miramar, the USN's Top Gun school moved, and, in 1996, personnel from MCAS El Toro and Marine Corps Air Facility Tustin were relocated to Miramar. On July 2, 1999, MCAS El Toro and MCAF Tustin were closed.

Miramar operates F/A-18 Hornets and KC-130 Hercules squadrons, as well as its CH-46E Sea Knight and CH-53E Super Stallion helicopters. The air station covers more than 23,000 acres.

Further reading: MCAS Miramar web site: www.miramar.usmc.mil.

Marine Corps Air Station New River

MCAS New River is located in New River, North Carolina, adjacent to Marine Corps Base Camp Lejeune and began operations in 1944, during World War II, as Peterfield Point, named after a Mr. Peter, on whose former tobacco field much of the station was built. The station was inactivated after the war, then reactivated as Marine Corps Air Facility Peterfield Point, Camp Lejeune, in October 1951, during the Korean War. In 1952, it was renamed Marine Corps Air Field New River and became home to Marine Air Group 26, a helicopter unit. Redesignated Marine Corps Air Station (Helicopter) New River during the Vietnam War in 1968, the station became a major operational airfield. In May 1972, Marine Aircraft Group 29 and supporting units were installed at the station, and in 1983, New River–based squadrons flew combat missions during the invasion of GRENADA. New River marines also fought in Operations Desert Shield and Desert Storm during the Persian Gulf War in 1990–91.

Currently, New River-based units provide direct helicopter support for Marine Forces, Atlantic, and the 2,600-acre facility is the USMC's premier helicopter air station.

Further reading: MCAS New River web site: www.newriver.usmc.mil.

Marine Corps Air Station Yuma

Located in Yuma, Arizona, MCAS Yuma is a major aviation training base. With access to 2.8 million acres of bombing and aviation training ranges, MCAS Yuma supports 80 percent of USMC air-to-ground aviation training. The station is home to Marine Aviation Weapons and Tactics Squadron 1, Marine Aircraft Group 13, Marine Wing Support Squadron 371, Marine Fighter Training Squadron 401, Marine Air Control Squadron 1, and Combat Service Support Detachment 16.

The origin of MCAS Yuma was as Fly Field, a U.S. Army facility established in 1928. In 1943, during World War II, it became Yuma Army Air Base, a training facility for USAAF pilots. Inactivated after the war, it was reactivated by the U.S. Air Force during the Korean War, on July 7, 1951, and was signed over to the USN on January 1, 1959. It became MCAS Yuma on July 20, 1962, and served primarily as a training base for pilots flying the F-4 Phantom, A-4 Skyhawk, and AV-8A Harrier. Today, MCAS Yuma is the busiest air station in the USMC, its primary mission to support aerial weapons training for the FLEET MARINE FORCE, Atlantic and Fleet Marine Force, Pacific, as well as for the USN. MCAS Yuma also serves as a base of operations for Marine Aviation Weapons and Tactics Squadron 1 and Marine Aircraft Group 13.

Further reading: MCAS Yuma web site: www. yuma.usmc.mil.

Marine Corps Base Camp Lejeune
MCB Camp Lejeune is located in Onslow County, North Carolina, and was established in September 1941 by the 1st Marine Division. Today, Camp Lejeune encompasses 246 square miles and is a base for active units as well as the USMC's largest training facility.

When it was established, the base was called Marine Barracks New River, North Carolina. It was given its present name toward the end of 1942, in honor of the 13th Commandant of the Marine Corps, Major General JOHN A. LEJEUNE. Camp Lejeune has not only trained thousands of marines, it was also the site of the development of USMC special operations; today it also serves for special training in riverine and urban operations.

Camp Lejeune includes satellite facilities at Camp Geiger, Camp Johnson, Stone Bay, and the Greater Sandy Run Training Area. Camp Johnson, today a key training base, was the first training facility for African-American Marines (when it was called Montford Point). Camp Geiger is devoted to marine combat training, and, during World War II, was home to the 1st Marine Division. The total population of Camp Lejeune is 150,000 people, including civilian employees.

Further reading: MCB Camp Lejeune web site: www.lejeune.usmc.mil.

Marine Corps Base Camp Pendleton
MCB Camp Pendleton is the USMC's major base in the west. Located north of San Diego, California,

it was established in March 1942 and named for General JOSEPH H. PENDLETON. During World War II, Camp Pendleton was headquarters for the USMC Training and Replacement Command.

Today, Camp Pendleton consists of 3,800 buildings and structures on 200 square miles. There are 14 family housing areas, six on-base public schools, and a 600-bed naval hospital. Each year more than 40,000 active-duty and 26,000 reserve military personnel from all services use Camp Pendleton's ranges and training facilities. Located here is the USMC's premier amphibious training base. The facility is also home to the First Marine Expeditionary Force and two of its major subordinate commands, the 1st Marine Division and 1st Force Service Support Group.

Further reading: MCB Camp Pendleton web site: www.pendleton.usmc.mil.

Marine Corps Base Camp Smedley D. Butler
Located on OKINAWA, at Camp Foster, MCB Camp Smedley D. Butler is responsible for the operation of all USMC facilities on the island, including Camps Schwab, Kinser, McTureous, Hansen, Courtney, and Foster, as well as Marine Corps Air Station Futenma. MCB Camp Smedley D. Butler is headquarters of the THIRD Marine Expeditionary Force and 3rd Division.

Further reading: MCB Camp Smedley D. Butler web site: www.mcbbutler.usmc.mil.

Marine Corps Base Hawaii
MCB Hawaii consists of 4,500 acres on the island of Oahu and includes Camp Smith, Kaneohe Bay, Marine Corps Training Area Bellows, Manana Family Housing Area, Pearl City Warehouse Annex, and Puuoloa Range Complex. MCB Hawaii maintains key operations, training, and support facilities. The mission of MCB Hawaii is to "support readiness and global projection" for the USMC. Its tenant units include U.S. Pacific Command; 3rd Marine Regiment; Commander Patrol and Reconnaissance Force Pacific; Fleet Marine Force, Pacific; Marine

Aircraft Group 24; Helicopter Antisubmarine Squadron Light 37; Special Operations Command, Pacific; Combat Service Support Group 3; Fleet Logistics Support Squadron 51; Joint Task Force–Full Accounting; First Radio Battalion; Fleet Aviation Specialized Operational Training Group Pacific Detachment Hawaii; Defense Logistics Agency–Pacific; USMC College of Continuing Education Satellite Campus; National Security Agency Central Security Service Pacific Headquarters; and 4th Force Reconnaissance Company.

Further reading: MCB Hawaii web site: www. mcbh.usmc.mil.

Marine Corps Base Quantico

Marine Corps Base Quantico, usually shortened to Quantico, stretches for five miles along the Potomac River in Virginia, occupying about 100 square miles. It is the major USMC base on the East Coast and is the location of the Development and Education Command, the principal educational arm of the USMC.

Quantico was established during World War I, in April 1917, when the expanding Marine Corps outgrew its two principal bases in Philadelphia and Washington, and was first occupied the following month by the 5th Marines. Between the world wars, Quantico became the site of the USMC schools. By 1944, during World War II, Quantico was almost exclusively used as a replacement training center. Today, although the Marine Barracks in Washington, D.C., remains the spiritual center of the USMC, Quantico is at the heart of day-to-day operations.

Further reading: MCB Quantico web site: www. quantico.usmc.mil.

Marine Corps Logistics Base Albany

Located in Albany, Georgia, MCLB Albany furnishes supplies for USMC forces east of the Mississippi River and to forces that are part of Fleet Marine Force, Atlantic. Marine Corps Logistics Base Barstow supplies USMC forces west of the Mississippi, in the Far East and Asia.

Further reading: MCLB Albany web site: www. ala.usmc.mil/base.

Marine Corps Logistics Base Barstow

Located in Barstow, California, MCLB Barstow was established as the Marine Corps Depot of Supplies during World War II, on December 28, 1942. In November 1978, the base received its present title of Marine Corps Logistics Base, reflecting its broad logistics support mission.

The Marine Corps Logistics Bases are comprised of three major components, Marine Corps Logistics Base Albany, Georgia; MCLB Barstow, California; and Blount Island Command, Jacksonville, Florida. MCLB Albany furnishes supplies for USMC forces east of the Mississippi and to Fleet Marine Force, Atlantic. MCLB Barstow supports USMC forces west of the Mississippi and in the Far East and Asia. Blount Island Command provides logistical support for the USMC Maritime Prepositioning Ships and the Norway Geo-Prepositioning programs (see MARITIME PREPOSITIONING SQUADRONS).

The Barstow base is comprised of three principal sites: Nebo, which encompasses 1,879 acres and functions as base headquarters; the Yermo Annex, encompassing 1,859 acres and serving as a storage and industrial complex; and a third site, of 2,438 acres, serving as a rifle and pistol range.

Further reading: MCLB Barstow web site: www. bam.usmc.mil.

Marine Corps Recruit Depots

Familiarly called "Boot Camp," MCRDs provide BASIC TRAINING for new marines. The USMC has two MCRDs, Marine Corps Recruit Depot Parris Island, South Carolina, and Marine Corps Recruit Depot San Diego, California. Male recruits from east of the Mississippi and all female recruits train at Parris Island, whereas male recruits from west of the Mississippi are sent to San Diego. Under special circumstances, training may also take place at the Marine Barracks, Washington, D.C., Marine Corps Base Camp Lejeune, or Marine Corps Base Quantico, Virginia.

Boot camp consists of 11 weeks of basic training, encompassing USMC history, close-order drill, the military Code of Conduct, and other USMC fundamentals. Recruits are conditioned physically, and they master a confidence course; they are trained in self defense, lifesaving, PUGIL STICK, individual combat training, and marksmanship.

See also DRILL INSTRUCTOR.

Marine Corps Recruit Depot Parris Island

"Parris Island" is one of the most famous places in the USMC. Located off the coast of South Carolina, it has served as "boot camp" for more than a million USMC recruits since 1915. Today, Parris Island delivers basic training to male recruits from the eastern United States and to all female USMC recruits, regardless of region.

Further reading: MCRD Parris Island web site: www.mcrdpi.usmc.mil.

Marine Corps Recruit Depot San Diego

MCRD San Diego has a twofold mission: recruiting marines from the Western Recruiting Region and delivering basic training to male recruits from the western United States. The depot is located in San Diego, California.

Further reading: MCRD San Diego web site: www.mcrdsd.usmc.mil.

basic training

Basic training, familiarly called "boot camp," is delivered at two locations, Marine Corps Recruit Depot Parris Island and Marine Corps Recruit Depot San Diego. Men who enlist west of the Mississippi are assigned to San Diego. Men who enlist east of the river are sent to Parris Island, as are female recruits, regardless of where they enlist.

USMC basic training consists of 12 weeks of training in addition to a week of processing. It begins with Receiving, which includes basic indoctrination in the Uniform Code of Military Justice, paperwork processing, getting the traditional "buzz" haircut, and receiving initial uniforms and field gear. During three to five days in Receiving, recruits are given the Initial Strength Test (IST). Failure to do two pull-ups, 35 sit-ups (in two minutes), and a 1.5-mile run in 13.5 minutes means assignment to the Physical Conditioning Platoon.

During week 1 of basic, the DRILL INSTRUCTOR commences the process of "forming" through "total immersion." This includes immersion in USMC vocabulary, military courtesy, and general discipline in addition to a Physical Training routine. Week 1 also includes an introduction to bayonet fighting and to the M16A2 rifle. Martial arts training was also added to the basic training program in 2000 and is introduced in week 1.

Week 2 continues the basics of close combat skills, including the use of the PUGIL STICK. Field first aid and academic classes on USMC values and

Trainees move to another stage of basic training on Parris Island.   *(U.S. Marine Corps)*

other subjects are also part of week 2, as is instruction on basic weapons handling.

Week 3 continues pugil stick exercise and other close combat training, more advanced classes on first aid and values, a 3-mile march (with packs), and the "Confidence Course"—an obstacle course.

Week 4 continues pugil stick and close combat training, as well as academic classes. Platoon drill is emphasized during this week as well.

Week 5 includes Combat Water Survival, a 5-mile hike, an examination on marine customs and courtesies, more first aid training and academics, and a major inspection.

Weeks 6 and 7 are devoted mainly to weapons training, including live-fire training with the M-16. In addition, recruits receive basic training in grenades and other types of weapons and, in week 7, take a 6-mile night march and run the Confidence Course a second time.

Week 8, called "Team Week," is devoted to various fatigue duties, such as work in the mess hall. It is followed during week 9 by training in the fundamentals of field firing and a 10-mile march.

Week 10 trains in the basics of patrolling, firing, setting up camp, and other field skills. Recruits are also given nuclear-biological-chemical training.

Week 11 begins with the Company Commander's Inspection and culminates in "The Crucible"—a 54-hour ordeal that includes food and sleep deprivation and some 40 miles of marching and problem solving as well as teamwork tests. When the Crucible is successfully completed, the DI presents each recruit with the USMC EMBLEM.

Week 12 is the final week and includes indoctrination in USMC history and other classes.

After basic training, graduates go on to further training at the SCHOOL OF INFANTRY. Those designated as infantry marines graduate from the school to their first permanent duty station, while non-infantry marines are assigned to the Marine Combat Training Battalion at the School of Infantry. MCT enhances combat skills and prepares marines for further training in the appropriate USMC "military occupation specialty" (MOS) school.

Basilone, John (1916–1945) *Marine Corps gunnery sergeant*
Born in Buffalo, New York, Basilone attended local parochial schools, then enlisted in the U.S. Army and served in the Philippines. In July 1940, he left the USA and enlisted in the USMC, serving in Cuba, at Marine Corps Base Quantico, and at Camp Lejeune before he was deployed with the 7th Marines to the South Pacific during WORLD WAR II.

In the Lunga area of Guadalcanal, on October 24, 1942, he took charge of two machine gun sections and was principally responsible for repulsing repeated Japanese attacks. Ultimately, his actions resulted in the destruction of an entire Japanese regiment. For this, Basilone was awarded the Medal of Honor.

While serving on Iwo Jima as a gunnery sergeant with the 27th Marines, Basilone single-handedly attacked and demolished a blockhouse under heavy fire. Although he succeeded in this mission, he was cut down by enemy fire. He was awarded the Navy Cross posthumously. A U.S. Navy destroyer was also named in Basilone's honor.

battalion   See ORGANIZATION BY UNITS.

beachhead
In an AMPHIBIOUS ASSAULT, the area of the enemy's shore where troops and equipment are landed. The first objective of the assault is to secure the beachhead, which then becomes the maneuver area from which the assault is pushed inland. During ongoing operations, the beachhead is the point at which supplies and reinforcements are landed. The beachhead serves as the main support base until a port or harbor is captured from the enemy. Supply operations into and out of the beachhead are the responsibility of a logistics officer known as the "beachmaster."

Belleau Wood
One of the great USMC triumphs of WORLD WAR I. The 4th Marine Brigade, attached to the army's

2nd Division, not only successfully repelled a German attack in this location on the Western Front (June 6, 1918), but also staged a determined counteroffensive at great cost (1,087 casualties) but with great effect. The marines repelled another counterattack and, on June 23, resumed the offensive, securing the entire woods by June 26. A grateful French commander renamed Belleau Wood *Bois de la Brigade de Marine,* and the Germans took to calling the marines "devil dogs" (after which the USMC adopted its English bulldog mascot).

bellhop

Derogatory term sailors sometimes apply to a marine, especially one serving aboard ship. Also called a "seagoing bellhop."

Biddle, William P. (1853–1923) *Marine Corps commandant*

The 11th COMMANDANT OF THE MARINE CORPS, Biddle received his officer's commission in 1875 and served in the SPANISH-AMERICAN WAR and the BOXER REBELLION. Subsequently, he was stationed in the Philippines and in PANAMA. He succeeded Commandant GEORGE F. ELLIOTT on February 3, 1911, and served until February 24, 1914, when he retired.

Bladensburg, Battle of

During the WAR OF 1812, this town in Maryland, five miles east of Washington, D.C., was the site of a one-sided skirmish, on August 24, 1814, between U.S. Army and raw militia troops on the one side and an invasion force of British regulars commanded by General Robert Ross on the other. Although Ross brushed aside the army and militia troops, who barely offered resistance, 400 U.S. Navy sailors and 103 marines used five pieces of naval artillery to block the road to Washington. Their position was ultimately hopeless, since they were vastly outnumbered, but they held the road long enough to give President James Madison and the government sufficient time to evacuate the capital. The marines and sailors repulsed three full-on infantry charges before they were finally flanked and forced to withdraw.

Once in Washington, Ross and his men put most of the public buildings to the torch.

Boeing PW-9   See AIRCRAFT, FIXED-WING.

Boomer, Walter E. (1938–   ) *Marine Corps general*

Born in Rich Square, North Carolina, Boomer took a B.A. from Duke University in 1960 and completed USMC Basic School the following year. He served with the 2nd Division at Marine Corps Base Quantico and was promoted to captain in 1966. He served in Vietnam during the VIETNAM WAR as commanding officer of a company in the 4th Marines during 1966. After his tour, in 1967, he

General Walter E. Boomer   *(U.S. Marine Corps)*

attended the Amphibious Warfare School, then became aide-de-camp (with the rank of major), assigned to the deputy chief of staff for plans in Washington, D.C. After attending the Armed Forces Staff College and taking the Short Advisors Course in 1971, he returned to Vietnam as an adviser to a South Vietnamese marine infantry battalion.

Boomer returned to the United States, where he received an M.S. degree in management and technology from American University, then was assigned to the U.S. Naval Academy in 1974, where he was chairman of the Department of Management. In 1977, Boomer was assigned as executive officer of the 3rd Marines in Hawaii, and in 1980 became commander of the 2nd Battalion of the 3rd Marines.

Boomer attended the Naval War College in 1980–81, then was assigned to the 4th Corps district in Philadelphia. Promoted to colonel in 1983, Boomer became director of the 4th Corps district. He was given command of the Marine Security Guard at Quantico in 1985, promoted to brigadier general the following year, and named director of public affairs at Marine Headquarters, Washington.

Boomer was given command of 4th Division in March 1989 and promoted to major general. The next year came promotion to lieutenant general and an appointment as commander of the Marine Central Command and the First Expeditionary Force. These he led during the PERSIAN GULF WAR (Operations Desert Shield and Desert Storm) during 1990–91.

After the war, Boomer became commanding general of Corps Combat Development Command at Quantico. He was promoted to general and assigned, on September 1, 1992, as assistant commandant. Boomer retired in 1994.

boot camp   See BASIC TRAINING.

Bougainville, Battle of

One of the Solomon Islands, Bougainville was occupied by Japanese forces early in WORLD WAR II. Operation Cherry Blossom was conceived by U.S. Navy planners to take Bougainville and use it for an air base from which to stage operations against Rabaul and NEW BRITAIN. The main Japanese base on Bougainville was located on the southern end of the island. Instead of attacking here, the 3rd Marine Division was landed at Empress Augusta Bay, a third of the way up the west coast of Bougainville, on November 1, 1943. The landing was preceded by intense naval and aerial bombardment, which knocked out Japanese naval and air strength on the island. Since few troops were positioned near Empress Augusta Bay, the USMC landing was almost unopposed, and the marines quickly established a perimeter. The army's 37th Division landed on November 8 and positioned itself on the marines' right flank. From here, USMC and USA forces advanced on the main Japanese position. Even while this action was proceeding, a fighter airstrip was quickly scratched out, followed by a bomber field.

By the end of December, the U.S. Army's Americal Division relieved USMC forces on Bougainville. In March 1944, the army had to resist two substantial Japanese assaults. Later, the army units were relieved by Australian troops, who continued to fight Japanese resistance until the very end of the war. Although Bougainville was never completely secured, it served from the end of 1943 to the end of the war as a base for American fighters and bombers.

Boxer Rebellion

Antiforeign rebels, covertly supported by the Empress Dowager, de facto ruler of China, attacked Europeans and Americans, including diplomats, in Peking (Beijing) and Tientsin in 1900. The rebels called themselves the "Righteous Fists of Harmony," which prompted Westerners to refer to them as the Boxers and the ensuing conflict as the Boxer Rebellion.

A small coalition of European and American military forces was sent to relieve the besieged diplomatic legations in Peking, to restore order,

Painting by Sergeant John Clymer (USMC) shows marines fighting the Boxers outside the Peking Legation, 1900. *(National Archives and Records Administration)*

and to put down the uprising. On May 24, 1900, Captain John Myers led a contingent of 54 marines and 5 sailors on a march to Peking. They arrived, with European troops, at the end of the month. The marines successfully held a position at the southwest corner of Legation Square and even counterattacked with good effect. The arrival of a multinational relief column, the 1st Marine Regiment, on August 13 enabled the liberation of all the legation buildings by August 14. The relief of Peking ended the Boxer Rebellion. Although greatly outnumbered initially, USMC losses were 17 killed and wounded.

Boyington, Gregory "Pappy" (1912–1988)
Marine Corps aviator

Most famous USMC aviator of WORLD WAR II, Boyington commanded Squadron 214, consisting mostly of novice pilots and known as the "Black Sheep" squadron. At 31, Boyington was the old man of the bunch and thus merited the nickname "Pappy." Piloting his F4U Corsair, Boyington personally shot down 14 Japanese aircraft in 32 days during the first combat tour of the squadron. He fought at GUADALCANAL, New Georgia, New Britain, and Rabaul before he was shot down and made a prisoner of war on January 3, 1944. He was liberated on August 29, 1945. Boyington received the Medal of Honor and retired from the USMC, a colonel, in 1947. His exploits became the basis of a popular television series, *Black Sheep Squadron*.

brig

USMC and USN term for a prison or other place of punitive confinement, either aboard ship or on shore.

Colonel Gregory "Pappy" Boyington (USMC)   *(U.S. Marine Corps)*

brigade   See ORGANIZATION BY UNITS.

brigadier general   See RANKS AND GRADES.

burp
U.S. Army slang for a marine.

Burrows, William Ward (1758–1805)
   Marine Corps commandant
Burrows was the first commandant of the U.S. Marine Corps, appointed by President John Adams on July 12, 1798, the day after Congress passed legislation creating the Marine Corps; traditionally, however, the marines have regarded SAMUEL NICHOLAS, captain of the CONTINENTAL MARINES, as the first commandant of the Corps and Burrows as the second. Burrows served from 1798 until March 6, 1804, when ill health forced his retirement.

Born in Charleston, South Carolina, on January 16, 1758, Burrows served in the AMERICAN REVOLUTION with the state troops of South Carolina and was commissioned a major at the time of his appointment as marine commandant. His command consisted of 881 officers, noncommissioned officers, privates, and musicians.

Burrows organized the marines primarily for service aboard some 25 navy vessels during the undeclared naval conflict generally called the Franco-American Quasi-War (1798–1800). Major Burrows was promoted to lieutenant colonel on May 1, 1800, but, as the Quasi-War wound down, he found himself embattled with a parsimonious Congress, which stinted on funds for the Corps and ordered a reduction in its already modest size. This made it very difficult for the commandant to recruit the caliber of personnel he wanted in what he intended to become an elite organization. Nevertheless, Burrows demanded high standards of professional performance and personal conduct from the officers and enlisted personnel he did manage to recruit. These standards stood the Corps in good stead when hostilities escalated with the BARBARY PIRATES and Congress authorized the expansion of the marines. As Burrows had fought the earlier reduction, now he presided over the expansion.

Commandant Burrows established a number of marine institutions, including the MARINE BARRACKS that still stand at Eighth and I Streets in Washington, D.C., and the first U.S. MARINE BAND, which he partially financed by securing contributions from his officers. Most important, his insistence on the highest possible standards of professionalism and character established a rigorous tradition that became a Marine Corps hallmark.

Butler, Smedley D. (1881–1940) *Marine Corps general*
Smedley D. Butler, nicknamed "Ol' Gimlet Eye," was one of two marines in the history of the Corps to receive *two* Medals of Honor (see also DALY, DANIEL). Born on July 30, 1881, in West Chester, Pennsylvania, he secured a marine commission as a

second lieutenant on May 20, 1898, by lying about his age. Sent to Cuba during the SPANISH-AMERICAN WAR, he arrived too late to see any action and returned to Washington, D.C., for a brief period of instruction. He was next assigned to the Marine Battalion, North Atlantic Squadron, with which he served until February 11, 1899. He was honorably discharged a few days later, on February 16, 1899, but quickly returned to the Corps, reentering with a commission as first lieutenant on April 8, 1899.

Butler was immediately assigned to duty with the Marine Battalion at Manila, Philippine Islands; then, from June 14, 1900, to October of that year, he served in China, during the BOXER REBELLION. He was breveted to the rank of captain for his heroism in action near Tientsin, during which he was wounded on July 13, 1900.

Butler returned to the United States in January 1901 and served variously ashore and at sea before he was promoted to major in 1909 and, in Decem-

Major General Smedley D. Butler (USMC)   *(U.S. Marine Corps)*

ber of that year, assigned to command the 3rd Battalion, 1st Marine Regiment in PANAMA. He was detached to command an expeditionary battalion to NICARAGUA on August 11, 1912, and participated in the bombardment, assault, and capture of Coyotepe, during October 12 to 31. He returned to Panama in November 1912 and, in 1914, was deployed with marines to Veracruz, Mexico, where he commanded the force that landed and occupied the city. For action here during April 21–22, he received his first Medal of Honor, going on to claim his second the very next year, for his bravery and leadership as commanding officer of detachments of the marines and sailors who repulsed Caco resistance at Fort Rivière, HAITI, on November 17, 1915.

In August 1916, Butler was promoted to lieutenant colonel and, during WORLD WAR I, commanded the 13th Marine Regiment in France. He emerged from the Great War with the Army Distinguished Service Medal, the Navy Distinguished Service Medal, and the French Order of the Black Star. Promoted to the temporary rank of colonel on July 1, 1918, and to temporary brigadier general on October 7, he reverted to permanent colonel on March 9, 1919, but was soon promoted to the permanent rank of brigadier general and was appointed commanding general of the Marine Barracks, Quantico, Virginia, serving in this capacity from 1920 to January 1924. Butler was the youngest general officer in the history of the Corps.

In January 1924, Butler was granted a leave of absence to accept the post of director of public safety of the city of Philadelphia, but, two years later, in February 1926, he returned to active duty as commandant of Marine Corps Base San Diego, California. In March 1927, Butler returned to China with the 3rd Marine Brigade, then came back to the States later in the year to resume command at Quantico. Promoted to major general on July 5, 1929, Butler was passed over for the post of COMMANDANT OF THE MARINE CORPS and, in disappointment, retired on October 1, 1931.

Always a maverick, Butler probably should not have been surprised that he was not named commandant. In 1935, he published *War Is a Racket,* a shockingly candid memoir that characterized the role of the marines in China and Central America as hired thugs protecting the interests of American big business. In addition to publishing this scathing book, Butler also exposed what he identified as a fascist/corporate cabal to overthrow President Franklin Roosevelt immediately after his inauguration in 1933.

Butler died at the Naval Hospital, Philadelphia, on June 21, 1940, after a brief illness.

C

C-12 Huron See AIRCRAFT, FIXED-WING.

camp

In contrast to a post—a permanent military installation—a camp is a temporary installation; however, note that some permanent USMC facilities include the word "camp" in their name, for example, Camp LeJeune.

See also BASES, CAMPS, AND OTHER INSTALLATIONS.

captain See RANKS AND GRADES.

Carlson, Evans F. (1896–1947) *Marine Corps commando*

Carlson was a pioneer of the concept of an elite ranger or commando force, which he led to great effect in WORLD WAR II.

A native of Portland, Oregon, Carlson first joined the U.S. Army in 1912, and attained the rank of sergeant by the time he was discharged in 1916 after serving in Hawaii and the Philippines. He reenlisted and was part of General John J. Pershing's Punitive Expedition against Pancho Villa later in 1916. During World War I, he served in the Argonne campaign, in which he was wounded. Commissioned a second lieutenant in May 1917, he was promoted to captain and served in the army of occupation.

In 1922, Carlson enlisted in the USMC as a private, but was soon commissioned (in 1923), based on his army experience. He served at Marine Corps Base Quantico, Puerto Rico, Pensacola, and Shanghai, then fought against insurgents in Nicaragua. His action leading a small unit earned him the

Brigadier General Evans Fordyce Carlson (USMC)
(U.S. Marine Corps)

40

Navy Cross—and doubtless inspired his interest in developing small-unit tactics.

In 1933, Carlson was assigned to the U.S. legation in Peking (Beijing), China, and began to learn Chinese. After a brief return to the United States, he was sent back to China in 1937, this time as a military observer during the Sino-Japanese War. During 1937–38, he studied guerrilla tactics with Chinese communist forces and was so struck by the dangers of Japanese aggression that he briefly resigned from the USMC to devote himself to lecturing on the topic.

Carlson reentered the USMC in 1941, on the eve of WORLD WAR II, at the rank of major. He was given command of the 2nd Marine Raider Battalion and shaped this unit into an elite commando/guerrilla force. "Carlson's Raiders" fought on Makin Island (August 1942)—an action for which Carlson, now a lieutenant colonel, won his second Navy Cross—and on GUADALCANAL. Carlson led his Raiders in classic small-unit actions during this pivotal 1942 battle.

Carlson functioned as an observer of the TARAWA invasion and served as a vital liaison between the overall commander and the commander on the ground. Carlson also ensured logistical continuity during the Guadalcanal campaign; he kept supplies flowing to the advanced and isolated USMC units. After Guadalcanal, Carlson was named assistant operations officer of the 4th Marine Division, charged with assisting with plans for the invasion of the MARSHALL ISLANDS early in 1944. Wounded in action on SAIPAN in June 1944, Carlson was forced to retire in July 1946 as a brigadier general.

Cates, Clifton B. (1893–1970) *Marine Corps commandant*

The 19th COMMANDANT OF THE MARINE CORPS, Cates was born and raised in Tennessee, graduated with a law degree from the University of Tennessee in 1916, then served in the MARINE CORPS RESERVE. With America's entry into WORLD WAR I, Cates was sent to France in 1918 and led a platoon of the 6th

Marines at BELLEAU WOOD and in other engagements. Wounded six times and gassed, Cates was decorated with the Navy Cross, the Silver Star, the Croix de Guerre, and the French Legion of Honor. He remained in the USMC after the war, serving on sea duty, then becoming a White House aide to the commandant of the Marine Corps. Later he served as aide-de-camp to the commander of the Pacific. Joining the 4th Marines at Shanghai in 1929, he served in China until 1932. Back in the States, he served in the War Plans section at USMC headquarters, then returned to China in command of a regiment. In 1940, he was given command of the USMC Basic School in Philadelphia.

During WORLD WAR II, Colonel Cates led the 1st Marines at GUADALCANAL, then returned to the United States in 1943 with the rank of brigadier general. He was given command of Marine Base Quantico, then returned to the Pacific front in 1944 as commander of the 4th Marine Division and led the successful attacks on TINIAN and then on IWO JIMA, in February 1945. Returning to the United States later in the year, he once again assumed command at Quantico.

Promoted to general in 1948, he was appointed commandant and immediately found himself obliged to fight for the future of the USMC, which was the victim of severe postwar cutbacks. Cates was highly successful in rallying congressional support for the USMC; this and the outbreak of the KOREAN WAR put an end to the cutbacks and prompted an expansion.

In 1952, at the conclusion of his four-year term as commandant, he requested continued active duty. To secure this, he accepted reversion to the rank of lieutenant general and took command at Quantico. When he finally retired on January 30, 1954, his four-star rank was reinstated.

CH-37 "Mojave"   See AIRCRAFT, ROTARY-WING.

CH-46 Sea Knight   See AIRCRAFT, ROTARY-WING.

CH-53D Sea Stallion   See AIRCRAFT, ROTARY-WING.

CH-53E Super Stallion   See AIRCRAFT, ROTARY-WING.

Chapman, Leonard F., Jr. (1913–   ) *Marine Corps commandant*

The 24th COMMANDANT OF THE MARINE CORPS, Chapman was raised in Florida and received an army commission after completing a University of Florida ROTC course; however, he entered the USMC in 1935, received artillery training, and served with the 10th Marines before he was sent to Hawaii in 1940. He was on sea duty during the early part of WORLD WAR II in the Pacific.

In 1942, Major Chapman was assigned as an artillery instructor at Marine Corps Base Quantico, and in 1944, as a lieutenant colonel, he took command of a battalion of the 11th Marines at PELELIEU. He continued as 4th Battalion commander at OKINAWA during April–July 1945.

After the war, Chapman served in the USMC Division of Plans, then in important positions at Quantico and Marine Corps Base Camp Pendleton. He took command of the 12th Marines in 1952, serving with them in Japan before going on to command Marine Barracks Yokosuka. After commanding the Force Troops of the FLEET MARINE FORCE Atlantic (1958–61), Chapman was promoted to brigadier general and was named deputy chief of staff at HEADQUARTERS MARINE CORPS, Washington, D.C. On January 1, 1968, as a major general, Chapman became assistant chief of staff. After WALLACE GREENE retired as commandant of the USMC, Chapman replaced him on January 1, 1968. Chapman was commandant during the first stages of U.S. troop withdrawal from Vietnam (see VIETNAM WAR). When he retired from the USMC on December 31, 1971, he was named director of the U.S. Immigration and Naturalization Service.

Chapultepec, Battle of

Chapultepec was a hilltop fortress two miles southwest of Belen Gate, one of the entrances to Mexico City. As General Winfield Scott's (USA) forces closed on the Mexican capital during the U.S.-MEXICAN WAR, Chapultepec was garrisoned by about 800 men and was heavily defended by artillery. The young students of an on-site military academy also participated in the defense of this position.

On September 13, 1847, a USMC battalion attached to the army's 2nd Brigade attacked Chapultepec from the south. Marines were part of a 40-man advance party that stormed the walls of Chapultepec during the initial assault. Simultaneously, marines captured Mexican artillery and neutralized it.

After Chapultepec fell, Mexico City followed, and marines were assigned mop-up operations on the day after the capital surrendered. USMC personnel raised the Stars and Stripes over the National Palace.

The USMC action at Chapultepec and Mexico City is commemorated in the "Halls of Montezuma" reference in the MARINE HYMN.

Château-Thierry

This French town, on the River Aisne, 60 miles northeast of Paris, was a principal objective of a German offensive late in WORLD WAR I. The 2nd Division took over defense of Château-Thierry from the battle-weary French on May 30, 1918. By June 6, the marines had stopped the German advance and commenced a counteroffensive at BELLEAU WOOD. With Belleau Wood, Château-Thierry demonstrated the extraordinary combat performance of the USMC.

Chemical Agent Monitor   See NUCLEAR-BIOLOGICAL-CHEMICAL EQUIPMENT.

chicken plate

Marine and army slang for a steel or ceramic insert worn inside a bullet-proof vest for added protection.

chief of naval operations (CNO)

The CNO is effectively the U.S. Navy's chief of staff. He or she commands the major USN headquarters and shore commands and activities as well as the operating forces of the USN. It is to the CNO (and the SECRETARY OF THE NAVY) that the COMMANDANT OF THE MARINE CORPS reports.

Choiseul Raid

Choiseul is one of the Solomon Islands in the Pacific, and in October 1943 during WORLD WAR II the little island became the target of a USMC paratroop landing. The battalion-strength raid was led by Colonel VICTOR KRULAK on October 27 and was intended to draw Japanese forces away from BOUGAINVILLE, the main objective of a combined USMC-USA assault. The marines knew they were greatly outnumbered—at least 4,300 Japanese occupied the island—but their objective was not to capture Choiseul, but merely to create a diversion.

This succeeded, although historians still dispute whether or not the raid was necessary, and many doubt that it caused the Japanese to modify their Bougainville positions. Nevertheless, the marines were successfully evacuated in November, and the operation is celebrated in USMC annals as an example of outstanding performance against a vastly superior enemy force—the kind of mission for which the USMC is specially trained and suited.

Chosin Reservoir, Battle of

On October 26, 1950, during the KOREAN WAR, the 1st Marine Division (attached to X Corps, USA) was transported to Wonson, on the east coast of the Korean Peninsula and assigned to attack the hydroelectric plant at Chosin. On November 2, while advancing along a rugged mountain road northwest of Hungnam, the 7th Marines made contact with Chinese forces. Nevertheless, by November 10, marines had reached the southern end of the

U.S. forces withdrew southward following the massive Chinese intervention in the Korean War. Shown here is Weapons Company, in line with Headquarters and Service Company, 2nd Battalion, 7th Marines, on November 27, 1950.   *(Naval Historical Center)*

Chosin Reservoir. Elements of this force moved west to Yudam-ni, where, on November 26, they were joined by the 5th Marines. In the meantime, the 1st Marines were thinly distributed to the rear, assigned to hold open the lines of communication to the advance marine positions. Thus strung out along a zone of action approximately 300 miles long, the marines were expected to effect a pincers action to flank North Korean forces in the area. Two adversaries intervened, however. The weather plunged below zero, and the Communist Chinese crossed the border in great numbers in a massive incursion into the war.

The Chinese attacks halted the U.S. advance to the Yalu River, then turned it. The thinly distributed marines found themselves under heavy attack and, as the great Eighth Army retreated, they were forced, in small units, to fight for their survival. They succeeded to a remarkable degree, but Chosin Reservoir is recorded in USMC annals as perhaps the most bitter fight of the Korean War.

Close Quarters Battle/Direct Action Program

The Close Quarters Battle/Direct Action Program consists of the following components: Individual Assault Kit, Assault Breacher's Kit, HAZMAT Assault Mask, Assault Vest, and Assault Suit. It is intended for use by Force Reconnaissance Companies; Marine Corps Security Force Battalions, Fleet Anti-terrorist Security Team (FAST) Companies, Special Operations Training Groups (SOTGs), Marine Security Guard (MSG) Units, and Military and Police Special Reaction Teams (SRTs).

The function of the Close Quarters Battle/Direct Action Program is to provide standardized personal, protective, and load-bearing capability for select Special Operations personnel. The Individual Assault Kit contains items required by the individual marine for the Direct Action, including climbing/rappelling equipment, individual protective apparel, personnel restraining devices, and load-bearing and accessory equipment. The As-

sault Breacher's Kit includes tools and equipment (other than munitions) to conduct mechanical and explosive forced entries into enclosed buildings and structures. Its components consist of mechanical entry devices, hand tools, firing devices, and safety equipment. The HAZMAT Assault Mask provides protection from toxic fumes that may be encountered during DA operations. This advanced mask incorporates enhanced communications and an expanded field of view. The Assault Vest combines combat load-bearing capabilities with enhanced torso ballistic protection. The Assault Suit provides a functional, durable, fire-retardant, protective outerwear that combines the most desirable features of the combat vehicle crewman/aviator suits.

The Close Quarters Battle/Direct Action Program package was designed using the input of marines who have performed the DA mission. It is intended to ensure that those performing the mission will have state-of-the-art equipment and that no improvisation of equipment will be necessary.

code talkers   See NAVAJO CODE TALKERS.

color sergeant of the U.S. Marine Corps

This noncommissioned officer commands the U.S. MARINE CORPS COLOR GUARD and also serves as the keeper of the Battle Color of the USMC—the official USMC flag. Special qualifications for the color sergeant include a height of at least 6 feet 4 inches and a White House security clearance. The color sergeant carries the National Ensign (U.S. flag) in ceremonies and the Presidential Color in all White House state functions and ceremonies. The color sergeant must use only one arm to carry the flag, whereas other military services permit both arms to be used.

Combat Rubber Raiding Craft   See

LANDING CRAFT.

Combat Service Support Schools (MCCSS)

The Marine Corps CSSS conducts formal resident training for commissioned officers and noncommissioned officers in logistics, motor transport, personnel administration, supply, and fiscal accounting and disbursing. The schools also conduct instructional management and combat water survival swim training.

MCCSSS is located at Camp Johnson, adjacent to Marine Corps Base Camp Lejeune, North Carolina. The individual schools include:

Combat Water Survival Swimming School

The Combat Water Survival Swimming School trains marine combat water survival instructors. The school works closely with the navy and the American Red Cross in developing appropriate advanced training.

Further reading: Web site: www.lejeune.usmc.mil/mccsss/schools/cwsss/cwsss.shtml.

Financial Management School

The Financial Management School provides six formal courses of instruction to marines as well as to Department of Defense civilian personnel: Financial Management Officer Course—Finance; Financial Management Officer Course—Comptroller; Advanced Finance Course; Financial Management Career Course; Basic Finance Technician Course; and Fiscal Budget Technician Course.

Further reading: Web site: www.lejeune.usmc.mil/mccsss/schools/fms/fms.shtml.

Instructional Management School

The Instructional Management School trains and educates the personnel who train and educate marines. Three sets of courses are offered:

1. The Formal School Instructor Course covers basic communication skills, preparation techniques, and adult learning, employing various teaching methods and instructional aids.
2. The Curriculum Developer Course focuses on the design and development of instructional materials, including conducting a learning analysis, writing learning objectives, test items, selecting a delivery system (method/media), media development, and constructing of both instructor and student outlines.
3. The Administrator Course addresses the management and supervision of instruction using the Systems Approach to Training (SAT), specially developed for the marines.

Further reading: Web site: www.lejeune.usmc.mil/mccsss/schools/ims/ims.shtml.

Logistics Operations School

The Logistics Operations School trains marines in organizational and intermediate motor transport maintenance, logistics and motor transport operations, maintenance management, landing support operations, and embarkation.

Further reading: Web site: www.lejeune.usmc.mil/mccsss/schools/los/los.shtml.

Personnel Administration School

The Personnel Administration School provides basic, intermediate, and advanced, resident, formal school instruction to marine personnel administrators, with special emphasis on combat service support. The Administrative Clerk Course and the Personnel Clerk Course are the entry-level offerings. Career-level courses are the Adjutant Course, Personnel Officer Course, Advanced Personnel Administration Course, Senior Clerk Course, and Reserve Administration Course.

Further reading: Web site: www.lejeune.usmc.mil/mccsss/schools/pals/pals.shtml.

Supply School

The Supply School designs, develops, conducts, and evaluates entry-level, intermediate, and advanced resident, formal education and training for officers and enlisted personnel assigned to the marine corps supply occupational field. The school offers the following courses of study:

Ground Supply Officer Course
Noncommissioned Officer Supply Course
Ground Supply Chief Course
Enlisted Supply Independent Duty Course
Basic Preservation and Packaging Course
Enlisted Supply Basic Course
Enlisted Warehouse Basic Course
Functional System Administrator Course
Enlisted Supply Basic Course (Reserve)
Ground Supply Officer Course (Reserve)

Further reading: Web site: www.lejeune.usmc.mil/
mccsss/schools/supplyschool.

combined arms team

A USMC and U.S. Army term for combat force in
which two or more arms are represented; for
example, aircraft providing close air support for
an infantry assault may be said to constitute a
combined arms team, as does (for instance) a team
that combines infantry, engineers, and defense
artillery.

commandant of the Marine Corps

The CMC reports to the SECRETARY OF THE NAVY and
THE CHIEF OF NAVAL OPERATIONS and is responsible
for the administration, discipline, organization,
training, and readiness of the USMC. The CMC is
a member of the Joint Chiefs of Staff.

communications equipment

Special communications equipment used by the
marines includes:

AN/TTC-42 (V)
Automatic Telephone Central Office

The AN/TTC-42 (V) Automatic Telephone Central
Office is an important component of USMC communications, providing automatic telephone
switching and satellite telephone subscriber service. It is an S-280 shelterized telephone central
office, which provides secure automatic switching
service (loop-to-loop, loop-to-trunk, and trunk-

to-trunk) as well as such subscriber service functions as loop and trunk hunting, precedence, and
preemption. These services are available to the
TRI-TAC family of 4-wire, digital subscribers
and non-secure voice terminals (DSVTs and
DNVTs) and to 4-wire digital trunks, including
both single-channel and Time Division Multiplexed (TDM) groups. The AN/TTC-42 will also
perform automatic switching for 4-wire analog
loops and trunks. Sophisticated communication
security used in the AN/TTC-42 includes the HGF-
93, HGF-94, KG-82, KG-93, and KG-94 protocols.
The USMC has 61 AN/TTC-42 (V) Automatic
Telephone Central Offices—at a unit cost of $2
million—allocated as of late 2003.

General characteristics of the system include:

Contractor: ITT Aerospace/Communications
Division
Length: 181 in
Width: 88.4 in
Height: 87 in
Weight: 5,525 lb
Displacement: 805.3 cu ft
Power: 115/230 volts, 50/60 hertz single-phase,
3 kilowatt; 30 ampere
Terminations: 280 circuits—180 via 7 mux
groups and 100 single-channel terminations
Circuits: 152 switched (loops and trunks) and
144 sole user
Trunks: 90 (up to 24 analog)
Multiplexed groups: four
Signaling modes: analog 4-wire DTMF, 4-wire
SF AC Supervised AUTOVON
Traffic (average): 650 calls/hr

SB-3865
Automatic Telephone Switchboard

The SB-3865 Automatic Telephone Switchboard is
a team-transportable, tactical, digital switching
system for voice and data communication across
secure as well as non-secure telephone lines. It provides automatic switching service (loop-to-loop,
loop-to-trunk, and trunk-to-trunk) and subscriber
service functions such as loop and trunk hunting,
precedence, and preemption. The USMC main-

tained 425 of the switchboards in its inventory as of 2004.

General characteristics of the SB-3865 Automatic Telephone Switchboard include:

Manufacturer: ITT Aerospace/Communications Division
Length, switch module: 20.7 in
Length, power module: 20.6 in
Width, switch module: 21.1 in
Width, power module: 17.8 in
Height, switch module: 19.6 in
Height, power module: 17.7 in
Weight, switch module: 99 lb
Weight, power module: 125 lb
Displacement, switch module: 3.5 cu ft
Displacement, power module: 3.5 cu ft
Power source: 120/208 VAC, 50/60 or 400 hertz single-phase, 480 watts, or 28 VDC, 304 watts
Terminations: 86 circuits per module (maximum of 96 per stack)
Circuits: 32 switched (loops and trunks) or 36 sole user
Trunks: 18 per module, 54 per stack maximum
Multiplexed groups: Three per module, nine per stack maximum
Signaling modes: analog 2-wire and 4-wire DTMF, 4-wire SF AC Supervised AUTOVON
Traffic: 130 calls/hr per module, 390 per stack maximum

Single-Channel Ground and Airborne Radio System (SINCGARS)

This USMC system provides the primary means of command, control, and communications (C^3) for the Ground Combat Element, Air Combat Element, and Combat Service Support Element of the MARINE AIR GROUND TASK FORCE (MAGTF). SINCGARS is capable of transmitting voice and analog or digital data up to 16 kilobytes per second. The system employs electronic counter-countermeasures to minimize vulnerability to enemy electronic warfare, and it provides secure communications with an integrated communications security (ICOM) device. This state-of-the-art sys-

tem replaces the AN/PRC-77 and VRC-12 series radios to provide improved reliability, availability, and maintainability. As of 2004, 25,390 of these $6,500 units were in the USMC inventory.

General characteristics of the SINCGARS tactical communications radio include:

Manufacturer: ITT Aerospace/Communications Division
Length: 10 in
Width: 10.7 in
Height: 3.4 in
Weight: 15.4 lb

company   See ORGANIZATION BY UNITS.

company clerk

In the USMC, a company clerk assists the master sergeant of the company. (In the army, he or she assists the first sergeant.) The company clerk is chiefly responsible for the day-to-day flow of paperwork and routine administrative procedures.

company grade officer   See RANKS AND GRADES.

Continental Marines

On November 10, 1775, the Continental Congress commissioned Robert Mullan, proprietor of the Tun Tavern in Philadelphia, to raise two battalions of marines under the leadership of SAMUEL NICHOLAS. On November 28, Nicholas was formally commissioned captain of the new force, called the Continental Marines, and although never officially appointed as commandant, he assumed that role as a practical matter. Today, the Tun Tavern is still considered the birthplace of the United States Marine Corps.

The Continental Congress authorized two battalions of marines, specifying that those recruited be good seamen, "able to serve to advantage by sea." Nicholas was soon promoted to major and, in

March 1776, under the overall command of the navy's John Paul Jones, Nicholas led 200 marines (and 50 sailors) in the first marine amphibious assault, landing on New Providence Island in the Bahamas. In a 13-day operation, the marines secured two forts, occupied Nassau, seized control of Government House, and captured 88 guns, 16,535 rounds of ammunition, and other supplies.

Nicholas and the marines next saw action in December 1776, when three companies (80 men) accompanied Washington's army in the successful Battle of Trenton. The marine companies remained with Washington in winter quarters at Morristown, New Jersey, until February 1777. In the spring, Washington formally incorporated some marines into artillery units of his Continental army, while Nicholas returned to Philadelphia and his shore-based marines were assigned to defensive duty in Delaware.

A small number of marines were deployed to New Orleans in January 1778 to keep British traders out of the port, and in April of that year, 20 marines were attached to service with John Paul Jones to sail on the *Ranger,* which raided the English coast. The marines participated in two raids, the first on British soil in some seven centuries. A handful of marines also accompanied Jones on the *Bon Homme Richard* during August 1779.

Continental Marines participated in a valiant but failed attack on Fort George in the Penobscot River in July 1779; they also served escort duty, assigned to guard a caravan of ox carts conveying a million silver crowns, loaned by France, from Boston's harbor to Philadelphia. In January 1783, Continental Marines formed the boarding party that seized the British ship *Baille* in the West Indies. This was the last military operation performed by the force.

At the conclusion of the American Revolution, Congress acted swiftly to disband the Continental army and the Continental navy. The Continental Marines was officially dissolved in June 1785, and it was not until July 11, 1798, that President John Adams signed the bill creating its successor organization, the United States Marine Corps.

corporal   See RANKS AND GRADES.

corps   See ORGANIZATION BY UNITS.

corpsman

In the USMC and U.S. Navy, a corpsman is an enlisted medic. With the dark humor typical of the military, the corpsman is often called a "corpse-man."

Cuban Rebellion

After the disputed presidential election of 1906, Cuba, independent from Spain following the SPANISH-AMERICAN WAR OF 1898, was on the brink of civil war. The outgoing Cuban president requested U.S. military aid. In response, 130 marines and sailors of the West Indies Squadron landed at Havana on September 13 to protect U.S. property. This force was followed by two USMC battalions to support a provisional government under the U.S. secretary of war, William Howard Taft. A second USMC regiment was landed on October 1. When units of the U.S. Army arrived later, the marine brigade was disbanded, save for the 1st Marine Regiment, which remained under army command and did not leave the island until 1909.

Marines returned in May 1912 to help quell a new rebellion. This provisional brigade consisted of two regiments. Once a new Cuban government regained control, the marines were withdrawn in late July.

Cushman, Robert E., Jr. (1914–1985) *Marine Corps commandant*

The 25th COMMANDANT OF THE MARINE CORPS, Cushman was born in St. Paul, Minnesota, and graduated from the U.S. Naval Academy in 1935. He attended Basic School, then was stationed with the 4th Marines in Shanghai in 1936. After serving in a number of stateside posts, Cushman was in command of the detachment aboard the battleship

Pennsylvania when it was attacked by the Japanese at Pearl Harbor on December 7, 1941.

During WORLD WAR II, Cushman, promoted to major, was assigned to the 9th Marines and, in May 1943, was given command of the 2nd Battalion. He led his command in combat on BOUGAINVILLE and GUAM, winning the Navy Cross for gallantry in repulsing a banzai charge on Guam.

Toward the end of the war, Cushman was stationed at Marine Corps Base Quantico and then was assigned to command the Amphibious War Branch, headquartered in Washington, D.C. He subsequently served on the staff of the commander of U.S. Naval Forces in the Atlantic and Mediterranean, then was assigned as director of plans and operations at the Armed Forces Staff College. In July 1956, Cushman was given command of the 2nd Marines at Marine Corps Base Camp Lejeune. During this period, he also served Vice President Richard M. Nixon as assistant for national security affairs.

In 1960, Cushman was appointed assistant commander of the 3rd Division, Okinawa, and in July 1962, now a major general, Cushman was named assistant chief of staff to the commandant of the USMC. Promoted to lieutenant general in 1967, Cushman became commander of III Marine Amphibious Force in Vietnam (see VIETNAM WAR).

During his two years as commander of III MAF, Cushman sharply disagreed with army general William Westmoreland, overall commander of U.S. forces in the theater, over the most effective use of the marines. Westmoreland wanted to use them as part of the so-called main force strategy, incorporating them in conventional massed assaults, whereas Cushman wanted to deploy the marines in separate hit-and-run raids and guerrilla-style actions and to have them work with South Vietnamese forces in furthering the so-called pacification of the rural villages.

Cushman left Vietnam and returned to the United States in 1969. He served as deputy director of the Central Intelligence Agency until he was appointed commandant on January 1, 1972. During his tenure, Cushman saw the last of the marines leave Vietnam and presided over the peacetime reduction of the Marine Corps to 194,000 marines. Although the Marine Corps was officially desegregated in 1949, de facto segregation persisted in some areas, especially in the Stewards Branch, which was all black. Cushman ordered an end to de facto and "voluntary" segregation throughout the corps.

Robert E. Cushman, Jr., retired as commandant in 1975 and died on January 2, 1985.

D

Daly, Daniel (1873–1937) *Marine Corps gunnery sergeant*

No less a figure than JOHN A. LEJEUNE, COMMANDANT OF THE MARINE CORPS, lauded Dan Daly as "the outstanding Marine of all time," and SMEDLEY D. BUTLER (with Daly, the only marine in history awarded *two* Medals of Honor) called him "the fightingest Marine I ever knew." Daly is perhaps best known for his rallying cry at WORLD WAR I's Battle of BELLEAU WOOD: "Come on, you sons of bitches, do you want to live forever?"

Born in Glen Cove, Long Island, New York, on November 11, 1873, the slightly built Daly (5 feet, 6 inches, 134 pounds) enlisted in the marines on January 10, 1899, eager to get in on the SPANISH-AMERICAN WAR. The fighting ended before he was out of boot camp, and he was deployed instead to shipboard service with the Asiatic Fleet. In 1900, he landed with the marines in China during the BOXER REBELLION and, in defense of the Tartar Wall, south of the American Legation, he held off a Boxer assault almost single-handedly. This action, on August 14, earned him his first Medal of Honor. His second Medal of Honor came 15 years later, when, on October 24, 1915, as a gunnery sergeant, he led a detachment of 35 marines against some 400 Caco insurgents in HAITI.

In addition to combat service in China and Haiti, Daly served in Panama, Cuba, Veracruz, Mexico, and Puerto Rico, in addition to various postings in the United States before the nation entered World War I. During this conflict, Daly served in France from November 4, 1917, to April 21, 1919, and saw combat in the Toulon Sector (March–May 1918), in the Aisne Operations (June 1918), and in the Château-Thierry Sector (June 1918). In this latter sector, he distinguished himself

Gunnery Sergeant Daniel Daly (USMC)   *(U.S. Marine Corps)*

at Belleau Wood, a battle in which a handful of marines successfully repulsed a major German offensive aimed directly at Paris. Daly went on to serve in the St. Mihiel Offensive (September 1918) and the Champagne Offensive (September–October 1918). He was wounded on June 21 and twice wounded on October 8, 1918.

Daly was the epitome of the marine noncommissioned officer. Repeatedly offered commissions, he turned them down, always expressing his desire to be an "outstanding sergeant" rather than a mediocre officer. Retired officially on February 6, 1929, with the rank of sergeant major, Daly spent the last years of his life as a Wall Street bank guard.

Dauntless bombers   See AIRCRAFT, FIXED-WING.

decorations and medals

Marines are eligible for decoration with the following medals and commendations. They are also eligible for many of the medals and decorations offered by the other services.

Marine Corps Expeditionary Medal

This medal is awarded to marines who have participated in operations against armed opposition on foreign territory. The medal, made of bronze, depicts a marine in full pack charging with bayonet through waves and onto the shore. The medal is suspended from a gold ribbon bearing three vertical red stripes, one at either end and in the middle.

Marine Corps Reserve Ribbon

The ribbon is presented to marines who have completed 10 years of service in the MARINE CORPS RESERVE. Ribbon is gold colored, with a narrow vertical stripe on each end.

Medal of Honor

The highest military honor in the United States, the Medal of Honor has been awarded 3,428 times in the nation's history and is presented by the president in the name of Congress to a person "who distinguishes himself or herself conspicuously by gallantry and intrepidity at the risk of his life or her life above and beyond the call of duty while engaged in an action against an enemy of the United States; while engaged in military operations involving conflict with an opposing foreign force; or while serving with friendly foreign forces engaged in an armed conflict against an opposing armed force in which the United States is not a belligerent party. The deed performed must have been one of personal bravery or self-sacrifice so conspicuous as to clearly distinguish the individual above his comrades and must have involved risk of life. Incontestable proof of the performance of the service will be exacted and each recommendation for the award of this decoration will be considered on the standard of extraordinary merit."

The marines have earned 295 Medals of Honor. The first was awarded to Corporal John F. Mackie for his actions on May 15, 1862, during the Civil War. The most recent was awarded to Lance Corporal James D. Howe for his actions in May 1970 at Quang Ngai, South Vietnam.

Marines are also eligible for the medals listed below, from the other services:

Combat Action Ribbon, Joint Meritorious Unit Award, Joint Service Achievement Medal, Meritorious Service Medal, Military Outstanding Volunteer Service Medal, National Defense Service Medal, NATO Medal–Former Republic of Yugoslavia, NATO Medal–Kosovo Operations, Navy Cross, Navy/Marine Corps Achievement Medal, Navy/Marine Corps Commendation Medal, Navy/Marine Corps Medal, Navy/Marine Corps Overseas Service Ribbon, Navy Occupation Service Medal, Philippine Defense Medal, Philippine Independence Medal, Philippine Liberation Medal, Philippine Presidential Unit Citation, Presidential Unit Citation, Prisoner of War Medal, Republic of Korea Presidential Unit Citation, Republic of Korea War Service Medal, Republic of Vietnam Campaign Medal, Republic of Vietnam Gallantry Cross with Palm, Southwest Asia Service Medal, United Nations Medal, United Nations Service Medal, Vietnam Service Medal, World War II Victory Medal.

Derna   See Barbary pirates; O'Bannon, Presley.

Desert Shield and Desert Storm   See Persian Gulf War.

Devereux, James P. S. (1903–1988) *Marine Corps general*

Devereux was the son of a military family and was born on post in Cuba. After attending the Army and Navy Preparatory School, Washington, D.C., he was sent to boarding school in Switzerland. He joined the USMC in 1923 and received his commission as a second lieutenant in 1925. His first overseas assignment was in Nicaragua during 1926–27. After sea duty, he became an officer of the legation guard in Peking (Beijing). During the 1930s, back in the United States, he was assigned to Marine Corps Base Quantico and then to the Coast Artillery School at the U.S. Army's Fort Monroe, Virginia. During the later 1930s, he served as an instructor at the Base Defense Weapons School, Quantico.

After brief sea service and service at Marine Corps Base San Diego, Devereux was posted to Pearl Harbor, Hawaii, in January 1941, then was sent to command the USMC detachment—449 marines—at Wake Island, little more than a way station for commercial seaplane flights via the Pan American Clipper.

After the outbreak of World War II in the Pacific, Wake Island was attacked by Japanese forces on December 11, 1941. Major Devereux commanded the remarkable, but ultimately hopeless, defense of the island. The marines surrendered to overwhelming numbers on December 23, and Devereux spent the rest of the war as a prisoner of war.

After World War II, Devereux was promoted to colonel, retroactive to November 1, 1942. He served in Washington, D.C., Quantico, and Camp Pendleton, retiring in August 1948 with the rank of brigadier general. After leaving the Marine Corps,

Devereux gained election to the U.S. House of Representatives.

Diver Propulsion Device (DPD)   See personal and miscellaneous equipment.

division   See organization by units.

Dominican Republic

With the assassination of Dominican dictator Leonidas Trujillo in May 1961, leftist political groups threatened to topple the government. USMC and USN forces were sent to the region in 1961 and 1963 to demonstrate support for what was deemed an anticommunist government. On each occasion, the show of force was sufficient to restore order. In 1965, however, a civil war erupted, and the government lost ground, including most of the capital city, Santo Domingo. The president hastily stepped down, and the United States feared that the Dominican Republic would go the way of Cuba. Accordingly, on April 28, 1965, 500 marines were sent to reinforce loyalist Dominican troops to secure landing areas for helicopters, so that U.S. and other nationals could be evacuated. Before the end of the month, three USMC battalions had been landed, with a fourth battalion held in reserve on board a waiting ship. When, on April 29, U.S. Army forces (82nd Airborne) arrived, command passed to an army general.

In light combat, nine marines died and 30 were wounded, but the rebels quickly backed down, the government forces retook Santo Domingo, an inter-American peace-keeping force was created by the Organization of American States, and a communist takeover of the nation was averted.

double trouble

Also known as "dual cool," the term describes a marine specially qualified as a SCUBA diver and as a paratrooper.

See also U.S. Marine Corps Reconnaissance Battalions.

Dragon Weapon System   See Antiarmor Weapons.

drill instructor

The DI is a noncommissioned officer who trains and oversees training of recruits during Basic Training. In the USMC, each recruit platoon is assigned three drill instructors, who are also called "Hats," after the distinctive campaign-style headgear the DI wears. Of the three drill instructors, one is senior and is distinguished by a black leather belt (so is called "Black Belt"; also, "Big Dad"). The senior DI is assisted by the "Second Hat"; together, they are in charge of instruction. The third DI ("Third Hat") deals with issues and matters of discipline.

The USMC DI is almost legendary for toughness; however, today's DI undergoes a rigorous 10-week training course and is forbidden from abusing recruits in any way. The term "drill sergeant," formerly interchangeable with "drill instructor," is now obsolete.

A drill instructor prepares his platoon for final drill competition.   *(U.S. Marine Corps)*

dual cool   See Double Trouble.

DUKW   See Amphibious Vehicles.

E

EA-6B Prowler See AIRCRAFT, FIXED-WING.

Elliott, George F. (1846–1931) *Marine Corps commandant*

Tenth COMMANDANT OF THE MARINE CORPS, Elliott attended the U.S. Military Academy at West Point for two years before he was commissioned a second lieutenant in the USMC in 1870. After serving in a variety of posts, he commanded a company during the SPANISH-AMERICAN WAR in 1898. The following year, he commanded a battalion at Cavite in the Philippines. He was appointed commandant of the USMC in October 1903, with the rank of brigadier general.

The USMC commanded by Elliott consisted of a mere 7,800 men, but, as a result of his lobbying President Theodore Roosevelt and Roosevelt's successor, William Howard Taft, the USMC was expanded. Equally important, its duties, often vaguely specified in the past, were clarified. Elliott retired in 1910.

embarked marines

While marines have always served aboard U.S. Navy ships in security and other roles, most marines sail as "embarked marines"—troops being transported for amphibious landing in a combat area.

emblem, USMC

The "Globe and Anchor" or "Corps Badge" is the official insignia of the USMC and features a spread eagle atop the world globe (Western Hemisphere) crossed by a fouled anchor. The eagle holds in its beak a scroll bearing the inscription SEMPER FIDELIS. The elements of the emblem acknowledge the USMC as an American maritime force (the eagle and the anchor) capable of global deploy-

The USMC emblem   *(U.S. Marine Corps)*

ment (the globe). The current emblem was designed in 1868 by General JACOB ZEILIN.

Eniwetok Atoll, Battle of

Eniwetok is a circular atoll located in the Marshall Islands and was the site of an important USMC engagement during WORLD WAR II. The 22nd Marines were assigned to take Engebi, northernmost of the Eniwetok islands, while the army's 106th Regiment landed on Eniwetok Island, at the south end of the atoll. When Engebi and Eniwetok had been secured, the large island between them, Parry, would be taken and occupied. The entire operation was code-named Catchpole.

The marines began by taking two tiny islands near Engebi and placing artillery on these. Fire was directed from this land-based position, as well as from U.S. Navy ships, against Engebi to prepare it for the USMC landing, which took place on February 19, 1944. The battle here lasted only six hours. All but 16 of the island's 1,200-man garrison were killed.

Operation Catchpole had assumed that Engebi was the most heavily defended of the islands. In fact, Eniwetok proved far more heavily defended, and a USMC battalion was deployed to assist the army regiment heavily engaged there. On February 21, Eniwetok was secured.

Now it was time to take Parry Island. However, while USN intelligence had concluded that the island was undefended, it was, in fact, occupied by a 1,300-man garrison. Nevertheless, supported by naval bombardment, a pair of USMC battalions took the island by February 22.

Possession of the Eniwetok atoll gave U.S. forces a valuable fleet anchorage and an air base from which operations against the Mariana Islands could be efficiently and adequately supported.

expeditionary force

This general term for an armed force assembled to accomplish a specific mission in a foreign country is also often used specifically to describe the USMC, which is above all an "expeditionary force," deployed to foreign countries to carry out a specifically defined mission.

Extreme Cold Weather Tent (ECWT)   See

PERSONAL AND MISCELLANEOUS EQUIPMENT.

F

F2A Buffalo   See AIRCRAFT, FIXED-WING.

F2H Banshee   See AIRCRAFT, FIXED-WING.

F2T Black Widow   See AIRCRAFT, FIXED-WING.

F4B Phantom II   See AIRCRAFT, FIXED-WING.

F4D Skyray   See AIRCRAFT, FIXED-WING.

F4F Wildcat   See AIRCRAFT, FIXED-WING.

F4U Corsair   See AIRCRAFT, FIXED-WING.

F6F Hellcat   See AIRCRAFT, FIXED-WING.

F8 Crusader   See AIRCRAFT, FIXED-WING.

F8C-5 Helldiver   See AIRCRAFT, FIXED-WING.

F9F-8 Cougar   See AIRCRAFT, FIXED-WING.

F/A-18A/C/CN Hornet   See AIRCRAFT, FIXED-WING.

F/A-18D Hornet   See AIRCRAFT, FIXED-WING.

Field Pack, Large, with Internal Frame (FPLIF)   See PERSONAL AND MISCELLANEOUS EQUIPMENT.

FIM-92A Stinger   See AIR DEFENSE ARTILLERY.

Financial Management School   See COMBAT SERVICE SUPPORT SCHOOLS.

fire base
A field combat base staffed by a company or platoon and used as a base from which patrols are sent out. Fire bases are sometimes established to provide security in a given area.

fire support base
An FSB is set up near a combat area to supply field combat units with logistical and artillery support. The FSB is not placed in the forefront of the front lines.

first lieutenant   See RANKS AND GRADES.

FJ1-FJ4 Fury   See AIRCRAFT, FIXED-WING.

flame thrower   See WEAPONS, INDIVIDUAL AND CREW-SERVED.

Fleet Marine Force

The FMF is the land assault component of the Navy Expeditionary Forces and consists primarily of marines. Currently, there are two principal FMFs: FMFLANT, assigned to the Atlantic and headquartered at Camp Lejeune, North Carolina, and FMFPAC, assigned to the Pacific and headquartered at Camp H. M. Smith, Hawaii.

Each FMF is organized into MARINE AIR-GROUND TASK FORCES (MAGTF) ranging in size from marine expeditionary units (MEU) of 1,000 to 4,000 marines, to marine expeditionary forces (MEF), comprising 30,000 to 60,000 marines. Currently, the total strength of each FMF is 89,000 marines.

forward observer

Artillery liaison officer attached to an infantry unit in the field for the purpose of directing artillery fire against the enemy.

Fuller, Ben H. (1870–1937) *Marine Corps commandant*

The 15th COMMANDANT OF THE MARINE CORPS, Fuller was born in Big Rapids, Michigan, and graduated from the U.S. Naval Academy at Annapolis in 1889. After a two-year cruise prior to his appointment as a USMC second lieutenant, Fuller served seven years at sea, then commanded a marine detachment aboard the *Columbia* in the West Indies during the SPANISH-AMERICAN WAR. He fought in the PHILIPPINE INSURRECTION, then in the BOXER REBELLION in 1900.

Major General Ben Hebard Fuller (USMC)   *(U.S. Marine Corps)*

In 1904, Fuller was assigned to command the USMC base at Honolulu, Hawaii. After serving in various other posts, he attended the Naval War College and was assigned to command the marine barracks in Philadelphia. He fought in SANTO DOMINGO in 1918–19, then served on the faculty of the Naval War College during 1920–22 before taking command of Marine Corps Base Quantico.

Fuller commanded the 1st Brigade in HAITI during 1924–25, and in July 1925 was named assistant commandant of the USMC. Promoted to major general, he became commandant in 1930, retiring early in 1934.

Functions Paper, The

Sometimes referred to as the "Key West Agreement," *The Functions Paper* was drawn up and agreed to in 1948 among the armed services and is the principal interservice agreement that defines the functions of each service. According to *The Functions Paper*, the USMC is to perform the following functions:

To provide Fleet Marine Forces of combined arms for service with the Fleet in the seizure or defense of advanced naval bases for the conduct of land operations necessary to the prosecution of a naval campaign.

To provide detachments and organizations for service on armed navy vessels as well as security detachments for the protection of navy property, bases, and naval stations.

To collaborate with the other services in developing doctrine, equipment, and techniques for amphibious operations.

To train and equip marine forces for airborne operations.

To collaborate and coordinate with the other services in developing doctrines, procedures, and equipment for marine airborne operations.

G

Gale, Anthony (1782–1843) *Marine Corps commandant*

Fourth COMMANDANT OF THE MARINE CORPS, Gale was born in Dublin, Ireland, and immigrated to the United States late in the 18th century. He was infamous for his hot temper, and in 1801 he killed a U.S. Navy officer in a duel. Despite this, Gale became commandant in 1819, appointed by the secretary of the navy to replace ARCHIBALD HENDERSON, who became acting commandant after the death of FRANKLIN WHARTON in 1818. His appointment was by virtue of his seniority within the Marine Corps.

Gale was quarrelsome—quarreling even with the navy secretary—and was a notorious imbiber. Court-martialed for his drunkenness and generally disreputable behavior in 1820, he unsuccessfully pleaded temporary insanity. President James Monroe dismissed him from the USMC, but directed that his pension be continued for life.

Geiger, Roy S. (1885–1947) *Marine Corps general*

Geiger commanded amphibious assaults on key Pacific islands during WORLD WAR II. Born in Middleburg, Florida, he graduated from John B. Stetson University in 1907 and took a law degree, but practiced for just a few months before enlisting in the USMC in November 1907. After only two years in the Marine Corps, he was commissioned a sec-

ond lieutenant and in 1915 was promoted to first lieutenant, having served at sea and in the Caribbean, the Philippines, and China. Promoted to captain in 1917, Geiger become the fifth USMC officer to complete pilot training. He served during

General Roy Stanley Geiger (USMC)   *(U.S. Marine Corps)*

WORLD WAR I in France as a major in command of a squadron of the 1st Marine Aviation Force.

After the war, Geiger served in HAITI as commander of the 1st Aviation Group, 3rd Marine Brigade, from 1919 to 1921. Transferred to Marine Corps Base Quantico in 1921, he attended and graduated from the U.S. Army's Command and General Staff School in 1925. Four years later, he graduated from the Army War College, and from 1929 to 1931 he commanded Aircraft Squadrons, East Coast Expeditionary Force, stationed at Quantico. In 1931 he was appointed officer in charge of aviation at HEADQUARTERS MARINE CORPS, Washington, D.C., serving there from 1931 to 1935.

Promoted to lieutenant colonel in 1934, Geiger commanded Marine Air Group One, 1st Marine Brigade, from 1935 to 1939, and then was sent to the Naval War College. Graduating in 1941, he was promoted to brigadier general and given command of the 1st Marine Air Wing, Fleet Marine Force, in September. With the outbreak of World War II, Geiger took command of the air wing on GUADAL-CANAL as soon as the island was captured. He served on Guadalcanal from September 1942 to February 1943, was promoted to major general, and returned to Washington as director of the Marine Division of Aviation. In November 1943, he succeeded General ALEXANDER A. VANDEGRIFT as commander of I Amphibious Corps (later redesignated III Amphibious Corps), which he led in the invasion of GUAM during July 21–August 10, 1944. Geiger was also in charge of the bloody invasion of PELELIU from September 15 to November 25, 1944, then went on to participate in the landing on OKI-NAWA from April 1 to June 18, 1945. In the Okinawa campaign, his corps was part of the Tenth Army, commanded by General Simon B. Buckner. When Buckner was killed in battle, Geiger assumed command of the Tenth Army until the arrival of General Joseph W. Stilwell on June 23. Thus Geiger became the only USMC officer ever to command a field army.

In July 1945, Geiger was appointed to command Fleet Marine Force, Pacific. After the war, in November 1946, he was assigned to a post in Washington, but soon fell ill. He died before receiving promotion to general, which Congress conferred posthumously in July 1947.

general   See RANKS AND GRADES.

Gilbert Islands, USMC assaults on

Early in WORLD WAR II, the Gilbert Islands, a widespread chain of several Pacific islands and atolls that was then a British colony, were seized from the British and occupied by the Japanese. MAKIN Island, one of the islands in the chain, was the site of a key Japanese radio station, which fell to a USMC raid in August 1942. While this raid was valuable, it also prompted the Japanese to beef up their defenses in the area, especially on Betio Island. This became the objective of an assault by the 2nd Division, USMC, in November 1943. After a battle of three days, the island fell to the marines. Simultaneously U.S. Army forces occupied Makin.

The action in the Gilberts was important in the Pacific war because it represented the first significant breach in Japan's outer defenses. It was the first step in the "island hopping" campaign that would constitute the war in the Pacific.

Glenn, John H., Jr. (1921–   ) *Marine Corps aviator, astronaut, U.S. senator*

Glenn was a distinguished USMC aviator, who achieved his greatest fame as an astronaut, the first American to orbit the Earth. Elected to the U.S. Senate in 1974, he became the oldest human being in space, when he volunteered for a Space Shuttle flight in 1998.

Born in Cambridge, Ohio, Glenn enlisted in the MARINE CORPS RESERVE in 1942 during WORLD WAR II and was subsequently designated an aviation cadet. After completing his flight training in March 1943, he shipped out to the Pacific in February 1944 and flew 59 missions in the Marshalls and Marianas with Fighting Squadron 155. He was sent back to the United States in February 1945, then served in GUAM after the war and on the North China patrol.

Colonel John H. Glenn, Jr. (USMC)   *(U.S. Marine Corps)*

After promotion to major in July 1952, Glenn took jet refresher training and, in February 1953, was ordered to Korea and assigned to Fighting Squadron 311. He flew 63 missions with that squadron and another 27 assigned to the USAF's 51st Fighter Wing. He shot down three MiGs.

On his return from Korea, Glenn went to the USN's Test Pilot School, completing his training in 1954 and working in advanced testing. His flight from Los Alamitos to New York in an F8U-1 Crusader on July 16, 1954, was the first coast-to-coast, nonstop supersonic flight in aviation history, which earned Glenn his fourth Distinguished Flying Cross.

Chosen as a Mercury astronaut in 1959, Glenn became the first American to achieve orbital spaceflight on February 20, 1962. Three years later, he retired from the USMC to enter business and to work as a civilian NASA consultant. Elected to the Senate from Ohio in 1974, he retired from the Sen-

ate in 1999, but in 1998 flew aboard Space Shuttle *Discovery* as "Payload Specialist 2" and the oldest person ever to fly in space.

Gray, Alfred M., Jr. (1928–   ) *Marine Corps commandant*

The 29th COMMANDANT OF THE MARINE CORPS, New Jersey-born Alfred M. Gray, Jr., enlisted in the USMC in 1950, served in the Pacific, then was commissioned a second lieutenant in 1952. He attended Basic School and the Army Field Artillery School before shipping out to the KOREAN WAR, where he served as an artillery officer with the 1st Division. He served a second Korean tour as an infantry officer with the 7th Marines before returning to the United States in December 1954.

From 1956 to 1961, Gray served in various stateside posts before moving to an assignment at GUANTÁNAMO BAY. He served in the VIETNAM WAR with the 12th Marines in 1965 and subsequently served in Vietnam with other outfits until his return to Washington in 1968 as a lieutenant colonel working on Department of Defense special projects. At Marine Corps Base Quantico, he helped to develop sensor technology.

In 1969, Gray returned to Vietnam for a second tour, specializing in surveillance and reconnaissance with I Corps. Subsequently, he served in intelligence and later attended the Command and General Staff School. In 1971, he commanded a battalion of the 2nd Division and was deployed to the Mediterranean. He was made commander of the 2nd Marines in April 1972 and then assistant chief of staff, G-3, 2nd Division.

After attending the U.S. Army War College in 1973, he was named to command the 4th Marines and simultaneously served as commander of Camp Hansen, Okinawa. In 1975, Gray returned to Vietnam, this time as deputy commander of the 33rd Amphibious Brigade, directing the U.S. evacuation of Southeast Asia.

Promoted to brigadier general in 1976, Gray commanded the 4th Amphibious Brigade and the Landing Force Training Command, Atlantic. In 1980, as a major general, he commanded 2nd

Division, Marine Corps Base Camp Lejeune. Promoted to lieutenant general in 1986, he commanded Fleet Marine Force, Atlantic; Fleet Marine Force, Europe; and II Amphibious Force. On July 1, 1987, promoted to general, he was appointed commandant of the USMC.

Greene, Wallace M., Jr. (1907–2003)

Marine Corps commandant

The 23rd COMMANDANT OF THE MARINE CORPS, Wallace M. Greene, Jr., was born in Burlington, Vermont, and graduated from the U.S. Naval Academy in 1930. Commissioned a second lieutenant in the USMC, he served in a variety of shore and sea duties before being posted to GUAM and Shanghai. Shortly before WORLD WAR II, he was stationed at GUANTÁNAMO BAY, Cuba. In 1941, he served in England as a military observer and also attended British amphibious warfare and demolition schools.

Greene was promoted to major and assigned in February 1942 as assistant chief of staff of the 3rd Marine Brigade, with which he sailed to Samoa. Late in 1943, he was sent to Hawaii as assistant chief of staff of V Amphibious Corps and was instrumental in planning the Marshall Islands campaigns. Early in 1944, as operations officer for the 2nd Division, Greene served in the SAIPAN campaign and in operations against TINIAN. He returned to Washington in October 1944 as operations officer, Division of Plans, Marine Headquarters.

After the war, Greene served in numerous staff positions, then attended the National War College and, in September 1955, was promoted to brigadier general and named assistant commandant at Marine Corps Base Camp Lejeune. He became base commandant in 1957, then was transferred to Washington, where he served as assistant chief of staff to the commandant of the Marine Corps. Promoted to major general, he became deputy chief of staff in 1958, then chief of staff in 1960. Greene was appointed commandant of the Marine Corps in 1964.

Greene oversaw operations in the DOMINICAN REPUBLIC in 1965 and the first major marine build-up in the VIETNAM WAR, at Da Nang, also in 1965. Greene presided over the deployment of marine forces during the early years of the war, until his retirement at the end of 1967.

Grenada invasion

Grenada is a small island nation (population 110,100) at the southern end of the Windward Islands chain in the West Indies. In 1979, a Marxist-Leninist coup led by Maurice Bishop, head of the radical New Jewel movement, overthrew the government. Subsequently, his pro-Cuban regime built a 9,800-foot-long airstrip, apparently for military purposes. The administration of Bishop proved short-lived; he was killed in a 1983 coup, which left Deputy Prime Minister Bernard Coard and General Hudson Austin in charge of the government. Sir Paul Scoon, Grenada's governor-general, secretly communicated with the Organization of Eastern Caribbean States (OECS), requesting aid in restoring order to the troubled country. The OECS, in turn, asked for U.S. military intervention, to which President Ronald Reagan enthusiastically agreed, citing a need to protect the approximately 1,000 American citizens in Grenada —most of them students at a local medical school.

Operation Urgent Fury was launched and included a naval battle group centered on the aircraft carrier *Independence,* as well as the helicopter carrier *Guam,* two USMC amphibious units, two Army Ranger battalions, a brigade of the 82nd Airborne Division, and special operations units. These massive forces landed on Grenada on October 25, 1983, and found themselves facing no more than 500 to 600 Grenadan regulars, 2,000 to 2,500 poorly equipped and poorly organized militiamen, and about 800 Cuban military construction personnel. The invading force seized the airport and destroyed Radio Free Grenada, a key source of government communications. Next, the U.S. nationals were evacuated, and Grenada was declared to be under U.S. military control by October 28.

Eighteen U.S. personnel died in the assault on Grenada, and 116 were wounded. Grenadan forces lost 25 dead and 59 wounded, while Cuban casualties were 45 dead and 350 wounded.

grunt

In the USMC and army, a grunt is an enlisted infantryman.

Guadalcanal

In WORLD WAR II, this southwest Pacific island became the site of a turning-point battle after Japanese forces began construction of an airfield on the island at the end of May 1942. This base posed a grave threat to the Allied supply line to Australia and New Zealand; therefore, Major General ALEXANDER VANDEGRIFT was ordered to lead two USMC regiments against it. The marines landed on August 7, 1942, taking the Japanese by surprise and capturing the airfield (renamed Henderson Field), but suffering an intense counterattack in return. The marines of the 1st Division held the island alone until the arrival of the 7th Marines in mid-September and the U.S. Army American Division and 2nd Marines in November, followed soon by

On Guadalcanal, a casualty from the front-line fighting is transferred from a makeshift stretcher before being taken through the jungle and downriver to a nearby hospital. *(Library of Congress)*

the U.S. Army's 25th Division. By February 1943, the remaining Japanese forces had been evacuated from Guadalcanal. Combined with the U.S. victory in the naval battle of Midway, Guadalcanal was a turning point in the Pacific war, marking an Allied shift to offensive warfare in this theater.

Guam

During WORLD WAR II, this U.S. Pacific possession in the Mariana Islands was taken by the Japanese on December 8, 1941. It had been defended by a badly outnumbered garrison of 125 marines and 271 sailors.

Operation Forager, the reconquest of Guam, commenced on July 21, 1944, and was a combined USMC and army operation. The island was declared secure on August 10, after virtually the entire 18,000-man Japanese garrison had been killed. Combined marine and army casualties were 7,714 killed and wounded. Securing Guam gave the U.S. Army Air Forces a key base from which B-29s could raid the Japanese home islands.

Guantánamo Bay

The United States has maintained a major naval base, with a USMC contingent, at Guantánamo Bay, Cuba, since December 1903. The base is the oldest U.S. base overseas and the only one in a communist country. It was leased by the United States in December 1903 as a coaling station for warships. The lease was reaffirmed by a 1934 treaty, which stipulates that the lease can be terminated only by the mutual consent of the United States and Cuba.

Since 1961, when President Dwight D. Eisenhower severed diplomatic relations with Cuba after Fidel Castro instituted a communist government there, the primary duty of the USMC contingent at Guantánamo has been to secure the base and patrol its 17.4-mile fence line.

Existing in essentially hostile territory, Guantánamo is wholly self-sufficient, with a desalination plant to provide fresh water and a generating plant to produce more than 800,000 kilowatt hours of electricity daily. The base is divided in two by Guantánamo Bay, which is 2.5 miles wide. The airfield is located on the leeward side, the main base on the windward side.

In 1991, USMC personnel were assigned the additional task of accommodating some 34,000 refugees who fled Haiti after a violent coup there. In May 1994, USMC and U.S. Navy personnel participated in Operation Sea Signal in support of Joint Task Force 160, tasked with providing humanitarian assistance to thousands of Haitian and Cuban migrants. The last Haitian migrants departed the base in November 1995, and the last Cuban refugees left on January 31, 1996.

In January 2002, USMC personnel took charge of "Camp X-Ray" at Guantánamo, a hastily constructed temporary prison compound for Taliban fighters captured during military action in Afghanistan following the September 11, 2001, terrorist attacks on New York and Washington. Following Operation Iraqi Freedom in 2003, some prisoners captured in Iraq have also been housed at Camp X-Ray.

gung-ho

A thoroughly committed, highly aggressive, extremely motivated soldier—a hard charger. The term *gung-ho* originated during WORLD WAR II with the USMC, which borrowed it from the Mandarin Chinese word gōnghō, meaning "to work together," but *gung-ho* has also found its way into the other services and into the civilian realm as well.

Gungi Marine

A "Gungi Marine" is the ideal marine, possessed not only of boundless courage and initiative, but also of good sense, good humor, and supreme competence. The term is doubtless related to GUNG-HO.

gunnery sergeant See RANKS AND GRADES.

gyrene

Slang for a marine, this term is widely used but of unknown origin. Since it rhymes with *marine,* it is reasonable to assume that it is a play on the word *marine* and may well be a combination of *G.I.* and *marine.* It may also be a combination of JARHEAD and "marine." Some have suggested that the word derives from *gyrinus,* the Latin term for tadpole, a reference to the amphibious mission of the USMC; this etymology seems farfetched, to say the least.

H

Hagaru-ri, breakout from

After the massive Communist Chinese incursion into Korea during the KOREAN WAR, which drove the marines out of their positions at the CHOSIN RESERVOIR, USMC units retreated to the town of Hagaru-ri. Chinese forces positioned themselves to the north, on high ground, and set up blocking forces along the route of retreat to Koto-ri. To prevent the capture of the marines, the order was given for the 7th Marine Division to attack to the south while the 5th Marines held Hagaru-ri. Simultaneously, a reinforced company of the 1st Marines, aided by British Royal Marines, would push northward from Koto-ri. The idea was to attack the Chinese forces from two directions and provide the marines at Hagaru-ri with a retreat route.

Although the 1st Marines and the Royal Marines were badly cut up, they managed to fight their way through, and, on December 1, 1950, were relieved by elements of the 7th Marines. This allowed the 5th and 7th Marines to make their break from Hagaru-ri on December 6. In a remarkable running fight, the USMC successfully evacuated the town, bringing all personnel and equipment out and reaching the safety of Koto-ri by December 7.

The breakout from Hagaru-ri is recorded in USMC annals as a classic withdrawal operation under extremely unfavorable conditions. Although the marines lost 730 killed and more than 3,600 wounded, their withdrawal had mauled the vastly superior Chinese forces, which were rendered incapable of pursuing the evacuated forces. The marines had transformed a costly encirclement and strategic retreat into an even more costly tactical defeat for the enemy.

Haiti

USMC action in Haiti first came in December 1914, when a USMC detachment was landed to secure the Haitian treasury during an uprising. In March 1915, two USMC companies were landed and advanced on Port-au-Prince, the Haitian capital, to restore order there. More marines followed, and by late August the total number of marines in country was 2,000. They fought pitched battles, including hand-to-hand combat in an abandoned French fort atop a 4,000-foot mountain, against insurgents called the Cacos.

With the defeat of the Cacos, the United States backed a new government friendly to its interests and established an indigenous Haitian Constabulary, commanded and trained by marines. When the Cacos reemerged in strength in March 1919, 1,000 marines of the 1st Brigade were landed to support the constabulary. During the summer, two marines and a Haitian constable penetrated the camp of the Caco leader, Charlemagne Peralte. The three killed Peralte. A new Caco leader emerged, and the 1st Brigade, now reinforced by the 8th Marines, began a systematic campaign against the Cacos. The rebellion ended in May 1920, when the

Marines from Lima Company, 3rd Battalion, 8th Marine Regiment, offload chairs at a local school in Haiti on May 11, 2004. The marines handed out nearly 30 desks, more than 100 chairs, and several tables to Escole Eu Venesuala (Venezuela School) as part of the Multinational Interim Forces effort to help the struggling Caribbean nation.   *(U.S. Marine Corps)*

new Caco leader was killed by a marine patrol. Marines remained in Haiti until 1934.

The USMC intervened in Haiti again after President Jean-Bertrand Aristide was overthrown in a military coup d'état. In 1994, marines were part of the U.S. military force that returned Aristide to office.

Han River Forts, Battle of the

Korea was long known as the "Hermit Kingdom" because of its intransigent, hostile posture toward any contact with foreigners. When a band of Koreans known as the Salee River pirates attacked and killed the crew of the shipwrecked USS *General Sherman*, the United States minister to China was sent to Seoul to negotiate a settlement. His escort consisted of an intimidating armada of five U.S. Navy warships, in advance of which a survey party was sent to chart the best passage up the Han River to Seoul. After the Koreans fired upon this party, the fleet commander, Admiral John Rodgers, demanded an apology. Receiving none, he sent a force of sailors and 109 marines under Captain McLane Tilton (USMC) to attack the ancient Han River Forts. The force landed near the first fort on June 10, 1871, and was bogged down in the mud. However, covered by naval bombardment, they assaulted the first fort, took it, and spiked its artillery. On June 11, the second fort fell, followed by the principal fort, known as the Citadel. Situated atop a 150-foot hill, the fort was a formidable objective for an assault, but the marines and sailors took it after a sharp hand-to-hand contest. Korean casualties were 243 killed; the marines lost two of their number.

The action at the Han River Forts made way for the U.S. minister, who negotiated at length with the Koreans, but failed to emerge with a treaty. Despite the absence of a document, the Koreans never attacked the Americans again.

Harpers Ferry

Harpers Ferry, Virginia (today, West Virginia), was, in 1859, the site of a federal arsenal. With 18 men, the radical abolitionist militant John Brown raided and captured the arsenal on October 16, 1859, with the object of arming slaves for a local slave revolt that, he hoped, would precipitate widespread slave revolts across the South.

Brown and his men, with hostages, holed up in a firehouse. No regular army detachment was available, so Lieutenant Israel Greene, with 86 marines, was ordered to Harpers Ferry from MARINE BARRACKS, Washington, D.C. On arrival, he was to turn over command to the senior army officer present, Colonel Robert E. Lee—who thus became the only U.S. Army officer ever to lead marines into combat.

On October 17, Lee deployed his marines in two storming parties, then sent his aide, Lieutenant J. E. B. Stuart, to parley with Brown in the hope of persuading him to surrender peacefully. When Brown refused, Lee ordered Lieutenant Greene to storm the firehouse. The battle lasted a mere three minutes. Greene wounded Brown, and his men killed all but four of Brown's followers. In the melee, four hostages, including the mayor of Harpers Ferry, were killed. One marine died.

Taken prisoner, Brown and his surviving followers were tried by the state of Virginia, which convicted them of murder and conspiracy to foment servile insurrection. They were hanged.

Harris, John (1793–1864) *Marine Corps commandant*

The sixth COMMANDANT OF THE MARINE CORPS, Harris was commissioned a second lieutenant in

Colonel John Harris (USMC)   *(U.S. Marine Corps)*

the USMC in 1814, saw no significant action in the WAR OF 1812, then served sea duty for most of the next two decades. He fought in the SECOND SEMINOLE WAR during 1836–37 and was breveted a major. Harris led a battalion in the U.S.-MEXICAN WAR, but reached the front too late to see action. He did serve in Mexico in the occupying forces.

Promoted to colonel in 1855, Harris became commandant at that rank in January 1859. He was commandant when a USMC detachment was ordered to HARPERS FERRY to quash John Brown's raid. Harris also commanded the USMC during the Civil War, until his death on May 12, 1864. He was widely criticized as too old and lethargic to lead the USMC in this great conflict.

hash marks

Hash marks are service stripes worn on the lower left sleeve of the uniform of an enlisted marine. Each stripe (hash mark) stands for four years of service.

hasty defense

Also called a hasty perimeter, a hasty defense is a defensive perimeter quickly set up under enemy fire. The art of the hasty defense relies heavily on existing terrain features to provide ready-made cover, since, by definition, creating a hasty defense allows no time for preparing formal defensive works.

HAWK   See AIR DEFENSE ARTILLERY.

Headquarters Marine Corps (HQMC)

HQMC is nominally located in Washington, D.C., but is physically accommodated in the Pentagon, with some offices at Marine Corps Base Quantico; the Navy Annex, Arlington; and Clarendon Center, Rosslyn, Virginia. HQMC is the USMC executive and includes the office of the COMMANDANT OF THE MARINE CORPS and all executive departments.

Henderson, Archibald (1783–1859) *Marine Corps commandant*

Fifth COMMANDANT OF THE MARINE CORPS, Henderson was born in Colchester, Virginia, and was commissioned a second lieutenant in the USMC in 1806. Promoted to captain in 1811, he served at sea during the WAR OF 1812 on board the USS *Constitution*. For his service, he was breveted major. Henderson also served at the Battle of NEW ORLEANS as commander of the USMC contingent in that celebrated victory of December–January 1814–15.

Henderson became USMC commandant in 1820, a period of crisis for the Marine Corps, which had suffered under the incompetent leadership of Henderson's predecessor, ANTHONY GALE, such that President Andrew Jackson agitated for its dissolution. Henderson spearheaded the effort to save the USMC, and he also led its reorganization through Congress in 1834. This put the USMC under the secretary of the navy, not the secretary of war, and increased its size.

In 1836, Henderson led the USMC contingent participating in the SECOND SEMINOLE WAR and emerged a brevet brigadier general, the first marine to hold that rank. Henderson did not personally lead troops in the U.S.-MEXICAN WAR, but he did secure presidential approval to increase the size of the USMC again and dispatched two battalions for service in the conflict. Henderson died in office in 1859, having served as a dynamic commandant for 39 years.

Heywood, Charles (1839–1915) *Marine Corps commandant*

Ninth COMMANDANT OF THE MARINE CORPS, Heywood was a native of Maine and received his commission as second lieutenant in 1858. While serving aboard a number of ships during the Civil War, he participated in the capture of Fort Clark and Fort Hatteras and commanded guns aboard USS *Cumberland* when it was sunk by the Confederate ironclad *Virginia (ex-Merrimack).*

After the war, Heywood continued to serve sea duty until he was given command of MARINE BARRACKS, Washington, D.C., in 1876. He commanded

Major General Charles Heywood (USMC) *(U.S. Marine Corps)*

the USMC in PANAMA in 1885. In 1891, Heywood was appointed commandant and introduced important personnel reforms, requiring fitness reports and promotion examinations, and establishing the School of Application, a training facility for new USMC officers. Heywood was commandant during the SPANISH-AMERICAN WAR and during subsequent action in the PHILIPPINE INSURRECTION, NICARAGUA, and again in Panama. Promoted to major general in 1902, he was the first USMC officer to hold that rank. He retired the following year, having presided over the first great period of USMC expansion, from 3,300 men at the time of the Spanish-American War to 7,600 men upon his retirement.

HH-1H Iroquois   See AIRCRAFT, ROTARY-WING.

higher

USMC slang for an officer more interested in advancing to the next rank than in proper command and welfare of his marines.

High-Mobility Multipurpose Wheeled Vehicle (HUMVEE)   See WHEELED VEHICLES.

history, overview of USMC

American Revolution through War of 1812

The CONTINENTAL MARINES, precursor of the USMC, was established early in the AMERICAN REVOLUTION, on November 10, 1775, by resolution of the Continental Congress. Two battalions of marines were authorized for service as landing forces with the newly born Continental navy. The size of the Marine Corps was no more that 300 to 400 men, and it was disbanded, along with the Continental navy, after the Treaty of Paris ended the war in 1783.

By the end of the 18th century, U.S. relations with its revolutionary ally France had deteriorated to the point that, in 1798, an undeclared naval war, often called the Franco-American Quasi-War, began. Anticipating the development of a full-scale war, the Congress reestablished the USMC on July 11, 1798. Marines formed a contingent of U.S. warship crews, their duties being to keep order aboard ship, to help man the guns, and to serve as boarding and landing parties.

Although the Franco-American Quasi-War petered out by 1800, U.S. shipping, like that of other "Christian" nations, was preyed upon in the opening years of the 19th century by the BARBARY PIRATES, state-sanctioned seaborne raiders operating from the coast of North Africa, especially Tripoli. Marines were instrumental in operations against the pirates on what the MARINE HYMN commemorates as the "Shores of Tripoli."

During the WAR OF 1812, the USMC served mainly aboard U.S. Navy ships and therefore participated in a number of brilliant tactical naval victories. On land, a small USMC contingent was part of the defense of Washington at the disastrous Battle of BLADENSBURG (Maryland), in 1813. While army and militia forces crumbled before the British advance on the capital, marines and

An MCAS Miramar CH-53 Super Stallion from Marine Heavy Helicopter Squadron 466, the Wolfpack, makes a pass hitting its target, allowing the pilots to complete their requirements for California Department of Forestry Certification. Once certified, the pilots are authorized to provide air support to ground fire fighters as they fight wildfires.   *(U.S. Marine Corps)*

sailors held fast, until they were flanked and overwhelmed by vastly superior numbers. Far more successful was USMC participation in the Battle of NEW ORLEANS in 1814–15, when a small contingent formed the very center of Andrew Jackson's defensive line.

U.S.-Mexican War

The major USMC action after the War of 1812 was during the Second Seminole War (1835–42), when the Corps was assigned to assist with the "removal" of the Seminoles from Florida and Georgia in accordance with the Indian Removal Act of 1830.

The next major conflict was the U.S.-Mexican War (1846–48), in which the USMC not only performed its traditional seaborne duties, but also served with General Winfield Scott (USA) in his advance on Mexico City in 1847. Marines successfully operated to seize Mexican seaports on both the Gulf and Pacific coasts before joining Scott's advance at Pueblo, Mexico. Their participation in the invasion of Mexico City is commemorated in the Marine Hymn reference to the "Halls of Montezuma."

Civil War

The USMC was involved in the earliest action commonly associated with the Civil War when, on October 18, 1859, under the command of Colonel Robert E. Lee (USA), a company of marines fought a three-minute battle to recover the U.S. arsenal at Harpers Ferry, Virginia (present-day West Virginia), which had been seized by militant abolitionist John Brown and a handful of followers. During the war itself, marines served mainly at sea, with the Union navy, but a USMC battalion did fight at the First Battle of Bull Run (July 21, 1861). Other USMC units saw action while serving with naval blockading squadrons at Cape Hatteras, New Orleans, Charleston, and Fort Fisher.

Post–Civil War Years

The USMC was by no means idle after the Civil War, but was landed in small parties to protect U.S. lives and property worldwide, in Egypt, Colombia, Mexico, China, Cuba, Formosa, Uruguay, Argentina, Chile, Haiti, Alaska, Nicaragua, Japan, Samoa, and Panama. The largest operation during this period was in Korea in 1871, against the so-called "Salee River pirates." In a "weekend war," marines captured 481 guns, 50 Korean battle standards, and neutralized the important Han River forts. Two marines were awarded the Medal of Honor, the first time this decoration had been presented to members of the service.

Spanish-American War and After

At the commencement of the Spanish-American War in 1898, the USMC consisted of fewer than 3,000 men. One of these men, Private William Anthony, serving as orderly to Charles D. Sigsbee, captain of the U.S. battleship *Maine,* rescued his skipper after the ship exploded in Havana Harbor. Thus, a U.S. marine was the very first hero of the war.

Marines attached to the U.S. Navy squadron commanded by Commodore George Dewey at Manila Bay landed to secure the Cavite Navy Yard and held this position for three months until the arrival of the U.S. Army.

As the USMC was the first to fight in the Philippines, so it was the first to land in Cuba. On June 10, 1898, a USMC battalion hit the beach at Guantánamo Bay and seized an advance base for the U.S. fleet. The Battle of Cuzco Well, four days later, was also a USMC victory.

After the war, marines fought in the Philippine Insurrection and the Boxer Rebellion. They also served elsewhere in China and in Nicaragua, Panama, the Dominican Republic, Cuba, Mexico (in the 1914 U.S. landings at Veracruz), and Haiti.

World War I

By the time of U.S. entry into World War I in April 1917, the USMC had already proven itself as a bold expeditionary force, especially effective in small-scale police actions. Army strategists, including the overall commander of the American Expeditionary Force, General John J. Pershing (USA), had strong doubts about the effectiveness and usefulness of the USMC in large-scale conventional warfare. These doubts were soon laid to rest by USMC performance in France, especially at Belleau Wood, Soissons, Saint-Mihiel, Blanc Mont, and the Meuse-Argonne. USMC aviation also got its start in World War I, providing close air support for Allied troops.

Of the more than 309,000 marines who served in France, about one-third were either wounded or killed in action.

Interwar Period

Like the other services, the USMC suffered severe cutbacks after World War I. Yet, under Major General JOHN A. LEJEUNE, 13th COMMANDANT OF THE MARINE CORPS, the USMC became neither demoralized nor complacent. It was during the interwar years that the Corps pioneered and developed the doctrines of AMPHIBIOUS ASSAULT and AMPHIBIOUS OPERATION that would prove critical to victory in the Pacific campaign of the war to follow.

World War II

Although the USMC would fight almost exclusively in the Pacific theater of WORLD WAR II, the 1st Provisional Marine Brigade (4,000 marines) was assigned to occupy and garrison strategically important Iceland, landing in July 1941, six months before the United States entered the war.

After the United States entered the war, following the Japanese attack on Pearl Harbor, December 7, 1941, marines were caught in the early defeats— in the Philippines and at GUAM and WAKE ISLAND —but would be instrumental in the amphibious operations that retook the islands of the Pacific, one by one, during the course of the war. GUADALCANAL, BOUGAINVILLE, TARAWA, NEW BRITAIN, KWAJALEIN, ENIWETOK, SAIPAN, GUAM, TINIAN, PELELIU, IWO JIMA, and OKINAWA were all hard-won USMC victories.

USMC strength at the beginning of World War II was 70,425 men. By war's end, this CORPS had grown to its historical maximum strength of 471,905. Almost 87,000 marines were killed or wounded in action; 82 were awarded the Medal of Honor.

Korean War

As the USMC developed amphibious doctrine and tactics between World War I and World War II, the Corps focused, after World War II, on developing "vertical envelopment" capability using helicop-

ters. However, the first major USMC operation of the KOREAN WAR (1950–53) was amphibious, as marines played a key role in the brilliant landing at INCHON in September 1950. Following the recapture of Seoul, marines participated in the UN advance to the CHOSIN RESERVOIR, then participated in the retreat and recovery that followed the entry of the Chinese Communists into the war in October and November 1950. Although an armistice was concluded in 1953, USMC ground forces were not completely withdrawn until 1955. Some 25,000 marines were killed or wounded in Korea.

Cold War Conflicts

The Cold War era saw an explosion of so-called brush-fire wars, the kind of insurgent and guerrilla conflicts that had long been the Corps's specialty. Between 1955 and 1963, marines were sent to intervene in conflicts in the Tachen Islands (port of Zhejian Province, China), in Taiwan, Laos, and Thailand, as well as, early on, in South Vietnam. Marines evacuated U.S. nationals from Egypt during the Suez crisis of 1956, and in July 1958, at the request of the government of LEBANON, a brigade-size USMC force landed there to stave off a communist coup.

In April 1965, a USMC brigade was landed in the Dominican Republic to protect Americans and evacuate those who wished to leave after a leftist uprising.

Vietnam War

The USMC entered the VIETNAM WAR (which began as a conflict between French colonial forces and Vietnamese nationalists shortly after World War II) in 1962, flying helicopter missions, providing ground reconnaissance, and furnishing advisers to the Vietnamese Marine Corps. However, the landing of the 9th Marine Expeditionary Brigade at Da Nang in 1965 was the beginning of the Corps's large-scale presence in the war; by the summer of 1968, following the Tet Offensive (see KHE SANH), USMC strength in Vietnam rose to its maximum of about 85,000. The following year, USMC withdrawal began as part of the process and policy of

"Vietnamization," the transition of responsibility for the war to South Vietnamese forces.

The last major USMC ground forces left Vietnam in June 1971, but USMC units played critical roles in the desperate, dramatic, and highly successful evacuation of Saigon in 1975 and were, in true marine tradition, the "last out" of the zone of combat. The Vietnam War was the longest conflict in USMC history. Over almost 10 years, 13,000 marines were killed and 88,000 wounded.

After Vietnam

Marines continued to play a major role in defending U.S. interests worldwide after the Vietnam War. In July 1974, USMC forces evacuated U.S. and foreign nationals from Cyprus during unrest there; from mid-decade on, the Corps figured with increasing importance in Europe, defending the northern flank of NATO. With the other services, the USMC played a leading role in developing the Rapid Deployment Force, a multi-service unit designed to provide flexible and timely military response to any crisis in the world. It was also during the post-Vietnam era that the MARITIME PREPOSITIONING SQUADRONS (MPSs) were developed to enhance rapid deployment capability.

In response to a growing number of terrorist attacks on U.S. embassies during the 1980s, marines landed in August 1982 at Beirut, Lebanon, as part of a multinational peacekeeping force. On October 23, 1983, a truck packed with 12,000 pounds of explosives crashed through the outer defenses of the USMC headquarters building at the Beirut airport, killing 241 marines and wounding 70 others. The tragic event was a demonstration of just how hazardous peacekeeping duty can be.

Grenada Invasion and Operation Just Cause

In October 1983, marines participated in a controversial but ultimately successful intervention in GRENADA, a mission to checkmate leftist forces there and to rescue some 1,000 U.S. nationals. Six years later, the marines were instrumental in Operation Just Cause, an invasion of Panama with the objective of taking into custody Panamanian dictator Manuel Noriega, who had been indicted on charges of international drug trafficking. The operation also supported the installation of a new Panamanian government.

Persian Gulf War

The invasion and annexation of Kuwait by Iraq in August 1990 triggered Operation Desert Shield and Operation Desert Storm—the PERSIAN GULF WAR. As part of a massive military force of a coalition of nations, including the United States, between August 1990 and January 1991, 24 USMC infantry battalions and 40 squadrons, more than 92,000 marines, deployed to the gulf.

Following an intensive air campaign beginning on January 16, 1991, the ground war commenced on February 24, and the 1st and 2nd Marine Divisions broke through Iraqi defenses to occupy Kuwait. Simultaneously, Marine Expeditionary Brigades pinned down Iraqi forces along the coast of Kuwait; by the morning of February 28, the Iraqi army had been effectively neutralized.

Somalia, Bosnia, and Rwanda

In December 1992, USMC forces landed in the African nation of SOMALIA, torn by war and famine, to participate in Operation Restore Hope, a humanitarian relief effort that often turned violent.

Simultaneously, half a world away, USMC aviators were participating in Operation Deny Flight, patrolling a no-fly zone over Bosnia-Herzegovina in an effort to control the outbreak of renewed violence there.

Two years later, in April 1994, USMC units were sent into Rwanda, Africa, to evacuate 142 U.S. nationals during intense civil unrest.

Recent Operations

Marines landed in Haiti in September 1994 as part of a U.S. force working to effect a peaceful transition of democratic government in that perpetually troubled nation. During the 1990s, marines also participated in domestic counternarcotics efforts, in battling an epidemic of wildfires in the American West, and in a variety of flood and hurricane relief operations.

Following the terrorist attacks on the United States on September 11, 2001, a contingent of marines was landed in southern Afghanistan, on November 26, becoming the first U.S. troops deployed on the ground in the "War on Terrorism," a campaign to kill or capture forces of the Taliban and al-Qaeda—both of them terrorist organizations—and to locate, capture, or kill Osama bin Laden, identified as the mastermind behind the attacks on the United States. As of 2005, USMC forces were continuing to serve in Afghanistan.

In 2003, marines participated in Operation Iraqi Freedom, the U.S. invasion of Iraq to remove Iraqi dictator Saddam Hussein from office. The fiercest marine action was the 21-day Battle of Fallujah, which cleared the city of insurgents and pro-Saddam loyalists.

General Thomas Holcomb (USMC) *(U.S. Marine Corps)*

hit the deck!

In the marines, as in the navy, a command meaning "Get up and get out of bed."

Holcomb, Thomas (1879–1965) *Marine Corps commandant*

Seventeenth COMMANDANT OF THE MARINE CORPS, Holcomb was born in New Castle, Delaware, and was commissioned a second lieutenant in the USMC in 1900. He served at sea and then was assigned as part of the legation guard of the U.S. minister at Peking (Beijing). Promoted to major in 1916, he fought in all the major USMC actions during WORLD WAR I and was highly decorated by the United States and France. Promoted to lieutenant colonel in 1920, he was assigned to command the USMC detachment at GUANTÁNAMO BAY, Cuba; then, after attending Command and General Staff School, he was assigned to command the USMC detachment at Peking.

From 1930 to 1932, Holcomb attended the Naval War College and Army War College, then was assigned to the Office of Naval Operations.

Promoted to brigadier general in 1935, he was given command of Marine Corps Base Quantico and then made commandant in 1936. He was jumped in rank to major general.

Holcomb oversaw the massive expansion of the USMC during WORLD WAR II, from 15,000 to 305,000 men, and in 1942 was promoted to lieutenant general, the first USMC officer to achieve that rank. Holcomb retired as commandant in April 1944, with the rank of general, and was named U.S. ambassador to South Africa. He served for four years in that post.

Horse Marines

This unit was formed from the legation guard at Peking (Beijing) late in the 1920s, ostensibly to facilitate the protection of U.S. lives and property there; however, the unit's function was chiefly ceremonial. When formed, the Horse Marines, who were trained and equipped in the manner of U.S. Army cavalrymen, numbered only 20 individuals. By the mid-1930s, the unit had grown to 50 men.

HRP Rescuer ("Flying Banana")   See
AIRCRAFT, ROTARY-WING.

Hue, action in and around

Hue was the old capital of Vietnam and, during the
VIETNAM WAR, remained a very important city. It
was a frequent target of North Vietnamese and
Vietcong attacks, and, during the infamous Tet
Offensive that began on January 31, 1968, Hue fell
to an overwhelming attack and was immediately
occupied by North Vietnamese forces.

Marines were sent to reinforce the beleaguered
South Vietnamese troops (ARVN) pinned down in
the city. The 1st Battalion of the 1st Marines were
the first to arrive and were soon reinforced by the
5th Battalion of the 5th Marines. Intense urban
fighting ensued, house to house. It was February 9

before the southern area of the city and environs
had been retaken.

On February 12, ARVN units joined the 1st
Battalion, 5th Marines in an attack on the central
city, approaching from the north. The battle raged
for 10 more days, again largely house to house.
Although the historical heart of the city was
destroyed in four weeks of combat, the marines
and ARVN forces retook it and dealt the North
Vietnamese and the Vietcong a costly tactical
defeat—one of many the communists suffered as a
result of the Tet Offensive. Yet, although Tet was a
tactical disaster for the North, it was for them a
strategic victory in that it intensified the antiwar
movement in the United States and essentially
broke the will of the American people to continue
prosecuting the war.

I

Improved ECWCS Fiberpile Shirt and Trousers   See PERSONAL AND MISCELLANEOUS EQUIPMENT.

Inchon

During the KOREAN WAR, Inchon, on the west coast of Korea near Seoul, was the site of a spectacular and daring amphibious landing of marines and army troops, the 1st Marine Division and the army's 7th Division. The challenge was to land on a strategically critical but geographically difficult inlet, subject to extreme tides. The marines made the initial landing at 6:30 A.M. on September 15, 1950, at the island of Wolmi-do. The marines secured this objective within two hours and set up blocking positions. Later in the day, additional USMC battalions landed on the western side of Seoul. Early the next day, September 16, all USMC elements linked up east of Inchon and readily defeated a North Korean counterattack. The army contingent landed on the 18th.

The Inchon landing put U.S. and UN forces in position to take the offensive against the invading North Koreans and drive them deep into their own territory.

indirect fire systems

The following indirect fire systems are either currently included in the USMC inventory or are of historical importance in the service.

Advanced Field Artillery Tactical Data System

AFATDS is a joint army–USMC automated fire-support command, control, and coordination system intended to control and coordinate all fire-support weapons in the field.

Built by Raytheon Systems, AFATDS replaces the army's TACFIRE command system, which was only partially automated. The fully automated AFATDS fire support system minimizes the sensor-to-shooter timeline and increases the hit ratio. The system provides fully automated support for planning, coordinating, and controlling mortars, field artillery cannon, rockets, guided missiles, close air support, attack helicopter, and naval gunfire.

AN/TPQ-36 Firefinder Radar

This mobile radar set is designed to locate—with first-round accuracy—hostile artillery and mortar fire. Secondarily, it can also be employed to register friendly fire. The principal features of the AN/TPQ-36 Firefinder Radar are its light weight, its compact size, and its high degree of mobility. The set can detect projectiles launched at any angle within selected 90-degree azimuth sectors over 360 degrees of coverage. This includes the capacity to locate simultaneous-fire weapons as well as weapons that fire in separate bursts or volleys. Additionally, the set can be used to register and adjust friendly fire. In this mode, the weapon location is computed and then used to direct counter-battery fires. The set can be used by the artillery battalions to locate hostile weapons, both mortars and short- to medium-range weapons.

The AN/TPQ-36 system consists of an operational control group, OK-398/TPQ-36, and an antenna transceiver group, OY-71/TPQ-36. The latest configuration, Version 8, developed by Toby Hanna Army Depot and Grumman Electronics, consists of a new Operations Control Group (OCG) using the army Lightweight Multipurpose Shelter (LMS) mounted on a M-1097 HMMWV. This vehicle tows the Antenna Transceiver Group (ATG) with the integrated Modular Azimuth Positioning System (MAPS) mounted on an M-116A2E1 trailer. The OCG is controlled by an operator located either within the shelter or at a remote location. The second M-1097 HMMWV carries a MEP-112A generator mounted on an M-116A2E1 trailer. Yet another vehicle carries the crew. As of late 2003, the USMC operated 22 AN/TPQ-36 Firefinder Radar units.

General characteristics of the system include:

Manufacturer: Hughes Aircraft Company
Length, shelter: 106 in
Length, antenna/transceiver: 181.1 in
Width, shelter: 82.7 in
Width, antenna/transceiver: 82.7 in
Height, shelter: 70.9 in
Height, antenna/transceiver (in operation): 145.7 in
Height, antenna/transceiver (in transit): 82.7 in
Weight, shelter: 2,400 lb
Weight, antenna/transceiver: 3,200 lb
Power requirements: 115/200 VAC, three-phase, four-wire, 400 hertz, 10 kilowatt
Support equipment required: two M923 five-ton trucks, two 10-kilowatt generators
Crew: nine enlisted marines

The radar sets are deployed with headquarters batteries in artillery regiments and in counter-battery radar platoons.

AN/USQ-70 Position Azimuth Determining System

The AN/USQ-70 Position Azimuth Determining System is an artillery inertial survey system designed to provide to firing elements rapid and accurate measurements in position, elevation, and azimuth. It is a highly mobile surveying system that uses an inertial measurement unit interfaced with a digital computer to provide an accurate means of performing artillery survey. The AN/USQ-70 consists of an inertial measurement unit, a control and display unit, the computer, the power supply, the installation kit, and the electrical cable set. Also required are the primary pallet, the battery box, and the transit case.

General characteristics of the AN/USQ-70 Position Azimuth Determining System include:

Manufacturer: Litton Industries
Weight: 539 lb, including primary pallet, battery box, and transit case
Transported by: Humvee or helicopter
Surveying accuracy, horizontal position error: 23 ft
Surveying accuracy, vertical position error: 9.8 ft
Surveying accuracy, azimuth: 0.4 mm
Power requirements: 961 watts, 40 amperes, 24 VDC

The system is used by Artillery Survey Sections in artillery regiments and battalions and by Unmanned Aerial Vehicle (UAV) units. Two crew members operate the system.

M-49 Telescope

The M-49 is a a 20-power observation telescope for daytime use. It is used for observing target areas and also for assessing the effectiveness of artillery fire. The telescope has no reticle, and is therefore not intended for use as a sighting device. The telescope is mounted on the M-15 Tripod and includes an objective assembly, body tube, prism housing assembly, and eyepiece assembly with focusing sleeve. The front end of the body tube, which extends three quarters of an inch beyond the objective, provides an integral and permanent sunshade.

The M-49 has long been used by the USMC, especially in scout or sniper sections of the infantry battalion. Marines use it to detect and identify targets.

General characteristics of the telescope include:

Manufacturer: IMO, VARO, and other vendors
Length: 13.5 in
Weight (without tripod): 2.75 lb
Magnification: 20x

M-90 Radar Chronograph

The M-90 Radar Chronograph measures the muzzle velocity of field artillery weapons by means of a Doppler radar system consisting of a radio-frequency antenna, transmitter-receiver, readout display, and mounting brackets semi-permanently mounted to each artillery weapon. The antenna and transmitter-receiver are mounted on a nonrecoiling part of the howitzer and are connected to the control and display unit by a 30-meter cable. The radar chronograph itself is powered by an external source of 18 to 30 volts DC. The M-90 provides muzzle velocity data to the Fire Direction Center (FDC), enabling it to compute accurate fire control solutions. Each artillery battery is assigned one M-90. The instrument's only limitation is that it is unable to measure muzzle velocities of rocket-assisted projectiles or basebleed projectiles (specially designed to reduce drag and thereby enhance in-flight velocity).

General characteristics of the M-90 Radar Chronograph include:

Length: 33 in
Width: 380 in
Height: 20 in
Weight (including transit case and accessories): 200 lb

M-94 Muzzle Velocity System (MVS)

The newly developed M-94 Muzzle Velocity System (MVS) is designed to replace the standard M-90 Radar Chronograph at the artillery battery level. Its function is to measure the muzzle velocity of field artillery weapons using Doppler radar in conjunc-

tion with digital signal processing. This will enable artillery batteries to eliminate gross range bias errors, a large contributing factor to artillery inaccuracies. This system will measure all types of field artillery rounds, including base-bleed and rocket-assisted projectiles—two types of rounds the M-90 cannot measure.

The system consists of an antenna, an antenna bracket assembly, remote display unit, antenna cable/cable reel, and a transport case. Its general characteristics include:

Velocity measuring range: 150–2,000 m/per second
Caliber range: 20 mm and up
Projectile types: conventional, base-bleed, sabot-discarding, rocket-assisted, tracer ammunition, deep cavity
Accuracy: Within 0.05 percent of the true muzzle velocity
Firing rate: 18 rounds/min
Power requirement: 18–33 VDC
Power consumption: 18 watts in standby mode, 30 watts in measure mode
Total weight: less than 100 lb

M-101A1 105-mm
Light Howitzer, Towed

The M-101A1 105-mm Light Howitzer, Towed is a light, towed, general-purpose field artillery weapon used as a contingency weapon during MARINE AIR GROUND TASK FORCE (MAGTF) deployments that require greater mobility than the heavier and bigger M-198 155-mm howitzer can provide.

The M-101A1 consists of the 105-mm howitzer cannon, an M-2-series recoil mechanism, and carriage. The weapon can be used for direct or indirect fire. The cannon consists of a tube assembly, breech ring, and locking ring and is mounted on the recoil sleigh assembly. The firing mechanism is a continuous pull (self cocking) type activated by pulling a lanyard. Operation is single-load, air-cooled; ammunition is semi-fixed. The carriage is of the single axle and split trail type, with the trails divided at emplacement and drawn together (and locked) during travel. The howitzer is towed from an integral drawbar.

The M-101A1 carriage consists of an equilibrator, shield, elevating mechanism, cradle, gear, elevating arcs, traversing mechanism, top carriage, wheels, and trails. The recoil mechanism is a constant hydropneumatic-type shock absorber, which decreases the energy of the recoil gradually and so avoids violent movement of the cannon or carriage. It is installed in the cradle of the carriage. The USMC has 248 of these weapons.

Other general characteristics of this light howitzer include:

Manufacturer: Rock Island Arsenal
Length: 19.5 ft
Width: 7.25 ft
Height: 5.66 ft
Weight: 4,980 lb
Bore diameter: 105 mm
Maximum effective range: 6.99 miles
Rate of fire, maximum: 10 rounds/min
Rate of fire, sustained: 3 rounds/min

M-198 155-mm
Medium Howitzer, Towed

The M-198 155-mm Medium Howitzer, Towed, provides field artillery fire support for all MARINE AIR GROUND TASK FORCE (MAGTF) units. The weapon is built of aluminum and steel, and is air transportable by CH-53E Super Stallion helicopter and KC-130 Hercules fixed-wing aircraft. The M-198 replaces the M-114A2, providing increased range, improved reliability, and enhanced maintainability. Moreover, the use of rocket-assisted projectiles greatly extends the range, lethality, and counterbattery fire of artillery battalions using this weapon. The M-198 fires all current and developmental 155 mm ammunition, and the USMC, as of late 2003, maintains an inventory of 541.

General characteristics of the M-198 155-mm Medium Howitzer, Towed, include:

Manufacturer: Rock Island Arsenal
Length, in tow: 40 ft, 6 in
Length, firing: 36 ft, 2 in
Width, in tow: 9 ft, 2 in

U.S. Marines cover their ears as a round is fired from an M-198 155-mm Medium Howitzer during exercise Rim of the Pacific '04 in the Hawaiian Islands, on July 14, 2004. *(Department of Defense)*

Height, in tow: 9 ft, 6 in
Weight: 15,758 lb
Bore diameter: 155 mm
Maximum effective range with conventional ammunition: 13.92 miles
Maximum effective range with rocket-assisted projectile: 18.64 miles
Rate of fire, maximum: 4 rounds/min
Rate of fire, sustained: 2 rounds/min
Crew: nine marines

M-224 60-mm Lightweight Mortar

The M-224 60-mm Lightweight Mortar provides USMC company commanders with an indirect-fire weapon. The mortar is a smooth-bore, muzzle-loading, high-trajectory weapon. Its cannon assembly is made up of a barrel, combination base cap, and firing mechanism, and its mount consists of a bipod and a base plate, which is provided with screw-type elevating and traversing mechanisms. A supplementary short-range sight is attached to the base of the cannon tube for firing on the move and during assaults. The weapon is equipped with a spring-type shock absorber to absorb recoil.

The M-224 60-mm Lightweight Mortar is the modern replacement for the WORLD WAR II–era M-2 and M-19 60-mm mortars. Whereas these weapons had an effective range of little more than one mile, the new weapon can reach targets at 2.17 miles, using improved long-range ammunition. The M-224 is also backward-compatible with older ammunition.

General characteristics of the M-224 include:

Length: 40 in
Weight: 46.5 lb
Bore diameter: 60 mm
Maximum effective range: 2.17 mi
Rate of fire, maximum: 30 rounds/min
Rate of fire, sustained: 20 rounds/min

M-252 81-mm Medium Extended Range Mortar

The M-252 81-mm Medium Extended Range Mortar was adopted by the USMC in 1986 and is a modified version of the standard British 81 mm mortar developed in the 1970s. It is the USMC weapon assigned to the mortar platoon of an infantry battalion. This crew-served, medium weight weapon is highly accurate and capable of great range—15,000 to 18,500 feet—and impressive lethality. The cannon has a crew-removable breech plug and firing pin, and a short, tapered muzzle lead-in that acts as a blast attenuator. The finned breech end facilitates cooling. The M-252 uses the standard M-64 mortar sight that is compatible with the USMC's M-224 60-mm Lightweight Mortar.

General characteristics of the M-252 81-mm Medium Extended Range Mortar include:

Length: 56 in (142.24 cm)
Weight, mortar assembly: 35 lb
Weight, bipod: 26 lb
Weight, base plate: 25.5 lb
Weight, sight unit: 2.5 lb
Weight, total: 89 lb
Bore diameter: 81 mm
Maximum effective range: 18,700 ft
Rate of fire, maximum: 33 rounds/min
Rate of fire, sustained: 16 rounds/min
Elevation: 45 to 85 degrees

Pack Howitzer 1923-E2

This highly mobile 75-mm gun began replacing the USMC's imported French 75s in 1930. Because the Pack Howitzer was relatively light and could be easily broken down for transportation, it was ideally suited to use in rough terrain and mountains and in amphibious campaigning. Operation required a crew of five. The weapon fired a 16-pound shell 10,000 yards. The Pack Howitzer was very extensively used in the Pacific during World War II.

Individual Tactical Load-Bearing Vest
(ITLBV)   See PERSONAL AND MISCELLANEOUS EQUIPMENT.

Infantry Fighting Vehicle   See WHEELED VEHICLES.

infantry shelter   See PERSONAL AND MISCELLANEOUS EQUIPMENT.

inspector-instructor

The inspector-instructor is a regular USMC officer assigned to MARINE CORPS RESERVE units to ensure that each unit has the benefit of current and coordinated professional training. The "I&I" provides training assistance as well as guidance to the reserve unit. Additionally, the I&I ensures that the unit is trained up to the standards set by the USMC.

Instructional Management School   See COMBAT SERVICE SUPPORT SCHOOLS.

Iran Hostage Crisis

In 1979, religious extremists backed a successful coup d'état against the secular, U.S.-allied government of the shah of Iran. In February, the U.S. embassy in the capital city of Tehran was stormed by insurgents. Using tear gas and birdshot, the 19 marines of the legation guard fought the attackers off, but, under repeated attack, were forced to surrender. Two marines were wounded, and one was held by the guerrillas for a week. Ultimately, all marines and embassy staff were released. However, after this incident, the embassy staff was reduced— as was the legation guard, to 13 marines. In the meantime, the U.S. government had decided to allow the deposed shah, a longtime ally, to undergo cancer treatment in an American hospital. This prompted a new attack on the embassy on November 4, 1979. USMC legation guards do not constitute a defensive force—their mission is to keep order within the embassy—and the corporal in charge of the guards ordered his men to hold fire. He determined that an attempt to defend the embassy was likely to cause more casualties. As a result, 61 Americans were taken prisoner. In January 1980, five secretaries and five marines were released. The rest of the prisoners became hostages for 444 days.

On April 11, 1980, President Jimmy Carter approved a plan to rescue the hostages. The plan called for all of the armed services to participate in the rescue force. This led to operational confusion, which was compounded by a series of mechanical failures with the helicopters, one of which crashed into a C-130 transport plane on takeoff, killing eight persons, including five marines. The rescue mission was aborted, and, the element of surprise having been lost, no further attempt was made.

Iwo Jima

This tiny Pacific island in the Bonin group assumed critical strategic significance in WORLD WAR II because of two Japanese airfields located there. Possession of these was important to Japan, but even more important to the United States; they could be used as bases for B-29 fighter escorts over Japan and as emergency landing fields for crippled B-29s returning from missions.

In early 1945, the Japanese positions were extremely well prepared on the island, with some 20,000 troops hunkered down in pillboxes, bunkers, and blockhouses, as well as volcanic caves. The V Amphibious Corps, consisting of the 3rd, 4th, and 5th Marine Divisions, landed on February 19, 1945, following extremely heavy USAAF and USN bombardment. Despite this softening-up operation, resistance to the invaders was very heavy. While the USMC inflicted staggering casualties on the Japanese defenders, it also sustained heavy losses. On February 22, a battalion of marines attained the key objective of Mount Suribachi, highest point on the island, and raised a small flag. Shortly afterward, a party raised a larger flag, which was the subject of a Pulitzer Prize–winning photograph and the inspiration for the IWO JIMA MEMORIAL in Washington, D.C., as well as becoming an unofficial symbol of the USMC.

However, the taking of Mount Suribachi hardly signaled the end of the battle. The major phase of combat occurred on the flatlands, which were most vigorously defended by the Japanese. Although a flag-raising ceremony was held on March 13, fighting continued, and it was not until the Japanese

Sergeant Michael Strank, Corporal Harlon H. Block, Private First Class Franklin R. Sousley, Private First Class Rene A. Gagnon, Private First Class Ira Hayes, and Pharmacist's Mate Second Class John H. Bradley (USN) raise the American flag over Mount Suribachi, Iwo Jima, February 19, 1945.   *(Arttoday)*

commander committed suicide (rather than surrender) on March 26 that the island was deemed secure. USMC casualties were 6,821 killed and 19,207 wounded. Japanese casualties were virtually total: nearly 20,000 defenders killed.

Iwo Jima Memorial

Officially the U.S. Marine Corps War Memorial, this bronze sculpture group is located in Arlington, Virginia, a short distance from Arlington National Cemetery. The monument is based on the famous Pulitzer Prize–winning photograph by combat photographer Joe Rosenthal depicting five marines and a U.S. Navy hospital corpsman (Sergeant Michael Strank, Corporal Harlon H. Block, Private First Class Franklin R. Sousley, Private First Class Rene A. Gagnon, Private First Class Ira Hayes, and Pharmacist's Mate Second Class John H. Bradley [USN]) raising the Stars and Stripes on Mount Suribachi, IWO JIMA, on February 19, 1945, during the extremely costly battle to take this Pacific island. It is intended to commemorate the sacrifices of all marines who have died in battle since the founding of the USMC in 1775. The memorial was completed in 1954 by artist Felix de Weldon and was financed privately. Its flag flies 24 hours.

J

jarhead

Slang term for a marine. Presumably, the term is a reference to the buzz-like haircut marines typically wear, which gives the human head a somewhat jar-like appearance.

Javelin   See ANTIARMOR WEAPONS.

Joint Service Combat Shotgun   See WEAPONS, INDIVIDUAL AND CREW-SERVED.

Joint Service Lightweight Integrated Suit Technology   See NUCLEAR-BIOLOGICAL-CHEMICAL EQUIPMENT.

Jones, James L. (1943–   ) *Marine Corps commandant*

The 32nd COMMANDANT OF THE MARINE CORPS, Jones was born on December 19, 1943, in Kansas City, Missouri, and was raised in France, returning to the United States to attend the Georgetown University School of Foreign Service, from which he earned a bachelor of science degree in 1966. The next year he was commissioned a second lieutenant in the USMC, completed Basic School in October 1967, and was ordered to South Vietnam, where he served as a platoon and company commander with Company G, 2nd Battalion, 3rd Marines. While serving in the VIETNAM WAR, he was promoted to first lieutenant in June 1968.

On his return to the United States in December 1968, Jones was assigned to Marine Corps Base Camp Pendleton as a company commander until May 1970. He was then posted to MARINE BARRACKS, Washington, D.C., again as a company com-

General James L. Jones (USMC)   *(U.S. Marine Corps)*

mander, serving in this assignment until July 1973. Promoted to captain in December 1970, he studied at the Amphibious Warfare School, Quantico, Virginia, during 1973–74, and in November 1974 was ordered to the 3rd Marine Division, OKINAWA, where he served as the commander of Company H, 2nd Battalion, 9th Marines, until December 1975.

From January 1976 to August 1979, Jones served in the Officer Assignments Section at HEADQUARTERS MARINE CORPS, Washington, D.C., and was promoted to major in July 1977. He subsequently became Marine Corps Liaison Officer to the U.S. Senate, receiving promotion to lieutenant colonel in September 1982, and serving as liaison until July 1984. Selected to attend the National War College in Washington, D.C., Jones graduated in June 1985 and was assigned command of the 3rd Battalion, 9th Marines, 1st Marine Division, Camp Pendleton, from July 1985 to July 1987, returning in August 1987 to Headquarters Marine Corps as senior aide to the commandant of the Marine Corps.

Promoted to colonel in April 1988, Jones was named military secretary to the commandant in February 1989 and the following year was assigned as commanding officer, 24th Marine Expeditionary Unit at Marine Corps Base Camp Lejeune, North Carolina. During his tour as commander, he participated in Operation Provide Comfort in northern Iraq and Turkey and was promoted to brigadier general on April 23, 1992.

In July 1992, Jones was named deputy director, operations and training, U.S. European Command, Stuttgart, Germany, then was reassigned as chief of staff, Joint Task Force Provide Promise, for operations in Bosnia-Herzegovina and Macedonia. In 1994, on his return to the United States, Jones was advanced to major general and was assigned to command 2nd Marine Division, Marine Forces Atlantic, Camp Lejeune. During 1996, Jones served as director, Expeditionary Warfare Division, Office of the Chief of Naval Operations and was subsequently named deputy chief of staff for Plans, Policies and Operations, Headquarters Marine Corps, Washington, D.C., and promoted to lieutenant general. After his promotion, Jones was assigned as military assistant to the secretary of defense, and, on June 30, 1999, he was promoted to general. The following month, he assumed the post of commandant.

K

KC-130 Hercules   See AIRCRAFT, FIXED-WING.

Kelley, Paul X. (1928–   ) *Marine Corps
commandant*

The 28th COMMANDANT OF THE MARINE CORPS, Kelley was born in Boston and was commissioned a second lieutenant after graduating from Villanova University in 1950. After serving at Marine Corps Base Camp Lejeune and Marine Corps Base Camp Pendleton, he was ordered to sea duty with the Sixth Fleet, then was stationed in Japan, where he became aide-de-camp to the deputy commander of FLEET MARINE FORCE, Pacific. After training at the army's Airborne Pathfinder School, Fort Benning, Georgia, Kelley saw service with the British Royal Marines as an exchange officer. He served in Aden, Singapore, Malaya, and Borneo before he returned to the United States as commanding officer of the Marine Barracks Newport, Rhode Island.

Kelley served in Vietnam (see VIETNAM WAR) in 1964 with the 3rd Amphibious Force. Promoted to lieutenant colonel, he returned to the United States in 1966 as USMC representative at Fort Benning. After attending the Air War College, Kelley was appointed military assistant to the commandant of the Marine Corps in 1969. The following year, as colonel, he returned to Vietnam in command of the 1st Marines, then brought the regiment back to Camp Pendleton in 1971.

In 1971, Kelley was appointed assistant to the director of the Joint Staff in Plans and Policy. In 1974, promoted to brigadier general, he was given command of the 4th Division and, in 1975, became director of the Development Center at Marine Corps Base Quantico.

Kelley became deputy chief of staff at HEADQUARTERS MARINE CORPS, Washington, D.C., in 1978 and, in 1981, was appointed to command the Rapid Deployment Joint Task Force, headquartered at MacDill Air Force Base. At this time, Kelley was promoted to general and, in July of 1981, was made assistant commandant of the Marine Corps. He was named commandant in 1983 and served until June 30, 1987.

Khe Sanh

During the VIETNAM WAR this village in South Vietnam's Quang Tri Province, near the Demilitarized Zone (DMZ), was a major USMC strong point from which marines attempted to control infiltration of South Vietnam from the north. Khe Sanh came under siege in February 1968 as part of the Tet Offensive and was successfully defended, although the 77-day siege was not broken until April. The position assumed a political importance far in excess of its actual strategic significance, as both sides came to see possession of it as vital to victory.

KLR 250-D8 Marine Corps Motorcycle

See WHEELED VEHICLES.

Korean War

The Korean War began on June 25, 1950, when Soviet-trained and Soviet-equipped troops of the North Korean army crossed the 38th parallel to invade South Korea, quickly overrunning the modest forces of that country.

Pursuant to his administration's policy of "containment"—using limited military action to confront and contain the spread of communism wherever it appeared—President Harry S. Truman mobilized U.S. forces. The supremely difficult objective of United Nations–sanctioned intervention in Korea was to prevent the spread of communism into the south and even, perhaps, to unify the nation, north and south, under a democratic government, while avoiding direct confrontation with the People's Republic of China or the Soviet Union. Such a "limited war" made victory difficult, but the alternative, an all-out war, was too risky to contemplate in an era of atomic weapons.

The first U.S. strikes were from the air, followed by U.S. Army divisions brought in from Japan and the Central Pacific and fighting under the aegis and authority of the United Nations. Post–WORLD WAR II demobilization had greatly reduced the strength and readiness of U.S. forces, which, initially, were badly outnumbered and compelled to fight a desperate holding action in the south.

In contrast to past interventions, there were no initial plans to use USMC forces in Korea; nevertheless, all MARINE CORPS RESERVE units were put on active status, and on July 7, 1950, the 6,500-man 1st Provisional Brigade was formed at Marine Corps Base Camp Pendleton. It arrived in Korea on July 12. Marine Air Group 33, flying the F4U Corsair, was also deployed. Although the theater commander, General Douglas MacArthur (USA), planned to hold the 1st Provisional Brigade for use in his daring landing at INCHON, he deployed it early to help defend Pusan. Incurring heavy losses, the marines nevertheless drove the North Koreans

back some five miles before the brigade was pulled back on September 5 preparatory to the Inchon operation.

The marines were a key part of the Inchon operation, which put UN forces in a position from which they drove the North Korean invaders back across the 38th parallel and, ultimately, deep into North Korean territory.

The UN counterattack was swift and successful. But warnings came from various military and political advisers that the action would surely provoke intervention from China as the counterattack neared the Yalu River and the Manchurian border. General MacArthur repeatedly dismissed the likelihood of such intervention, but it in fact occurred in October and November 1950. Marine units now functioned to protect the rear and flanks of the retreating army forces in what proved to be some of the hardest, most bitter fighting of the war. The enemy was not only the North Koreans and Chinese, but the northern winter, which dropped temperatures to some 20 degrees below zero.

Early in 1951, the retreat was halted south of the 38th parallel. By June 1951, peace talks were under way, and UN forces were used mainly in a defensive strategy, which proved costly to the communists, yet also frustrating to American military commanders, who believed that politicians and diplomats were denying them victory. Marine operations during the rest of the war, from June 1951 until the truce declared on July 27, 1953, focused on attacking and seizing certain strategic strong points in order to keep them from falling to the enemy. It was a heartbreaking and difficult mission.

When the shooting ceased on July 27, 1953, UN forces had achieved at least one of Truman's original policy objectives: Intervention had "contained" communism north of the 38th parallel. This did little to moderate the frustration of some U.S. military commanders, who felt that genuine victory had been withheld. Nevertheless, the intervention had succeeded in containing communism without triggering a third world war.

Krag-Jorgenson Rifle   See WEAPONS, INDIVI-
DUAL AND CREW-SERVED.

Krulak, Charles C. (1942–   ) *Marine Corps commandant*

The 31st COMMANDANT OF THE MARINE CORPS, Krulak was born in Quantico, Virginia, and graduated from the U.S. Naval Academy at Annapolis in 1964. He graduated from the Amphibious Warfare School in 1968 and was awarded a master's degree from George Washington University in 1973. Krulak also graduated from the Army Command and General Staff College (1976) and from the National War College (1982). In addition, Krulak saw combat in the VIETNAM WAR and was commanding officer of the Special Training Branch at Marine Corps Recruiting Depot San Diego and commanded the Counter Guerrilla Warfare School at OKINAWA.

Krulak was company officer at the U.S. Naval Academy in 1970 and, from 1973 to 1976, commanded the Marine Barracks at the North Island USMC Air Station. From 1983 to 1985, Krulak was commanding officer of the 3rd Battalion, 3rd Marines, then served in various staff positions, before receiving appointment as plans officer in the FLEET MARINE FORCE in 1982. After serving as deputy director in the White House Military Office beginning in 1987, he was given command of the 10th Marine Expeditionary Brigade in 1989, then made assistant divisional commander of the 2nd Division. Named to command the 6th Marine Expeditionary Brigade in 1990, Krulak went on to assignment as assistant deputy chief of staff for manpower in August 1991. Promoted to major general in 1992, he was named commander of the Combat Development Command at Marine Corps Base Quantico in August 1992. As a lieutenant general, Krulak was appointed to command Fleet Marine Force, Pacific, in July 1994; promoted to general the following year, he was named commandant of the Marine Corps on June 30, 1995.

Krulak, Victor H. (1913–   ) *Marine Corps general*

A Denver native, Krulak graduated from the United States Naval Academy with a commission as a second lieutenant in the USMC in May 1934. In 1936, he was assigned to the 6th Marines at Marine Corps Base San Diego, then was stationed the next year at Shanghai with the 4th Marines. After his return to the United States, he attended the junior course at Marine Corps Base Quantico and was assigned to the 1st Brigade.

Krulak was appointed to the staff of the Amphibious Corps, Atlantic, in April 1941 and was promoted to captain. He was then transferred to the staff of Major General Holland "Howlin' Mad" Smith in September 1942, when the Amphibious Corps was moved to San Diego. After taking parachute training in February 1943, Krulak was shipped out to New Caledonia in the Pacific, where he assumed command of the 2nd Parachute Battalion. As a lieutenant colonel, Krulak led his unit in action at Vella Lavella (September) and on CHOISEUL Island (October). He was decorated with the Navy Cross for Choiseul, but had to return to the United States for treatment of wounds suffered during the assault.

After light duty at the Division of Plans in Washington, D.C., Krulak joined the 6th Division in October 1944 as assistant chief of staff for operations. In this capacity, he participated in planning and directing the invasion of OKINAWA. For his contribution to this invasion, Krulak received the Legion of Merit.

In the postwar USMC, Krulak was given command of the USMC Research Section and was appointed assistant director of the Senior School at Quantico. He assumed command of the 5th Marines at Marine Corps Base Camp Pendleton in June 1949, was promoted to colonel, and became assistant chief of staff for operations of the FLEET MARINE FORCE, Pacific. In 1951, he was named chief of staff, Fleet Marine Force, Pacific.

Promoted to brigadier general in 1956, Krulak was named assistant commander of the 3rd Divi-

Lieutenant General Victor H. Krulak (USMC)   *(U.S. Marine Corps)*

sion, stationed at Okinawa. He subsequently returned to Quantico as director of the Educational Center there and was promoted to major general in November 1959. Shortly after this, he was appointed to command Marine Corps Recruit Depot San Diego, then became, in 1962, special assistant to the director for counterinsurgency

under the Joint Chiefs of Staff. This appointment made Krulak the obvious choice for chief of the Joint Staff Mission to Vietnam in January 1963. Krulak became an important figure in U.S. military policy with regard to Vietnam, and he favored a strategy of pacification rather than the all-out confrontation strategy advocated by the army.

Krulak's final command was as commander of Fleet Marine Force, Pacific; although he was a candidate for COMMANDANT OF THE MARINE CORPS, he retired in 1968 before any such appointment was made.

Kwajalein, Battle of

A large atoll among some 90 islands in the Marshall Islands, Kwajalein was the focus of an important U.S. assault and invasion during WORLD WAR II. The objective was Kwajalein, largest of the atoll islands, and the twin islands of ROI-NAMUR. On February 1, 1944, two regiments of the USMC 4th Division landed on Roi-Namur. Roi was quickly secured, but the marines met stubborn resistance on Namur, which was not taken until February 2.

While the marines defeated the Japanese on Roi-Namur, the army's 7th Division captured a number of small islands to put them in position to attack Kwajalein, which fell after a three-day battle.

Kwajalein Atoll provided ample anchorage for U.S. Navy ships mounting attacks against the Marianas, while Roi became the base for a bomber airfield.

L

lance corporal   See RANKS AND GRADES.

landing craft

Strictly speaking, landing craft include any sea-going craft used in landing operations. This entry also includes the broader range of assault craft used by the marines.

Air-Cushion Vehicles

Air-cushion vehicles travel at high speeds over water, ground, or marshy surface on a cushion of air generated by the vehicle and trapped beneath it in a flexible-skirted chamber. The marines (as well as the navy and army) use these vehicles for amphibious assaults and, sometimes, to move troops and equipment from ship to shore.

The marines employ the following air-cushion vehicles:

Landing Craft, Air Cushion (LCAC)

LCACs transport weapons systems, equipment, cargo, and personnel of marine assault elements from ship to shore and across the beach. The LCAC is a high-speed, over-the-beach, fully amphibious landing craft capable of carrying a payload of 60–75 tons at speeds in excess of 40 knots. A hovercraft, the LCAC can operate in waters regardless of depth, underwater obstacles, shallows, or adverse tides. It can operate inland, clearing obstacles up to 4 feet, regardless of terrain or topography. The craft

A U.S. Navy Landing Craft, Air Cushion, more commonly known as LCAC, loaded with Marines and their equipment from 3rd Marine Regiment, heads toward the beach during amphibious assault training. *(Department of Defense)*

operates on mud flats, sand dunes, ditches, marsh-lands, riverbanks, wet snow, and slippery and icy shorelines.

Developed by the marines and navy during 1977–81, the LCAC was authorized for full production in 1987. The craft are operated by the navy for the landing of marines. General characteristics of the LCAC include:

Builder: Textron Marine and Land Systems; Lockheed Aircraft; Avondale Gulfport Marine

Power plant: four Avco-Lycoming gas turbines, 12,280 horsepower; two shrouded reversible-pitch propellers; four double-entry fans for lift

Length: 88 ft

Beam: 47 ft

Displacement, fully loaded: 200 tons

Capacity: 60 tons (75-ton overload)

Speed: 40+ knots, with payload

Armament: two 12.7-mm machine guns; gun mounts support a wide variety of weapons

Crew: five

Range: 200 miles at 40 knots, with payload; 300 miles at 35 knots, with payload

Personnel capacity: 24 marines

LACV-30

The LACV-30 is the most versatile hovercraft operated by the navy. It may be used in a variety of roles, including patrol of intercoastal, harbor, and inland waterways and for search and rescue, but the marines generally employ it for personnel and cargo transport in landing assault scenarios.

The LACV-30 maneuvers on snow, desert, ice, slush, marshes, river beds, and swamps. It can operate in rough seas. Payload is 30 tons, with more than 1,600 square feet of cargo deck. General characteristics include:

Length, overall: 76.5 ft

Beam, overall (on cushion): 36.9 ft

Height, overall (on cushion): 28.11 ft

Height, cargo deck (on cushion): 7.1 ft

Cargo deck: 51 ft by 32 ft

Cruise speed: 45 mph

Payload, maximum: 30 tons

Main propulsion: two Pratt and Whitney ST6-76 Twin Packs (gas turbines)

Propellers: two 9-foot-diameter variable-pitch propellers

Lift fans: two 7-foot-diameter centrifugal fixed-pitch fans

Fuel capacity: 2,240 gal

Before the advent of air-cushion craft, the marines used an array of conventional landing craft. Some are still in use.

Landing Craft, Personnel (LCP)

The LCP was developed by the USMC in conjunction with the Eureka Tugboat Company (New Orleans) in 1940. The original boats were 36 feet long and capable of carrying 36 fully equipped marines. Although some had gas engines, most were diesels, capable of making eight knots. Wood hulled and with plywood gunwales, the LCPs were not very durable and were replaced by a new generation of LCP, the LCP(R), in mid-1942. The most important innovation was a forward ramp for easier and faster troop unloading. Early in 1943, the LCP(R) was replaced by the landing craft, vehicle, personnel (LCVP) and the landing craft vehicle, tracked (LVT).

Landing Craft, Tank (LCT)

The LCT originated in England, and a U.S. version, LCT, Mk-5, entered service late in 1942. The ship was 112 feet long and could carry five 25-ton or four 40-ton tanks for an AMPHIBIOUS OPERATION and in an AMPHIBIOUS ASSAULT. An improved Mk-6 appeared in 1944. Although slow, making a top speed of only 7 knots, the ships were used extensively in the Pacific to transport and land tanks.

Landing Craft, Vehicle Personnel (LCVP)

The landing craft, vehicle personnel (LCVP) replaced the landing craft, personnel (LCP) in 1943 for amphibious assault. Like the earlier craft, it was 36 feet long and made of wood, but it was armored and had an armored ramp. Its 225-horsepower engine drove it at 9 knots, a knot better than the LCP. LCVPs were built in profusion—25,358 by the end of the war—and they were used by the USMC and USA, in both the Pacific and European theaters.

In addition to major landing craft, the marines employ a variety of specialized small craft for landing assault purposes. These include:

Combat Rubber Raiding Craft

The CRRC, or "Rubber Duck," is a raft used by the USMC as well as by army units (Green Berets and Rangers) and Navy SEALs for clandestine insertions and extractions. The raft is 15 feet long and 6 feet wide and can hold five troops with equipment. The CRRC is normally powered by a 55-horsepower outboard motor, which will move the raft at 20 knots over a range of 65 miles.

Riverine Assault Craft (RAC)

The USMC uses the Riverine Assault Craft (RAC) as an inland and coastal waterway patrol craft. Its assigned missions typically include armed escort; command, control, and communications; transport; armed reconnaissance; and pursuit and interception.

The Riverine Assault Craft is fast, very maneuverable, and highly survivable in the river environment, enabling it to direct fire support and to conduct command/control, armed escort, electronic warfare, pursuit/intercept, and scout/patrol missions. It can serve as an effective platform for a wide array of military and commercial communication and electronic systems as well as crew-served weapons systems.

The craft features an aluminum hull and is powered by twin inboard, 300-horsepower Cummins turbo diesels, which are connected to Hamilton water jets. Fore and aft gun tubs may mount either the M-2 50-caliber Heavy Machine Gun or the Mk-19 40-mm Grenade Machine Gun. Medium machine guns may also be mounted, on pintles that are fixed to the port and starboard gunwales.

The Riverine Assault Craft is crewed by four marines and can additionally transport as many as 15 combat-loaded marines. It has a very shallow draft, which enables it to operate in as little as 8 inches of water while on plane and 30 inches of water while moving slowly or stopped. The craft's transport trailer may be towed by a 5-ton cargo truck.

General characteristics of the Riverine Assault Craft (RAC) include:

Length: 35 ft
Beam: 9 ft, 2 in
Draft: 30 in (8 in on plane)
Displacement, empty: 13,600 lb
Displacement, full load: 16,400 lb
Speed, maximum: 43 mi per hr
Speed, cruise: 31 mi per hr
Acceleration from cruise to 40 miles per hour: 10 sec
Range: 400 mi
Fuel endurance: 8 hr
Power: twin 300-hp Cummins diesel engines driving Hamilton 271 waterjets
Crew: four to five
Troop lift capacity: a combat-loaded USMC rifle SQUAD, consisting of 10 to 15 marines
Communications: military HF/VHF/UHF RAY-90 Marine band transceiver
Navigation: R40X Radar; V820 Depth Finder; Raystar 920 GPS; RayNav 780 LORAN-C; Fluxgate Compass; Magnetic Compass
Armament: fore and aft gun tubs capable of mounting 7.62-mm, 50-caliber or 40-mm automatic weapons; port and starboard pintle mounts for 7.62-mm machine guns
Transportability: Amphibious Ship, CH-53E Super Stallion, KC-130 Hercules C-141 (or larger transport aircraft), 5-ton truck

Landing Operations Doctrine

Published by the U.S. Navy in 1938, *Landing Operations Doctrine* was a revision of a USMC document, *Tentative Manual for Landing Operations*, published in 1934. The original document and its revision embodied the amphibious warfare doctrine that would dominate U.S. assault operations in the Pacific during WORLD WAR II and put the USMC front and center as the service of choice for amphibious assault operations. The U.S. Army based its field manual, *Landing Operations on Hostile Shores,* on the USMC document and the USN revision of it.

Landing Vehicle, Tracked (LVT and LVT[A])
See AMPHIBIOUS VEHICLES.

Laser Rangefinder AN/GVS-5   See PERSONAL AND MISCELLANEOUS EQUIPMENT.

LAV-25   See AMPHIBIOUS VEHICLES.

leatherneck
This nickname for a marine is as old as the USMC itself and comes from the leather collar or stock prescribed in 1776 by the U.S. Navy as part of the marine uniform. The idea behind the leather stock was utilitarian—to ward off saber blows to the neck—but it was never practical for this purpose. Moreover, it was singularly uncomfortable. Despite its questionable utility and the discomfort it caused, the leather stock remained a part of the USMC uniform until after the CIVIL WAR. The nickname survived well beyond that period and was especially current during WORLD WAR II.

Lebanon
USMC forces were first dispatched to this small Middle Eastern nation in 1958 at the request of the Lebanese president, who was threatened by a Syrian-backed revolution. Three battalions were deployed, later reinforced by an army unit. The withdrawal of U.S. forces began after an election on July 31, 1958, restored stability. The withdrawal was completed in October.

In 1982, the U.S. deployed 800 marines of the 32nd Marine Amphibious Unit to operate with French and Italian troops as UN peacekeepers in Lebanon. The 32nd was relieved by the 24th on October 30, 1982. By this time, marines and other UN forces were the frequent targets of warring factions contending for control of Lebanon, particularly in the capital city of Beirut. On October 23, 1983, a truck packed with 12,000 pounds of explosives crashed through the outer defenses of the USMC headquarters building at the Beirut airport. The suicide bomber detonated the explosives, killing 241 marines and wounding 70 others; simultaneously, another bomber attacked a building housing French paratroops, killing 58.

Despite this tragedy, the USMC presence was maintained in Lebanon until February 7, 1984, when President Ronald Reagan announced the withdrawal of all marines except for a small force charged with guarding the embassy.

Legation Guards   See U.S. MARINE CORPS SECURITY GUARD BATTALION.

Lejeune, John A. (1867–1942) *Marine Corps commandant*
The 13th COMMANDANT OF THE MARINE CORPS, Lejeune was a Cajun born and raised in Pointe Coupee Parish, Louisiana. He graduated from Louisiana State University and, subsequently, the U.S. Naval Academy (1888), cruised as a navy midshipman for two years, then was commissioned a second lieutenant in the USMC. During the SPANISH-AMERICAN WAR, Lejeune commanded the marine contingent serving aboard the USS *Cincinnati*. In November 1903, as a major, he landed at Colón, Panama, to protect the newly created Panamanian government, which the United States supported, largely to ensure the future construction of the Panama Canal.

Lejeune commanded 3,000 marines in the occupation of VERACRUZ, Mexico, to oppose the Huerta regime in 1913 and support the installation of Venustiano Carranza as president. Four years later, Lejeune commanded the 2nd Division during WORLD WAR I and participated at SAINT-MIHIEL and the Meuse-Argonne. On his return to the United States in 1919, Lejeune served as commandant of Marine Corps Base Quantico until, in Jan-

Lieutenant General John A. Lejeune (USMC)   *(U.S. Marine Corps)*

uary 1920, he was named commandant of the USMC. He served in this post for nine years, retiring in 1929 to become superintendent of the Virginia Military Academy. Shortly before he died, he was promoted to lieutenant general on the retired list. Marine Corps Base Camp Lejeune, North Carolina, is named in his honor.

lieutenant colonel   See RANKS AND GRADES.

lieutenant general   See RANKS AND GRADES.

Light Armored Vehicle–Command and Control (LAV-C2)   See AMPHIBIOUS VEHICLES.

Light Armored Vehicle–Logistics (LAV-L)
See AMPHIBIOUS VEHICLES.

Light Armored Vehicle–Mortar (LAV-M)
See AMPHIBIOUS VEHICLES.

Light Armored Vehicle–Recovery (LAV-R)
See AMPHIBIOUS VEHICLES.

Logistics Operations School   See COMBAT SERVICE SUPPORT SCHOOLS.

M

M-1 .30-caliber Carbine See WEAPONS, IN-
DIVIDUAL AND CREW-SERVED.

M-1A1 Main Battle Tank See TRACKED
VEHICLES.

M-1 Mine-Clearing Blade System See
TRACKED VEHICLES.

M-2HB Browning Machine Gun See
WEAPONS, INDIVIDUAL AND CREW-SERVED.

M-3A1 Antitank Gun See ANTIARMOR
WEAPONS.

M-9 Armored Combat Earthmover (ACE)
See TRACKED VEHICLES.

M-9 Personal Defense Weapon See WEAP-
ONS, INDIVIDUAL AND CREW-SERVED.

M-16A2 Rifle See WEAPONS, INDIVIDUAL AND
CREW-SERVED.

**M-17 Lightweight Decontamination
System** See NUCLEAR-BIOLOGICAL-CHEMICAL
EQUIPMENT.

**M-21 Remote-Sensing Chemical Agent
Automatic Alarm** See NUCLEAR-BIOLOGICAL-
CHEMICAL EQUIPMENT.

**M-40/42 Chemical/Biological Protective
Masks** See NUCLEAR-BIOLOGICAL-CHEMICAL EQUIP-
MENT.

M-40A1 Sniper Rifle See WEAPONS, INDIVI-
DUAL AND CREW-SERVED.

M-47 Dragon II See ANTIARMOR WEAPONS.

M-49 Telescope See INDIRECT FIRE SYSTEMS.

M-60 Machine Gun See WEAPONS,
INDIVIDUAL AND CREW-SERVED.

**M-60A1 Armored Vehicle-Launched
Bridge (M60A1 AVLB)** See TRACKED VEHICLES.

M-82 Special Application Scope Rifle (SASR) See WEAPONS, INDIVIDUAL AND CREW-SERVED.

M-90 Radar Chronograph See INDIRECT FIRE SYSTEMS.

M-94 Muzzle Velocity System (MVS) See INDIRECT FIRE SYSTEMS.

M-101A1 105-mm Light Howitzer, Towed See INDIRECT FIRE SYSTEMS.

M-151 TOW See ANTIARMOR WEAPONS.

M-198 155-mm Medium Howitzer, Towed See INDIRECT FIRE SYSTEMS.

M-203 40-mm Grenade Launcher See WEAPONS, INDIVIDUAL AND CREW-SERVED.

M-224 60-mm Lightweight Mortar See INDIRECT FIRE SYSTEMS.

M-240G machine gun See WEAPONS, INDIVIDUAL AND CREW-SERVED.

M-249 SAW See WEAPONS, INDIVIDUAL AND CREW-SERVED.

M-252 81-mm Medium Extended-Range Mortar See INDIRECT FIRE SYSTEMS.

M-1911A1 .45-caliber Pistol See WEAPONS, INDIVIDUAL AND CREW-SERVED.

M-1917A1 Browning Machine Gun See WEAPONS, INDIVIDUAL AND CREW-SERVED.

M-1918 Browning Automatic Rifle (BAR) See WEAPONS, INDIVIDUAL AND CREW-SERVED.

M-1919A4 Browning Machine Gun See WEAPONS, INDIVIDUAL AND CREW-SERVED.

M-1919A6 Browning Machine Gun See WEAPONS, INDIVIDUAL AND CREW-SERVED.

M-1921 and M1928A1 Thompson Submachine Gun See WEAPONS, INDIVIDUAL AND CREW-SERVED.

M-1941 Johnson Light Machine Gun See WEAPONS, INDIVIDUAL AND CREW-SERVED.

major See RANKS AND GRADES.

major general See RANKS AND GRADES.

Makin, Battle of
Located in the GILBERT ISLANDS, Makin Atoll was the site of a key Japanese radio station (on Butaritari Island) early in WORLD WAR II. Colonel EVANS CARLSON led his 2nd Raider Battalion against the island on October 17, 1942, destroying the radio station and wiping out the Japanese garrison there almost to a man.

While this early USMC triumph was most welcome—and elimination of the radio station an important tactical victory—the raid had an important but adverse strategic effect. It alerted the Japanese to the need for strengthening island defenses, and it made the situation in the Pacific that much more difficult for the navy, army, and Marine Corps.

Mameluke Sword

Worn by USMC officers, the Mameluke Sword copies the pattern of the swords used by Muslims in North Africa and Arabia at the time of the successful USMC assault on Tripoli in 1805 during the Tripolitan War. Lieutenant PRESLEY NEVILLE O'BANNON received a Muslim-style sword from the governor of Tripoli in token of the governor's surrender. (The engagement is commemorated in the MARINE HYMN as the "shores of Tripoli.") A cross hilt and

An original Mameluke Sword from the 1800s   (U.S. Marine Corps)

ivory grip distinguish the ceremonial weapon, which is carried on parade and, occasionally, to denote the officer of the day.

The Mameluke Sword is reserved for officers' wear. Staff noncommissioned officers wear an NCO Sword whenever dress blues are worn. Additionally, sergeants may wear the NCO Sword for drill with troops, parades, reviews, and ceremonies. While the Mameluke Sword is distinctive to the USMC, the NCO Sword is identical to the U.S. Army infantry officer's sword.

See also BARBARY PIRATES.

Mariana Islands Campaign

The Marianas are 14 islands some 1,500 miles east of the Philippines. Three of the islands in the group, SAIPAN, TINIAN, and Rota, had been administered by Japan since the end of WORLD WAR I. Guam, the largest of the Marianas, was a U.S. possession. Guam fell to Japanese invasion on December 8, 1941, and Saipan figured as the main Japanese base.

As a result of the U.S. "Island-hopping" campaign strategy in the Pacific, Saipan was isolated by mid-1944. Therefore, on June 15, 1944, the 2nd and 4th Marines combined with the army's 27th Division to land on Saipan, which was secured after very heavy fighting on July 9.

After Saipan was taken, the 3rd USMC Division and 1st USMC Brigade made an assault on Guam on July 21. This, too, proved a very hard fight, but with the aid of the army's 77th Division, the island was retaken on August 10.

The final Marianas objective was Tinian, which the United States wanted as a base for B-29 bomber operations against the Japanese mainland. Tinian was captured on August 1 by the USMC's 2rd and 4th Divisions.

Marine Aircraft Group 36

Marine Aircraft Group (Helicopter Transport) 36 was commissioned at Marine Corps Air Facility, Santa Ana, California on June 2, 1952. On March

16, 1959, "Helicopter Transport" was dropped from MAG 36's designation and, in August 1965, the unit was deployed to Vietnam during the VIET-NAM WAR, the first complete Marine Aircraft Group to arrive in the combat zone. Operating from an air facility at Ky Ha, MAG 36 provided resupply, troop lifts, air strikes, recon inserts and extracts, and medical evacuation for allied troops in the southern I Corps area. In the fall of 1967, MAG 36 moved to Phu Bai, and in early 1968, the unit was heavily involved in defending against the Tet Offensive. MAG 36 was redeployed from Vietnam to Marine Corps Air Station Futenma on November 4, 1969, and subsequently redeployed detachments to Thailand and Vietnam to provide combat air refueling for USMC fighter/attack aircraft.

In April 1975, MAG 36 participated in Operation Eagle Pull, the emergency evacuation of American civilians from Cambodia. Then, during April 29–30, the unit evacuated more than 7,000 people from Saigon, South Vietnam, during the general evacuation of the capital.

Since the Vietnam War, MAG 36 has supported USMC fleet operations in the Pacific Theater.

Marine Air Ground Task Force Training Command

Formerly the Marine Corps Air Ground Combat Center (MCAGCC), the command was redesignated Marine Air Ground Task Force Training Command (MAGTF) on October 1, 2000. MAGTF began on August 20, 1952, as Marine Corps Training Center at Twentynine Palms, California, for live-fire training. Originally, the center was used primarily for artillery training, then evolved into a combined-arms training facility, a kind of "combined-arms exercise college" for the USMC.

Today, MAGTF is operated under the Training and Education Command.

Marine Assault Climbers Kit   See PERSONAL AND MISCELLANEOUS EQUIPMENT.

Marines of the Second Reconnaissance Battalion practice their rappelling from a UH-1 Huey helicopter at the Marine Corps Air Ground Task Force Training Center, Twentynine Palms, California.   *(Department of Defense)*

Marine Aviation Weapons and Tactics Squadron One

MAWTS-1 is part of the Training and Education Command and provides standardized advanced tactical training and certification of unit instructor qualifications in support of Marine aviation training and readiness. The squadron also provides assistance in the development and employment of aviation weapons and tactics for the USMC.

Special Weapons Training Units (SWTUs) were formed in the 1950s to provide training for USMC attack squadrons, which were assigned to carry special weapons. During the 1960s, conventional weapons delivery was added to the curriculum and the SWTUs were redesignated as Marine Air Weapons Training Units, MAWTULant at Cherry Point, North Carolina, and MAWTUPac at El Toro, California. In 1976, a USMC study group recommended establishment of the Weapons and Tactics Training Program (WTTP) for all of Marine aviation, including development of a graduate-level Weapons and Tactics Instructor (WTI) Course. Consolidated WTI courses were then conducted at Marine Corps Air Station Yuma, Arizona, by a combined MAWTU staff in May 1977 and February 1978. These proved so successful that Marine Aviation Weapons and Tactics Squadron One was commissioned at Yuma on June 1, 1978.

Since its commissioning, MAWTS-1 has conducted two WTI courses per year and now produces more than 300 WTI graduates annually. In June 1983, an Aviation Development, Tactics, and Evaluation Department (ADT&E) was established to coordinate the MAWTS efforts in developing and evaluating tactics and hardware in all functional areas of Marine Corps aviation. In 1988, a Ground Combat Department was added to encourage increased participation during the WTI course by infantry, artillery, and armor officers. Other MAWTS-1 courses embedded within WTI include the Intelligence Officers Course; Aviation Ground Support and Logistic Officers Course; the Rotary Wing Crew Chief Course; and KC-130 Navigator Course; KC-130 Loadmaster Course; KC-130 Flight Engineer Weapons Course; Tactics Instructor Course; and the MACCS Enlisted Weapons and Tactics courses. An advanced curriculum includes the Tactical Air Commanders Course, MEU/SPMAGTF ACE Commanders Course, and the MAWTS-1 Commanders Course. MAWTS-1 personnel conduct a Mobile Training curriculum consisting of the MEU ACE Training Course, the MAGTF Aviation Integration Course, and the Marine Division Tactics Course.

MAWTS-1 maintains liaison with the aviation and tactics schools of the USN, USA, and USAF, as well as the armed forces of certain Allied nations.

Marine Barracks

The term has two meanings. It may denote the ceremonial and special security unit assigned to Washington, D.C., and located at 8th and I Streets (often nicknamed "8th and Eye"). The oldest USMC post, it includes the residence of the COMMANDANT OF THE MARINE CORPS. It is considered the "spiritual home" of the USMC.

"Marine Barracks" also refers to a special guard unit assigned to ensure the internal security of major U.S. Navy shore stations, including the protection of USN nuclear weapons.

Marine Corps Air Ground Combat Center
See MARINE AIR GROUND TASK FORCE TRAINING COMMAND.

Marine Corps Air Station Beaufort   See
BASES, CAMPS, AND OTHER INSTALLATIONS.

Marine Corps Air Station Cherry Point
See BASES, CAMPS, AND OTHER INSTALLATIONS.

Marine Corps Air Station Futenma   See
BASES, CAMPS, AND OTHER INSTALLATIONS.

Marine Corps Air Station Iwakuni   See
BASES, CAMPS, AND OTHER INSTALLATIONS.

Marine Corps Air Station Miramar   See
BASES, CAMPS, AND OTHER INSTALLATIONS.

Marine Corps Air Station New River   See
BASES, CAMPS, AND OTHER INSTALLATIONS.

Marine Corps Air Station Yuma   See BASES,
CAMPS, AND OTHER INSTALLATIONS.

Marine Corps Base Camp Lejeune   See
BASES, CAMPS, AND OTHER INSTALLATIONS.

Marine Corps Base Camp Pendleton   See
BASES, CAMPS, AND OTHER INSTALLATIONS.

Marine Corps Base Camp Smedley D. Butler   See BASES, CAMPS, AND OTHER INSTALLATIONS.

Marine Corps Base Hawaii   See BASES,
CAMPS, AND OTHER INSTALLATIONS.

Marine Corps Base Quantico See BASES, CAMPS, AND OTHER INSTALLATIONS.

Marine Corps Combat Development Command

MCCDC had its origin in the MARINE CORPS SCHOOLS established at Marine Corps Base Camp Lejeune in 1920. The MCCDC is the intellectual core of the USMC and is the central agency responsible for training, concepts, and doctrine development for the USMC. In addition to the Marine Corps University and the Marine Corps Schools, MCCDC consists of 10 divisions: Requirements; Concepts and Plans; Warfighting Integration; Doctrine; Training and Education; Studies and Analysis; Coalition and Special Warfare; War Gaming and Combat Simulation; Marine Corps Presentation Team; and Science and Innovation.

Marine Corps Combat Identification Program (MCCIP)

Fratricide, death by friendly fire, has always been a major problem on the battlefield, and it has become even more pressing as the tactical nature of warfare grows more complex. Under the oversight of the Joint Combat Identification Office (JCIDO), the Marine Corps Combat Identification Program provides ground-to-ground and air-to-ground identification of friendly and unknown (hostile or neutral/noncombatant) forces in the battle space. The program uses an active millimeter wave (MMW) question and answer system for target interrogation, validation, and identification prior to engagement. In the ground-to-ground format, the system consists of an installation kit (A-kit) and the BCIS equipment set (B-kit). These kits consist of an Interrogator Antenna, Transponder Antenna, Ballistic Armor Housing, Comm Unit Display Interface, and the Display/Interface Mount. The narrow-beam, directional Interrogator Antenna is bore sighted to the main weapon system on long-range, direct-fire armored platforms. The omnidirectional Transponder Antenna

is mounted on all high fratricide-risk armored platforms deployed forward of the battle area. The air-to-ground system consists of a BCIS pod mounted to the AIM-9 Sidewinder missiles fired from rotary-wing and fixed-wing aircraft. The Marine Corps Combat Identification Program (MCBIP) provides to platform gunners and commanders a visual and/or audio signal that identifies potential targets, day or night, and in all weather conditions. The object is to use currently available technologies to reduce or prevent fratricide. The advantage of the Marine Corps Combat Identification Program (MCBIP) is that the components can be assembled off the shelf and fielded immediately.

General characteristics of the Marine Corps Combat Identification Program (MCBIP) include:

Manufacturer: TRW/Magnavox
Probability of correct target identification: 90 percent under all battlefield conditions (99 percent objective)
Target engagement time: > 1 sec
Multiple interrogations/responses: ≥ 3 simultaneous
Maximum effective range (minimum-maximum), ground-to-ground: 500 ft–18,000 ft
Maximum effective range (minimum-maximum), air-to-ground: 500 ft–26,000 ft
Discrimination between targets: >+/– 22.5 mils in azimuth or > 800 ft in range
Reliability: 1,242 hr (threshold) to 2,760 hr (objective)

Marine Corps Expeditionary Medal See DECORATIONS AND MEDALS.

Marine Corps Intelligence

Marine Corps Intelligence, also called Marine Corps Intelligence Activity (MCIA), supports USMC acquisition policy and budget planning and programming, and provides pre-deployment training and force contingency planning for requirements that are not satisfied by theater, other service, or national capabilities. MCIA works in conjunction with Naval Intelligence and Coast Guard Intelligence at the National Maritime Intelligence Center in Washington, D.C., and at Marine Corps Base Quantico, Virginia.

Marine Corps Logistics Base Albany   See
BASES, CAMPS, AND OTHER INSTALLATIONS.

Marine Corps Logistics Base Barstow   See
BASES, CAMPS, AND OTHER INSTALLATIONS.

Marine Corps Recruit Depot Parris Island
See BASES, CAMPS, AND OTHER INSTALLATIONS.

Marine Corps Recruit Depots   See BASES,
CAMPS, AND OTHER INSTALLATIONS.

Marine Corps Recruit Depot San Diego
See BASES, CAMPS, AND OTHER INSTALLATIONS.

Marine Corps Reserve
The Marine Corps Reserve began in 1916 with three officers and 33 enlisted men, but did not commence in earnest until passage of the Naval Reserve Act of 1925 and the Naval Reserve Act of 1938. By the end of WORLD WAR II, when the USMC reached its historical maximum strength of 471,000, 70 percent of marines were reservists. Today, the USMCR, like other military reserve forces and the National Guard, is fully integrated in all military planning.

The USMCR is composed of three classes and one special category.

Fleet Marine Corps Reserve constitutes Class I and is composed of former regular enlisted marines with at least 20 years of service in the reg-

ular marines. This class may be employed as needed without further training. Class I reservists remain in this class until they have completed 30 years of combined regular and reserve service.

Selected Marine Corps Reserve constitutes Class II and, like Class I marines, can be instantly assimilated into regular service. Most Class II marines have six months of training with a six-year military obligation and attend semimonthly or monthly drills and annual training.

Individual Ready Reserve (Class III) consists of physically qualified marines who are not assigned to Class I or Class II. These personnel are available for mobilization in time of war or national emergency. They do not participate in the level of unit training engaged in by Class II members.

In addition to the three basic classes of reservists, a Limited Assignment (Overage) Category allows certain USMCR officers with special qualifications to serve as needed in special mobilization assignments.

Marine Corps Reserve Ribbon   See DECO-
RATIONS AND MEDALS.

Marine Corps Schools
Marine Corps Schools is headquartered at Marine Corps Base Quantico and is under the command of the president of Marine Corps University, who reports to the commanding general of MARINE CORPS COMBAT DEVELOPMENT COMMAND. The schools include:

♦ Marine Corps War College: a top-level school that annually convenes a class of 12 colonels, including peers from other services
♦ School of Advanced Warfighting: provides a year of advanced training for graduates of the Command and Staff College
♦ Command and Staff College: provides a nine-month course for majors and lieutenant colonels

- Amphibious Warfare School: provides career-level instruction for captains to prepare them for company-level command and battalion-level staff work
- Command and Control Systems Course: a specialized Amphibious Warfare School curriculum for communications and intelligence officers
- Basic Communications Officer Course: to qualify for the communications specialty
- Officer Candidate School: provides enlisted marines with basic officer training; graduates become commissioned USMC officers
- Staff Noncommissioned Officers' Academy: provides advanced NCO training
- Basic School: provides further training for newly commissioned officers and certain enlisted personnel

Marine Corps Supply

Marine Corps Supply services furnish logistics support for the USMC. The USMC maintains a central inventory control point (ICP) at Marine Corps Logistics Base Albany, Georgia, where all procurement is centralized. Processing of all requisitions goes through this ICP. Additionally, the inventory control point is responsible for cataloging all USMC items; for provisioning, which means providing necessary support, maintenance, and repair items for all USMC equipment and equipment systems; for providing technical services and support; and for providing publications necessary to supply functions.

In addition to the ICP, the USMC maintains remote storage activities. The two principal RSA are at Albany and at Marine Corps Logistics Base Barstow, California. The USMC also maintains numerous smaller RSAs to ensure that supply needs are met anywhere they occur.

Marine Expeditionary Brigade (MEB)   See
ORGANIZATION BY UNITS.

Marine Expeditionary Force (MEF)   See
ORGANIZATION BY UNITS.

Marine Expeditionary Unit (MEU)   See
ORGANIZATION BY UNITS.

Marine Forces
The USMC is currently deployed in seven "Forces," as follows:

- Marine Forces Atlantic (MARFORLANT), headquartered in Norfolk, Virginia
- Marine Forces Europe (COMMARFOREUR), headquartered in Stuttgart, Germany
- Marine Forces Korea (USMARFORK), headquartered in Seoul, South Korea
- Marine Forces Pacific (MARFORPAC), headquartered at Camp Smith, Hawaii
- Marine Forces Reserve (MFR), headquartered at Marine Corps Base Quantico, Virginia
- Marine Forces South (MARFORSOUTH), headquartered in Broward and Dade Counties, Florida
- Marine Forces Unitas (MARFORUNITAS), which works in cooperation with the military of various Latin American nations

Marine Helicopter Squadron One
Established in December 1947 as an experimental unit to test and evaluate helicopters and tactics, Marine Helicopter Squadron One (HMX-1) was subsequently also tasked with providing all helicopter transportation for the president of the United States overseas and within the United States. HMX-1 also provides helicopter transportation for the vice president, members of the cabinet, and foreign dignitaries, under the direction of the White House Military Office. In addition, HMX-1 provides emergency evacuation and other support as directed by the COMMANDANT OF THE MARINE CORPS.

MARINE ONE is the call sign used when the president is on board any HMX-1 helicopter; however, the primary presidential helicopter is the Sikorsky VH-3D Sea King.

Marine Hymn

The Marine Hymn is the anthem of the USMC and came into use shortly after the Civil War. Its melody is a close approximation of a marching song from Jacques Offenbach's (1819–80) opera *Genviève de Brabant* and its lyrics are anonymous.

> *From the Halls of Montezuma*
> *To the Shores of Tripoli,*
> *We will fight our country's battles*
> *In the air, on land and sea.*
> *First to fight for right and freedom*
> *And to keep our honor clean,*
> *We are proud to claim the title*
> *of United States Marine.*
>
> *Our flag's unfurled to every breeze*
> *From dawn to setting sun.*
> *We have fought in ev'ry clime and place*
> *Where we could take a gun.*
> *In the snow of far-off Northern lands*
> *And in sunny tropic scenes,*
> *You will find us always on the job—*
> *The United States Marines.*
>
> *Here's health to you and to our Corps,*
> *Which we are proud to serve.*
> *In many a strife we've fought for life*
> *And never lost our nerve.*
> *If the Army and the Navy*
> *Ever look on Heaven's scenes,*
> *They will find the streets are guarded*
> *By United States Marines.*

Marine One

The call sign used when the president of the United States is on board of one of the helicopters of MARINE HELICOPTER SQUADRON ONE. (Compare "Air Force One," the call sign of any USAF aircraft when the president is on board.)

President George H. W. Bush enters Marine One on the South Lawn of the White House. *(George H. W. Bush Library)*

Maritime Prepositioning Squadrons (MPSs)

The USMC maintains three permanent MPSs, on station in the eastern Atlantic; at Diego Garcia, in the Indian Ocean; and off the Mariana Islands in the Central Pacific. These floating squadrons stand at readiness to meet crises quickly. They consist of transport vessels preloaded with supplies, ready to receive marines for rapid deployment.

Marshall Islands Campaign

The Marshall group consists of atolls some 1,500 miles southeast of SAIPAN. Following WORLD WAR I, the League of Nations gave the Japanese a mandate over the principal atolls of Jaluit, Mili,

Maloelop, Majuro, Wotje, KWAJALEIN, and ENIWE-TOK. Well before WORLD WAR II, the Japanese exploited their mandate by building airfields on islands in these atolls, so that they were very well established in this strategic location.

The first U.S. strike against the Marshalls was at Kwajalein: a landing by the USMC's 4th Division on February 1, 1944, at ROI-NAMUR, while the army attacked Kwajalein Island. Engebi Island, in the Eniwetok Atoll, was struck next, on February 19, and on February 22, marines secured Parry Island, also a part of the Eniwetok Atoll.

The successful completion of the Marshall Islands Campaign put U.S. forces in an excellent position to press the next campaign, against the MARIANA ISLANDS.

mascot

The official mascot of the USMC is the English bulldog. The mascot dates from 1918 and World War I, when German soldiers, overwhelmed by the fighting prowess of the marines, called them *Teufelhunden,* or "devil dogs."

master gunnery sergeant   See RANKS AND GRADES.

master sergeant   See RANKS AND GRADES.

Mayaguez incident

On May 12, 1975, the *Mayaguez,* a U.S.-flagged container ship, was stopped by a Cambodian gunboat while en route from Hong Kong to Thailand. The ship was compelled to anchor off Koh Tang, a jungle island some 30 miles from the Cambodian port of Kampong Som, to which the 39 crew members were taken and temporarily held.

In response to the seizure of the *Mayaguez,* President Gerald Ford ordered a military operation to retake the vessel and free the crew. The U.S. Air Force, U.S. Navy, and USMC participated in the joint operation, in which marines boarded the abandoned *Mayaguez* on May 15, while the destroyer escort *Wilson* intercepted Cambodian boats transporting the prisoners from Kampong Som and freed them. In the meantime, more marines attacked Koh Tang, but were pinned down by heavy resistance and had to be evacuated on May 16.

Although the mission was a success—the *Mayaguez* recovered, the crew freed—it was costly: 11 marines, two sailors, and two airmen were killed; 41 marines, two sailors, and seven airmen were wounded. Three USAF helicopters were destroyed and another 11 damaged.

MC-5 Static Line/Free-Fall Ram Air Parachute System (SL/FF RAPS)   See PERSONAL AND MISCELLANEOUS EQUIPMENT.

McCawley, Charles G. (1827–1891) *Marine Corps commandant*

The eighth COMMANDANT OF THE MARINE CORPS, McCawley was born in Philadelphia and was commissioned in the USMC in 1847. Directly upon his commissioning, McCawley participated in the amphibious invasion of VERACRUZ during the U.S.-MEXICAN WAR, then went on to fight through to the invasion of Mexico City. He was breveted captain at the Battle of CHAPULTEPEC.

McCawley served in the Civil War, commanding a battalion that participated in the capture of Port Royal, South Carolina, and in the unsuccessful attempts to take the forts defending Charleston in 1863. As a result of his heroic actions in an unsuccessful assault on Fort Sumter on September 8, 1863, McCawley was breveted major.

After the war, McCawley served in Washington and was appointed commandant in 1876. He generally raised the standards for USMC enlistment and reformed the organization of the Marine Corps. In 1882, he managed to ensure that a certain number of U.S. Naval Academy graduates would be available for service as USMC officers, thereby greatly increasing the quality of the organization's officer corps. McCawley is also fondly remembered for assigning JOHN PHILIP SOUSA as leader of the U.S. MARINE BAND. McCawley retired, with the rank of colonel, on January 29, 1891.

Medal of Honor   See DECORATIONS AND MEDALS.

MEU (SOC) Pistol   See WEAPONS, INDIVIDUAL AND CREW-SERVED.

Midway, Battle of

Midway is a coral atoll lying 1,134 nautical miles to the northwest of Honolulu. A U.S. possession since 1867, Midway was garrisoned by three USMC units, the 6th Defense Battalion and two air squadrons, on the eve of WORLD WAR II. On June 4, 1942, Japanese forces began operations against Midway, intending to capture it. USMC pilots, vastly outnumbered, flew obsolescent F2A Buffalos and a few new F4F Wildcats against Zeros and got the worst of it. Aerial attacks on two Japanese aircraft carriers were to no avail. Nevertheless, the marines held their positions until the main U.S. Navy force was in position and the final phase of the Battle of Midway got under way on June 6. The great naval battle would be costly to both sides, but would prove the turning point of the war in the Pacific. After Midway, U.S. forces assumed the offensive and remained on the offensive through the end of the war.

Mitchell PBJ   See AIRCRAFT, FIXED-WING.

Mk-19 40-mm Machine Gun, MOD 3
See WEAPONS, INDIVIDUAL AND CREW-SERVED.

Mk-48 Power Unit and Mk-14 Container Transporter Rear Body Unit   See WHEELED VEHICLES.

Mk-48 Power Unit and Mk-15, Recovery/Wrecker Rear Body Unit   See WHEELED VEHICLES.

Mk-48 Power Unit and Mk-16, Fifth-Wheel Semi-trailer Adapter Rear Body Unit   See WHEELED VEHICLES.

Mk-48 Power Unit and Mk-18 Self-loading Container and Ribbon Bridge Transporter   See WHEELED VEHICLES.

Mk-155 Mine Clearance Launcher   See WHEELED VEHICLES.

Mobile/Unit Conduct of Fire Trainer (M/U-COFT)   See TRACKED VEHICLES.

Modular Sleeping Bag (MSB)   See PERSONAL AND MISCELLANEOUS EQUIPMENT.

MP-5N Heckler and Koch 9-mm Submachine Gun   See WEAPONS, INDIVIDUAL AND CREW-SERVED.

Mundy, Carl E., Jr. (1935–   ) *Marine Corps commandant*

The 30th COMMANDANT OF THE MARINE CORPS, Mundy was born in Atlanta, graduated from Auburn University in Alabama, and was commissioned a USMC second lieutenant in 1957. After service at sea and as a Basic School instructor, Mundy served in the VIETNAM WAR during 1966–67 as an operations officer and executive officer with the 3rd Battalion, 26th Marines and as intelligence officer in III Amphibious Force. After his return to the States, Mundy served in a variety of staff positions, culminating in a promotion to brigadier general and assignment as director of personnel at HEADQUARTERS MARINE CORPS in 1982.

Mundy subsequently commanded 4th Amphibious Brigade, then became director of operations for the USMC. Promoted to major general in 1986 and lieutenant general in 1988, he served as deputy chief of staff and deputy to the Joint Chiefs before assuming command of FLEET MARINE FORCE, Atlantic. After promotion to general in 1991, he was named commandant.

N

Navajo code talkers

The need for rapid but secure communications is always important in war and was especially urgent in the Pacific during WORLD WAR II, where rapid movement and surprise tactics were of critical value against the Japanese.

Philip Johnston, the son of a missionary to the Navajos and one of the very few non-Navajos who spoke the language, was a veteran of WORLD WAR I who knew that Native American languages, especially Choctaw, had been used during that war to encode messages. He believed that the Navajo language would be ideal for secure communications in World War II. The language is unwritten and extremely complex. Its syntax, qualities of intonation, and its dialectical variety render it wholly unintelligible to those who lack either lifelong exposure or extensive training. At the time of World War II, it was estimated that fewer than 30 non-Navajos—none of them Japanese—could understand Navajo.

With all of this in mind, Johnston met with Major General Clayton B. Vogel, commanding general of Amphibious Corps, Pacific Fleet, early in 1942 and presented his idea. Johnston agreed to conduct tests under simulated combat conditions. The tests demonstrated that Navajos could encrypt, transmit, and decrypt a three-line message in 20 seconds. Cipher machines of the period required a half-hour to perform the same task. Thoroughly impressed, Vogel recommended to the COMMANDANT OF THE MARINE CORPS that the USMC recruit 200 Navajos.

The first 29 Navajo recruits reported for BASIC TRAINING in May 1942. Working at Marine Corps

Two of the Navajo code talkers of World War II
(National Archives)

Base Camp Pendleton, this first contingent created the Navajo code, quickly accomplishing the task of developing a dictionary and inventing many words for military and technological terms. This dictionary, including all code words, had to be committed to memory during the training of the so-called code talkers. After completing that training, the code talker was sent to a USMC unit in the Pacific. His principal mission was to transmit orders and information relating to tactics and troop movements over field telephones and radios. Secondarily, the code talkers served as messengers. They participated in every assault and campaign the USMC conducted in the Pacific from 1942 to 1945, including GUADALCANAL, TARAWA, PELELIU, and IWO JIMA, and they served in all six USMC divisions as well as in USMC Raider battalions and parachute units. The Japanese never succeeded in breaking the code.

As of 1945, some 540 Navajos had enlisted in the USMC, of whom 375 to 420 were trained as code talkers. Their contribution went largely unheralded until September 17, 1992, when the code talkers were officially recognized by a special permanent exhibition at the Pentagon. A highly fictionalized account of the code talkers was presented in the 2002 film *Windtalkers.*

naval relations

While both the U.S. Navy and U.S. Marine Corps are regulated by and subordinate to the Department of the Navy, they are separate, although intimately partnered, services. Neither service is subordinate to the other.

Neville, Wendell C. (1870–1930) *Marine*
Corps commandant

Nicknamed "Whispering Buck," Neville was born in Portsmouth, Virginia, and graduated from the U.S. Naval Academy in 1890. He cruised for two years as a navy midshipman, then was commissioned a second lieutenant in the USMC. He served with distinction in the SPANISH-AMERICAN WAR, receiving

the Brevet Medal, at the time the highest decoration the USMC awarded. He next saw action in China, during the BOXER REBELLION, then served in the Philippines, Cuba, NICARAGUA, PANAMA, and Hawaii.

Neville, as lieutenant colonel, led the 2nd Marines during the U.S. invasion of VERACRUZ, Mexico, in 1914, and received the Medal of Honor for his actions. During WORLD WAR I, as colonel, Neville fought in major battles, including BELLEAU WOOD and Soissons. He was promoted to major general on his return to the United States in 1919 and assigned as assistant commandant, then as commander of the Department of the Pacific. Appointed commandant in 1929, he died in office a year later.

New Britain, Battle of

Located in the Bismarck chain in the Solomon Sea, opposite New Guinea, New Britain was occupied by the Japanese early in WORLD WAR II. With Rabaul, it figured as an important Japanese air base and harbor. In support of the campaign against Rabaul, the USMC's 1st Division landed on New Britain at Cape Gloucester on December 26, 1943. Landing on two beaches, the marines fought through the torrential rains of the monsoon, captured the airfield, then pursued the retreating Japanese, flushing them from the highlands to the coast, and then pushing them along the coast toward Rabaul.

Although Japanese resistance was tough, as it always was, the chief adversaries in the New Britain battle were the rugged terrain of the island's highland area and the relentless monsoon rains.

New Georgia, Battle of

Located northwest of GUADALCANAL, New Georgia Island had a Japanese airfield at a place called Munda, which, acting in concert with the army's 43rd Division, the USMC's 4th Raider Battalion secured in June 1944.

While the 43rd Division made the principal landing on New Georgia, the marine raiders, on June 21, landed separately on the north end of the island and took Viru Harbor. They advanced southward to secure the harbor at Bairoko with the purpose of sealing off the Japanese retreat from Munda. The marines were thwarted by Japanese resistance and rugged jungle terrain. In the meantime, the 43rd Division had to take up a position short of Munda, and two additional army divisions were called in to take the airfield.

Although the airfield was secured as an important U.S. base, much of the Japanese garrison evacuated to Kolombangara Island and thereby escaped annihilation.

new man rule

An unwritten rule in USMC procedure directing that replacements take the point, or advance position, in a ground operation.

new meat

A new replacement assigned to a USMC combat unit. He or she may be subject to the new man rule.

New Orleans, Battle of

The Battle of New Orleans, commanded on the American side by Andrew Jackson, is remembered as one of the few great American land victories of the WAR OF 1812, even though it took place after the signing of the Treaty of Ghent, which ended the war. (The slow pace of transatlantic communications in the early 19th century kept the news of peace from both sides.)

Jackson led a combination of regular army troops and miscellaneous militia forces in his successful defense of New Orleans against a veteran British force led by General Edward Pakenham. However, a force of 400 marines under the command of Major Daniel Carmick also played an important role in Jackson's victory. A portion of the USMC force was deployed in five gunboats, which challenged the British landing. Most of the force was positioned in the center of Jackson's line of defense.

The first British attack was a probe on December 28, 1814, which was aimed directly at the marines' sector. The marines held their ground and repelled the probe. Eleven days after this initial assault, Pakenham unleashed his main attack, a formed charge by 3,500 men. The action was as stupid as it was gallant, and 2,300 British troops were either wounded or killed. Pakenham was among the slain. As for Jackson, he was full of praise for the small USMC contingent, which had contributed significantly to the victory.

Nicaragua

The U.S. Marine Corps was first sent to intervene in Nicaragua in 1852 and then again in 1854, when three landings were made in the Bluefields area to protect U.S. lives and property during one of many uprisings that followed independence from Spain in 1821. A Conservative regime brought a modicum of peace to the nation from the 1860s until 1893, when José Zelaya, a Liberal militant, seized power. He maintained control until 1909, after a Conservative revolution erupted against his regime. A provisional USMC regiment of 750 was landed to aid the Conservatives; after the situation was stabilized, the marines were withdrawn in September 1910.

In 1912, Liberal forces reemerged and seized much of the southeastern portion of the country. Three hundred fifty marines were landed in May 1912 and were eventually reinforced by 780 more. Very rapidly, the marines seized the initiative and suppressed the rebels. They then withdrew, except for a contingent of 100 legation guards.

After an interval of about 10 years of relative stability, the Liberals rose in revolt yet again, in 1922, but a coalition government was formed by 1924 and the prospects for peace looked hopeful. Perhaps unwisely, the legation guards were withdrawn, which triggered renewed fighting in the Bluefields region. Marines were landed again in 1926 and more in January 1927. The United States also supplied arms to the government, and the entire 5th Marines arrived, reconstituting in-country the 2nd Brigade. The show of force reinstated the Conservatives. When the charismatic Liberal leader Augusto Sandino persisted in fighting the Conservative regime, the United States backed the formation of a Guardia Nacional, which collaborated with the marines in a campaign against the so-called Sandinistas during 1928. The marines continued to participate in combat against the Sandinistas until 1931, when President Herbert Hoover withdrew them. By this time, a Conservative government, friendly to the United States and under the dictatorship of Anastasio Somoza (head of the Guardia Nacional), had been installed. Somoza treacherously captured Sandino under the pretext of truce talks and ordered his execution in 1934.

Nicholas, Samuel (1744–1790) *Marine Corps commandant*

The Continental Congress commissioned Philadelphia-born Samuel Nicholas captain of the CONTINENTAL MARINES on November 28, 1775, a few days after this service was created. Although he was not

Major Samuel Nicholas (Continental Marines)
(U.S. Marine Corps)

officially called commandant, he served effectively in that capacity during the AMERICAN REVOLUTION and is generally honored by marines as the first COMMANDANT OF THE MARINE CORPS.

In the spring of 1776, Nicholas, promoted to major, led the first marine amphibious assault, landing 200 marines and 50 sailors at New Providence, Bahamas, where he captured important forts and appropriated much-needed supplies. He next led 80 marines (three companies) in George Washington's triumphant assault on Trenton on December 26, 1776.

Nicholas and his marines remained with Washington until early 1777, when Nicholas was sent to Philadelphia and the marines were used for defensive duty in Delaware. Nicholas was the senior marine commander throughout the American Revolution. With peace, however, the Continental Marines was disbanded, and Nicholas retired to civilian life.

nuclear-biological-chemical equipment

Nuclear, biological, and chemical weapons have become increasingly significant battlefield threats in recent years. The following equipment is included in the Marine Corps inventory.

Chemical Agent Monitor

The Chemical Agent Monitor is a handheld device for monitoring chemical agent contamination on personnel and equipment, primarily in a post-attack situation. The device is simple to operate, having only two controls, an on/off push-button switch and a mode-select push-button switch, which selects the blister or nerve-agent mode of operation.

The Chemical Agent Monitor detects vapors of chemical agents by sensing molecular ions of specific mobilities—time of flight—and uses advanced timing and microprocessor technologies to reject incorrect inferences. This enables the unit to detect and to discriminate between vapors of nerve or blister agents and also to display the relative concentration of either. The USMC instrument is also capable of detecting and discriminating among other agents.

General characteristics of the device include:

Length: 17 in
Width: 4 in
Height: 7 in
Weight: 5.5 lb
Agent concentration detectability: 0.1 mg/m^2
Response time: under 60 sec for 0.1 mg/m^2 of
  agent

In the modern battlefield environment, chemical agents have become an increasingly important threat, and monitors will become more and more common in the field.

M-17 Lightweight Decontamination System

NBC (Nuclear-Biological-Chemical) weapons are a heightened risk in the battlefield of the 21st century, making it critical that USMC field forces have rapid access to effective decontamination apparatus. The Lightweight Decontamination System is a compact, lightweight, entirely portable decontamination system consisting of a 7.3-horsepower engine, a self-priming pump for drawing and pressurizing water, a fan assembly to deliver combustion air to the heater, a water heater, a self-priming pump for the heater fuel system, and a small generator to supply electricity for ignition and safety control functions. The system is transportable by ¾-ton trailer, 1¼-ton cargo truck, cargo aircraft, and, as a sling load, by helicopter.

The system provides pressurized water at temperatures up to 248° Fahrenheit at a rate of up to 9 gallons per minute. It draws water from any natural source up to 30 feet away and 9 feet below pump level. The system incorporates an additional 3,000 gallon water-storage tank in case of a lack of natural water sources. The system is also saltwater resistant.

By 2004, the USMC had fielded almost 3,000 units. General characteristics of the M-17 Lightweight Decontamination System include:

Main unit dimensions—
Length: 40.2 in
Width: 23.2 in

Height: 33.9 in
Weight: 360 lb

Accessory kit dimensions—
Length: 41.8 in
Width: 20.5 in
Height: 15.4 in
Weight: 143 lb

Water bladder dimensions—
Height: 5.8 ft when full
Weight: 70 lb
Capacity: 1,580 gal
Water temperature: up to 248°F
Water delivery rate: 9 gal/min
Setup time: under 30 min

M-21 Remote-Sensing Chemical Agent Automatic Alarm

The USMC employs the Remote Sensing Chemical Agent Automatic Alarm as a two-man-portable, automatic scanning, passive infrared sensor to detect nerve and blister agent vapor clouds. The sensor measures changes in the infrared energy emitted from remote objects or from a cloud formed by the agent.

The M-21 Remote Sensing Chemical Agent Automatic Alarm is a stand-alone, tripod-mounted, chemical agent overwatch system intended for use in a defensive role. Components of the system include the detector, tripod, the M-42 remote alarm unit, transit case, power cable assembly, and a standard military power source. The unit may be used for reconnaissance and surveillance missions to search areas between friendly and enemy forces for chemical agent vapors and to provide advance detection and warning of chemical hazards. The most desirable use of the unit is deployment in pairs—two reconnaissance teams—so that one alarm can be used in the overwatch position while the other reconnaissance team is on the move.

The remote warning can be transmitted by two methods. A hardwire can be run to the M-42 alarm, or a digital signal can be transmitted from the M-21 via an RS-232 cable. This latter arrangement provides a capability to link with the Marine Corps Hazard Warning System/Network.

General characteristics of the M-21 Remote Sensing Chemical Agent Automatic Alarm include:

Length, operational configuration: 20 in
Width, operational configuration: 48 in
Height, operational configuration: 51.5 in
Weight, operational configuration: 66 lb
Length, storage/shipping configuration: 31 in
Width, storage/shipping configuration: 30 in
Height, storage/shipping configuration: 22 in
Weight, storage/shipping configuration: 117 lb
Power requirements: 120 watts at 21 to 30 volts
Chemical agent detection range: 1.86 to 3.1 mi
Instantaneous field of view, vertical: 1.5 degrees
Instantaneous field of view, horizontal: 60 degrees
Chemical agent spectral range: 800 to 1,200 cm^{-1}
Mean time between operational-mission failures: 277 hours

M-40/42 Chemical/Biological Protective Masks

The M-40/42 series of chemical/biological protective masks replaced three earlier models, the M-17 (general purpose), M-25 (vehicle crewman), and M-9 (heavy duty) masks, to provide respiratory, eye, and face protection against field concentrations of chemical and biological agents. The M-40/42 masks are effective against chemical and biological agent vapors, aerosols, toxins, and radiological fallout particles.

The masks consist of a silicone rubber face piece with an in-turned peripheral face seal and rigid binocular lens system. A face-mounted gas and aerosol filter canister may be mounted on either the left or the right cheek. Each filter is effective against a maximum of 15 nerve, choking, and blister agent attacks and against a maximum of two blood agent attacks. Biological agents do not degrade the filter.

The masks are available in small, medium, and large sizes to ensure a proper fit. They afford unobstructed and undistorted forward vision, and cor-rective lenses may be obtained and fitted into the mask. The mask also permits intelligible speech, does not interfere with hearing, and provides for a drinking capability while being worn. Microphone air adapters are provided for combat vehicle and aircraft applications. Because of all these features, the mask may be worn continuously for up to 12 hours.

The M-40/42 Chemical/Biological Protective Masks afford the following protection probabilities:

95 percent effective against 5,000 mg-min/m³
75 percent effective against 20,000 mg-min/m³
50 percent minimum probability of achieving no more than .002 percent penetration of *Bacillus globigii*

The breathing resistance of the mask is no greater than 55 millimeters of water at 85 liters per minute.

Portable Collective Protection System

The Portable Collective Protection System is an uncontaminated, positive-pressure shelter for use in a chemical/biological environment. The system consists of the protective shelter, a support kit, and a hermetically sealed filter canister. The shelter is a tent and fly. The tent floor and the fly are made of a Saranaex composite material. The tent is supported by an aluminum structure, and when overpressure is applied, the shelter provides protection from liquid and vapor chemical agent penetration as well as biological agent penetration. An integral airlock allows decontamination of entering personnel.

The system's support kit contains all the accessories required for deployment of the system, including the motor/blower assembly that supplies air to the system and the flexible ducts that guide the air to and through the hermetically sealed filter and then to the shelter. The filter canister consists of a hermetically sealed aluminum canister containing a gas filter and a particulate filter.

The system provides an uncontaminated, positive-pressure shelter for use as a command and control facility or as a rest and relief facility for up to 14 marines at a time. The tactical plan is to provide about four hours of rest and relief per day.

General characteristics of the Portable Collective Protection System include:

Operational configuration: 300 sq ft
Storage/shipping configuration, length: 9 ft
Storage/shipping configuration, width: 2.5 ft
Storage/shipping configuration, height: 3.4 ft
Storage/shipping configuration, weight: 673 lb
Air supply rate: supplies 200 cubic feet/min of clean air to the shelter
Temperature range: −25 to 120°F
Filter effectiveness: particulates, 0.3 microns or larger

Saratoga Chemical Protective Overgarment

The Saratoga suit was developed in the 1990s to replace the long-standard Overgarment 84 (OG-84) to provide improved and enhanced protection against chemical and biological agents. This protective outerwear is intended as part of a system to cover the entire body, feet, hands, and face. It is effective against chemical agent vapors, aerosols, and droplets, as well as all known biological agents.

The suit consists of a coat and trousers. The coat has a full-length zippered opening that is covered by a single protective flap. It also incorporates an integrated hood as well as hook and pile sleeve closures. The trousers may be adjusted by waist tabs. The trousers are held up by suspenders, and there are closures on the lower outside section of each leg. The suit can be worn over the duty uniform or undergarments and is wearable in all environments and conditions. It is not degraded by fresh or salt water, and it is fully launderable. The suit is intended to be used with appropriate gloves, boots, and mask.

The Saratoga suit uses spherical carbon technology to provide effective body protection from all known chemical/biological warfare agents while offering excellent flow conditions for body heat dissipation. This makes the Saratoga suit more comfortable than previous protective overgarments. The outside layer of material is cotton ripstop, which has been corpel treated. The suit comes in small, medium, large, and x-large sizes, and, as of 2004, the USMC had an inventory of 654,000 suits; however, the Saratoga suit is schedule to be replaced by the Joint Service Lightweight Integrated Suit Technology, which is already being acquired by the USMC.

General characteristics of the Saratoga Chemical Protective Overgarment include:

Protection period: 24 hours
Durability: 30 days continuous wear
Concentration resistance: 10mg/m^2 challenge for chemical agents and any challenge (battlefield) for biological agents
Length: size dependent
Width: size dependent
Height: size dependent
Weight: approximately 4.7 lb
Maximum effective temperature: 120°F
Storage life: 13 years

O

O'Bannon, Presley (1776–1850) *Marine Corps lieutenant*

O'Bannon was one of the first high-profile heroes of the USMC. Born in Fauquier County, Virginia, he was commissioned a second lieutenant in the USMC in 1801 and quickly rose to first lieutenant. In 1804, he was attached to the naval fleet that President Thomas Jefferson ordered to the Mediterranean to combat the BARBARY PIRATES. O'Bannon commanded a small USMC detachment, and led seven marines from this unit in company with a mixed force of European mercenaries and Arabs against the fortified town of Derna on April 27, 1805. O'Bannon's marines penetrated the enemy defenses, making way for the Arab troops to attack and defeat the soldiers of the bey of Tunis. This accomplished, O'Bannon raised the Stars and Stripes over the fort at Derna—the first time the American flag had been raised on foreign soil. The capture of Derna had little effect on the outcome of the war against the Barbary Pirates, since the bashaw of Tripoli had already agreed in principle to a favorable treaty with the United States; however, it was a dramatic vindication of the honor and effectiveness of the USMC.

O'Bannon's successful operation is alluded to in the MARINE HYMN—"the shores of Tripoli"—and is commemorated by the marine officer's MAMELUKE SWORD, a stylized replica of the ornate weapon reputedly presented to O'Bannon by the bey of Tripoli, Yusuf Hamet (who had been exiled by his brother, the bashaw).

Lieutenant Presley Neville O'Bannon (USMC)
(U.S. Marine Corps)

OE-1 Bird Dog   See AIRCRAFT, FIXED-WING.

Okinawa

Largest of the Ryukyu Islands, Okinawa was stubbornly defended by the Japanese during WORLD WAR II, largely because it was recognized that possession of the island would put the Americans in an ideal position from which to invade Japan itself.

The actual landing on Okinawa—by Tenth Army and the USMC III Amphibious Corps (consisting of the 1st and 6th Divisions)—was made on Easter Sunday, April 1, 1945, and met with only light opposition. Indeed, by April 21, resistance in the northern part of the island had been overcome; the main fighting took place in the south and consumed far more time than had been anticipated, ending only in late June. USMC casualties included some 2,938 killed (army and navy combined KIA were 12,500). Japanese losses were astronomical by comparison, 110,000 killed, 7,400 taken prisoner. An estimated 80,000 civilians on the well-populated island lost their lives. Capture of the island provided air bases for unremitting B-29 bombing raids against Japanese cities, as well as a staging area for a planned invasion that was made unnecessary by the dropping of two atomic bombs in August 1945.

Operation Just Cause   See PANAMA.

Operation Starlight

During the VIETNAM WAR, Operation Starlight was the first major U.S. operation against the Vietcong. The 7th Marines, the 3rd Marines, and a battalion of the 4th Marines attacked the 1st Vietcong regiment on the Van Tuong Peninsula. The USMC elements deployed both overland and amphibiously, supported by AD-4s as well as by naval bombardment, to envelop the Vietcong within a pincers movement.

The operation stepped off on August 19, 1965, and was a great success, resulting in the destruction of an entire enemy regiment.

organization, administrative and by major commands

As of 2004, the Marine Corps consisted of approximately 173,000 men and women, including 42,000 members of the MARINE CORPS RESERVE. In addition, the Corps employs approximately 18,000 civilian support workers.

The marines operate under the control of the Department of the Navy and secretary of the navy, to whom the COMMANDANT OF THE MARINE CORPS directly reports. The commandant presides over Operating Forces and a Supporting Establishment. The heart of the Corps, the Operating Forces consist of three elements: Marines Corps Security Forces, Marine Security Guard Battalion, and the Fleet Marine Forces. The Supporting Establishment, about 28,000 marines, is responsible for recruiting, for systems development and testing, and for developing doctrine, tactics, and techniques.

Within the Operating Forces, the U.S. MARINE CORPS SECURITY FORCE consists of about 5,000 marines and is responsible for shipboard security and for the security of onshore establishments. The Marine Corps Security Guard Battalion provides legation guards to 128 embassies worldwide. (see U.S. MARINE CORPS SECURITY GUARD BATTALION). Fleet Marine Forces are the major warfighting element of the Corps and are deployed as needed in Marine Air Ground Task Forces. These MAGTFs include Marine Expeditionary Forces (MEFs), Marine Expeditionary Units (MEUs), and Special Purpose MAGTFs, all of which vary in size as required for a particular mission.

organization by units

Operationally and tactically, the marines are organized into the following units, listed in order of ascending size and scope of responsibility:

Fire Team

A fire team is an informal tactical group, usually consisting of four marines and constituting one-third of a squad.

Squad

A marine squad is usually commanded by a sergeant or staff sergeant and composed of three fire teams, each fire team typically consisting of four men. The total strength of the Marine Corps squad is 13, including the commander.

Platoon

A low-level infantry unit, a marine platoon (beginning in the WORLD WAR II era) consists of three squads. There are three platoons to a company. The strength of a contemporary platoon is not fixed, but varies depending on the nature of the unit; however, a World War II marine rifle platoon generally consisted of 76 men.

Company

In the marines and in the army, a company is a unit of troops under the command of a captain and consists of a headquarters section and two or more platoons. A company consists of 140 or more personnel and is the basic element of a battalion. Conventionally, companies within the battalion are assigned alphabetic names (Company C, or Charlie Company, for example), although independent companies are assigned numerical names (3rd Communications Company).

Battalion

Until the expansion of the marines during WORLD WAR I, the battalion was the largest organizational unit in the service, varying in size from 150 men to 300. World War I introduced the brigade and regiment. Each brigade at this time consisted of 9,300 men and was divided into two regiments, each of which consisted of four battalions, with 1,160 men each. During World War II, the battalion was reduced to 881 men, which remains more or less the strength of this unit currently.

Regiment

A traditional unit term no longer officially used by the marines or the army (having been supplanted in both by the brigade), "regiment" is still used unofficially in deference to tradition.

Brigade

Brigades were unknown in the marines before a reorganization of the Corps in 1913, at which time a brigade consisted of two regiments. During World War I, a marine brigade was large, at 9,300 men. In World War II, the brigade was upgraded to divisional status, and in the VIETNAM WAR, the brigade concept was revised as the Marine Expeditionary Brigade, which consists of about 16,000 marines.

Marine Expeditionary Brigade (MEB)

The Marine Expeditionary Brigade (MEB) was a mainstay of marine deployment beginning in the 1950s and was employed in the KOREAN WAR, Vietnam War, and the PERSIAN GULF WAR. The MEB was eliminated throughout the Marine Corps during the early 1990s, but was reactivated, one MEB within each Marine Expeditionary Force (MEF), as of January 1, 2000. The MEB was seen as a force structure that had the capability of responding rapidly and with great flexibility to crises and trouble spots. The MEB supports such marine doctrines as Operational Maneuver From the Sea, which calls for strike capability 220 miles inland with fast-moving and sustainable forces, and also in urban combat; the marines believe that access by sea offers the best early-entry force into most urban areas.

The Amphibious MEB embarks aboard navy ships to destinations throughout the world, where it can make an amphibious assault, take a beachhead, and open a lane to project offensive combat power ashore.

The Amphibious MEB consists of more than 4,000 marines. A Maritime Prepositioning Force MEB can be much larger—greater than 16,000 marines—and large enough to project offensive combat power throughout its theater of operation. This would be used as a land-based force.

The Marine Expeditionary Brigade (MEB) is a Marine Air-Ground Task Force (MAGTF) built around a reinforced infantry regiment, an aircraft group, and a Brigade Service Support Group (BSSG). It is commanded by a brigadier general. As a marine expeditionary force, it is capable of rapid deployment via amphibious shipping or strategic airlift. The MEB deploys with 30 days of supplies, so that the MEB is intended as the forward echelon of the MEF.

The Ground Combat Element (GCE) of an MEB is normally an infantry regiment reinforced with selected division units. The Aviation Combat Element (ACE) is a task-organized marine aircraft group that includes varied aviation capabilities as well as antiair warfare capabilities, as required by the situation.

The Combat Service Support Element (CSSE) is a Brigade Service Support Group (BSSG) organized to provide maintenance support, front-line haul transportation, expeditionary vertical and horizontal construction, supply support, medical collecting and clearing, and landing support functions.

Division

The division was the largest marine unit at the beginning of World War II and consisted of two brigades for a total of 16,000 men per division. When the marines were reorganized during the 1980s into Marine Air Ground Task Force units, divisions operated within the larger units.

Marine Air Ground Task Force (MAGTF)

The MAGTF is a combined armed force consisting of a command element, a ground combat element, an aviation combat element, and a combat service (support) element. MAGTFs are established on an as-needed basis to accomplish specific missions, then disbanded on completion of the mission. There are currently four types of generic MAGTFs. The Marine Expeditionary Brigade (MEB) is explained above. The other three generic MAGTFs are the Marine Expeditionary Force (MEF), Marine Expeditionary Unit (MEU), and the Special Purpose Force (SPF). The strength of the MAGTFs is flexible; the largest, as in the Persian Gulf War, may contain up to 100,000 marines.

Marine Expeditionary Force (MEF)

The largest MAGTF, an MEF consists of 30,000 to 60,000 marines under the command of a lieutenant general. There may be one or more infantry divisions and an aircraft wing. The MEF is highly self-sustaining, capable of remaining in combat without resupply for 60 days.

Marine Expeditionary Unit (MEU)

The MEU is a MAGTF consisting of 1,000 to 4,000 marines, typically an infantry battalion and a composite aircraft squadron, under the command of a colonel. The MEU is the basic building-block unit of a MAGTF.

Special Purpose Force (SPF)

The smallest generic MAGTF, the SPF consists of 100 to 1,000 marines and/or navy SEALs. The SPF typically responds to crises in foreign locations, and they are often the first U.S. military personnel on the scene. Often, they are used in unconventional operations.

Corps

Spelled with a capital C, "The Corps" is a synonym for the United States Marine Corps. Spelled with a lowercase C, the corps is an organizational unit that was too large for the small USMC until the middle of World War II, when the first USMC corps was organized following the Battle of GUADALCANAL in 1943. By the end of the war, the marines fielded two amphibious corps. After the war, the term *corps* was not used, but the function of a corps was assumed first by the III Marine Amphibious Force (during the Vietnam War era) and then, during the 1970s and 1980s, by Marine Air Ground Task Forces.

Marine Corps Aviation

Marine Corps aviation units use two special organization terms. A *squadron* is the basic marine aviation unit, which generally consists of aircraft of a single type. The marine squadron consists of two or more *flights,* which are generally defined as a group of aircraft and crews assigned a common mission.

OV-10 Bronco   See AIRCRAFT, FIXED-WING.

Oxygen Transfer Pump System   See PERSONAL AND MISCELLANEOUS EQUIPMENT.

P

Pack Howitzer 1923-E2   See INDIRECT FIRE SYSTEMS.

Panama

In 1988, Panama's strongman dictator, Manuel Noriega, was indicted in absentia by a U.S. federal grand jury for drug trafficking. Pursuant to the indictment, Presidents Ronald Reagan and George H. W. Bush employed economic and diplomatic sanctions in an effort to pressure Noriega into resigning. After these attempts failed, and amid deteriorating U.S.-Panamanian relations, USMC and U.S. Army reinforcements were deployed to U.S. installations in Panama during the spring of 1989. This show of force did not prompt Noriega to step down; after a coup attempt against him failed in October 1989, Noriega issued a "declaration against the United States," which was followed by several incidents of harassment against U.S. nationals in Panama. The most severe incident was the shooting of an off-duty USA officer by Panamanian troops. This brought about, on December 19, 1989, the creation of a U.S.-sponsored alternative government for Panama, led by President Guillermo Endara. Early the next morning, December 20, Operation Just Cause was launched.

The operation began with an air assault (by then-new USAF F-117 Stealth fighters) against the barracks of the Panamanian Defense Force (PDF). U.S. Army Rangers were given responsibility for the main ground action, while marines guarded the entrances to the Panama Canal and other U.S. defense sites located in the Canal Zone. Rangers, reinforced by marines, advanced on the central Canal Zone, attacking en route the Commandancia, headquarters of Noriega and the PDF. Marines of the elite Task Force Semper Fi secured a six-mile area southwest of Panama City, encompassing the U.S. Naval Station, Howard Air Force Base, the Arraijan Tank Farm, and the Bridge of the Americas. Other units took and held Torrijos International Airport.

The fighting in Panama City was conducted house-to-house over a five-day period, as marines hunted down PDF troops and sought Noriega. In the meantime, a civil-affairs army Ranger battalion assisted President Endara in establishing order. The Rangers quickly created a new Panamanian police force, the Panama Public Force, to preserve civil order after U.S. troops withdrew. As for Noriega, he was not located until January 1990, when he was arrested and transported to the United States for trial. On April 10, 1992, Noriega was convicted on eight counts of cocaine trafficking, racketeering, and money laundering. He was sentenced to 40 years' imprisonment.

Casualties included 190 PDF soldiers killed and 124 wounded; 5,313 were taken prisoner. Nineteen American troops were killed and 303 wounded, including one marine killed and two wounded. The total number of marines deployed in Operation Just Cause was only 600 out of a total military force of 24,000.

Parachutist Individual Equipment Kit

(PIEK)   See PERSONAL AND MISCELLANEOUS EQUIPMENT.

Parris Island   See BASES, CAMPS, AND OTHER INSTALLATIONS.

Pate, Randolph McCall (1898–1961) *Marine Corps commandant*

The 21st COMMANDANT OF THE MARINE CORPS, Pate was born in Port Royal, South Carolina, and saw his first military service in the U.S. Army, as an enlisted soldier during WORLD WAR I. After the war, he attended Virginia Military Institute, graduating in 1921 and receiving a commission as a second lieutenant in the MARINE CORPS RESERVE. Pate served in SANTO DOMINGO (1923–24) and China (1927–29), then was posted in the United States.

By the outbreak of World War II, Pate was a lieutenant colonel and took command as chief of logistics at GUADALCANAL. Later, he served as deputy chief of staff, FLEET MARINE FORCE, Pacific, and, after the war, became director of the Marine Corps Reserve and commandant of the Marine Corps Educational Center at Marine Corps Base Quantico.

As a major general, Pate commanded the 1st Marine Division during the KOREAN WAR in 1953, just before the armistice. He was appointed commandant in 1955 and personally commanded marines sent to Egypt during the Suez Crisis of 1956. Pate retired, a general, on December 31, 1959.

PBY-5A Catalina   See AIRCRAFT, FIXED-WING.

Peleliu

An island in the Palau group of the western Carolines, Peleliu held important Japanese positions, which were attacked in September 1944 during WORLD WAR II. The 1st Marine Division, III Amphibious Corps, invaded, only to find that the number of Japanese defenders had been grossly underestimated. A 72-hour campaign had been envisioned; the assault actually lasted from September 15 to October 22 and exacted 1,300 USMC deaths. Army units, which were called in to reinforce the USMC invasion, suffered 827 casualties.

Although the Battle of Peleliu turned out to be one of the hardest fought in the Pacific war, the island proved of little strategic value.

Pendleton, Joseph H. ("Uncle Joe") (1860–1942) *Marine Corps general*

A native of Rochester, Pennsylvania, Pendleton was a U.S. Naval Academy graduate (1882), served two years at sea, then was commissioned a second lieutenant in the USMC. He served in U.S. posts, at sea, and twice in Sitka, Alaska, before being posted to the Philippines. Promoted to major, he commanded the USMC base on Guam before assuming command of a USMC base at Bremerton, Washington, during 1906–09. After serving again in the Philippines, Pendleton assumed commands at Portsmouth, New Hampshire, and in NICARAGUA. In 1913, now a colonel, Pendleton led an expeditionary force at GUANTÁNAMO BAY.

Pendleton served in various U.S. commands until June 1916, when he led marines against rebels in SANTO DOMINGO. Promoted to brigadier general, he became acting military governor there until his return to the United States in October 1918, when he was appointed to command Marine Corps Recruit Depot Parris Island. In 1919, he assumed command of the advanced force base at San Diego, California, and in 1922 was appointed commanding general of the Department of the Pacific. He was promoted to major general in 1924 and retired later in the year, as commander of the 5th Brigade. Marine Corps Base Camp Pendleton, San Diego, is named for him.

Penobscot Bay Fiasco

During the AMERICAN REVOLUTION, 700 British troops and three Royal Navy men of war were deployed to Penobscot Bay at the mouth of the Penobscot River in Maine to build a fort and naval base from which operations could be directed against upper New England. A combined force of CONTINENTAL MARINES and Massachusetts State Marines was put at the head of a 900-man Patriot army to attack the British fort and drive out the garrison.

The marine elements of the Patriot force landed on July 28, 1779, easily neutralized the light opposition they encountered, and occupied the high ground before the still-incomplete British fort. At this point, however, the militia commander caught up with the marines, and a dispute over command ensued. This delayed the Patriot advance just 500 yards short of the fort. During this interval, a British frigate hove into sight, prompting the Patriot commander to order a general withdrawal against the vigorous objection of the marines. In this way, a magnificent opportunity was lost. The militia commander was subsequently convicted by a court-martial of dereliction of duty.

Persian Gulf War

On August 2, 1990, the Iraqi army, at the time the fourth largest ground force in the world, invaded Kuwait pursuant to a proclamation of annexation. Within a week, Kuwait had fallen to Iraq, and the United States worked through the United Nations to assemble a large coalition of nations to compel Iraq's dictator, Saddam Hussein, to withdraw from Kuwait.

U.S. military forces began a buildup in the Middle East on August 7, 1990, in response to a Saudi request for military aid to defend against possible Iraqi invasion. Dubbed Operation Desert Shield, the buildup included the 7th Marine Expeditionary Brigade, followed by the 4th Marine Expeditionary Brigade, and the 1st Marine Expeditionary Brigade, bringing USMC presence during Desert Shield to 30,000. A call-up of USMC RESERVES added another 31,000. The USMC presence included ground troops as well as the 1st and 2nd Air Wings. The total USMC presence was a small por-

tion of the 450,000 troops that would ultimately constitute the coalition forces arrayed against the Iraqi invaders.

Saddam Hussein defied a series of UN resolutions ordering his withdrawal from Kuwait. The UN set a withdrawal deadline of January 15, 1991. When this deadline elapsed, Operation Desert Shield became Operation Desert Storm—and the Persian Gulf War began on the morning of January 16 with a massive air campaign. The air war continued for five weeks and some 88,000 missions, which devastated Iraqi defenses. Then, on "G Day," February 24, 1991, the ground war was commenced with a marine attack from the extreme right of the coalition line. Two USMC divisions rapidly breached the Iraqi defenses, and by the end of that first day of the ground war, the marines had destroyed three Iraqi divisions.

At 4:30 in the morning of February 25, marines engaged in the largest tank battle in their history. Victory was total, and the Iraqi tanks completely destroyed. By the 27th, marines had liberated Kuwait City.

As spectacular as the USMC operations were, they represented a small part of the war. Coalition forces were on the verge of totally destroying the armed forces of Saddam Hussein when President George H. W. Bush, declaring that the objective of liberating Kuwait had been attained, announced that hostilities would cease at 8 A.M., February 28.

Despite his overwhelming military defeat, Saddam Hussein remained absolute dictator of Iraq. In 2003, as a result of the U.S. invasion of Iraq in Operation Iraqi Freedom, Saddam was driven from office, but marines and army forces were then faced with a long insurgency, which included resistance by Saddam loyalists.

personal and miscellaneous equipment

Important Marine Corps personal and miscellaneous equipment includes survival gear, parachute equipment, and equipment for operating in special environments. (Also see NUCLEAR-BIOLOGICAL-CHEMICAL EQUIPMENT.)

AN/PSN-11 Precision Lightweight GPS Receiver (PLGR)

The AN/PSN-11 Precision Lightweight GPS Receiver (PLGR) provides precise geopositioning and timing for USMC ground units. It is a small, handheld, Global Positioning System (GPS) receiver that incorporates selective availability/antispoofing (SA/A-S) and antijam capability. Like all GPS devices, it provides precise positioning and timing solutions based on signals received from GPS satellites. Five channels are available, and the unit is capable of Precision Code (P Code) and Y Code (encrypted P Code) reception. Positioning solutions may be displayed in latitude, longitude, military grid reference system, Universal Transverse Mercator, British National Grid, or Irish Transverse Mercator Grid coordinates. Containing 49 map datums, the PLGR can be programmed to support navigation.

Specifications of the unit include:

Length: 9.45 in
Width: 4.23 in
Weight: 2.75 lb

AN/PSS-12 Metallic Mine Detector

The AN/PSS-12 Metallic Mine Detector is employed to locate land mines during minefield breaching, road sweep, and follow-on clearance operations. It is a lightweight, handheld metallic mine detector capable of detecting very small metallic objects, including small firing pins in plastic and wooden mines. The detector can detect mines in fresh or salt water as well as mines and other metallic objects buried up to 20 inches in the ground.

The AN/PSS-12 is considered a state-of-the-art, world-class mine detector that is especially well suited to detecting the often very small amounts of metal used in the construction of modern land mines. As of 2004, the USMC had 547 of the units in its inventory, most of them deployed with combat engineer battalions, engineer support battalions, and Marine wing support squadrons.

General characteristics of the AN/PSS-12 Metallic Mine Detector include:

Manufacturer: Schiebel Instruments, Inc.
Power supply: 4 1.5-volt batteries
Operating time: 70 hr
Weight, in transport case: 13.7 lb
Mine detector alone: 8.5 lb
Materials: telescopic pole consists of an inner plastic tube and outer aluminum tube

Diver Propulsion Device (DPD)

Marine reconnaissance underwater combat divers currently engage in closed-circuit underwater diving, an expanded operational role that requires divers to use additional equipment to complete their missions. The DPD enhances the performance and survivability of the combat diver in amphibious reconnaissance operations by propelling the diver at a speed of 1 knot. Power is provided by rechargeable gel-cel lead oxide batteries connected to two drive motors, the batteries furnishing sufficient power to propel the diver about as long as his oxygen supply lasts. The DPD enables divers to conduct long-range "Over-The-Horizon" (OTH) operations. With the aid of the DPD, the diver can conserve his energy; moreover, the DPD also serves as a platform for real-time intelligence collection, while decreasing the possibility of detection by allowing the diver to stay submerged.

General characteristics of the Diver Propulsion Device (DPD) include:

Manufacturer: Coastal Systems Station
Weight: 165 lb
Speed: 1 knot
Endurance: 200 min

Field Pack, Large, with Internal Frame (FPLIF)

The field pack is a key piece of equipment for any infantry marine. The modern FPLIF is an internal frame pack that offers 6,800 cubic inches of storage space. It incorporates a detachable 2,500-cubic-inch patrol pack and an internal compartment for stowage of the sleeping bag. Water resistant, it is adjustable and is designed to complement the normal center of gravity to promote comfortable and efficient movement for the wearer.

The new FPLIF was designed to remedy the deficiencies of the large traditional "Alice Pack" by increasing storage capacity, enhancing comfort and mobility, and keeping all gear protected from the environment. The versatile pack can hold all additional gear needed in a cold weather environment.

General characteristics of the Field Pack, Large, with Internal Frame (FPLIF) include:

Length: 30 in
Width: 21 in
Weight: 8 lb
Area: 4.375 sq ft
Volume: 3.64 cu ft
Stowage: 3.64 cu ft
Color: woodland camouflage

Improved ECWCS
Fiberpile Shirt and Trousers

The Improved ECWCS Fiberpile Shirt and Trousers were developed to provide marines with a flexible, comfortable means of staying warm in temperatures ranging from +40° to −25° Fahrenheit. The shirt is a front-opening jacket with long sleeves, hand-warming packets, two breast pockets, and a zip-up collar. The trousers are bib type, with built-in suspenders featuring quick-release fasteners and a full-length side zipper for easy donning and removal. Both the shirt and trousers are made of 100 percent polyester fleece. Models come in a variety of weights and insulation thicknesses.

The ECWCS was designed to reduce the uncomfortable bulk of traditional USMC extreme cold weather garments. Fleece is a commercially available fabric choice that is light in weight, water resistant, quick drying, and noted for its high level of comfort. The shirt and trousers together weigh only .6 pounds.

Extreme Cold Weather Tent (ECWT)

The Extreme Cold Weather Tent (ECWT) is a self-standing shelter capable of accommodating four marines to sleep, dry wet clothing, and prepare meals in extreme cold-weather environments. The ECWT is a domelike structure that incorporates a waterproof opaque fly sheet. It is especially designed for maximum stability in high winds and durability in generally harsh environmental conditions. The design includes a vestibule entrance area with sufficient space for two men to shed their packs and cold weather clothing before entering the tent body. Assembly can be accomplished by one person.

The Extreme Cold Weather Tent (ECWT) represents a major improvement over the previous tent used in extreme cold weather, which was constructed simply by putting five Norwegian tent sheets together. These tended to freeze when wet, becoming stiff and difficult to handle. To erect this type of tent, it was necessary to dig out the snow inside and tie the external liner to a tree. The self-standing dome-style tent is much more efficient in all respects.

General characteristics of the Extreme Cold Weather Tent (ECWT) include:

Length, erected: 102 in
Length, stored: 28.5 in
Width, erected: 110 in
Width, stored: 14.5 in
Height, erected: 55 in
Height, stored: 13 in
Storage volume: 3.1 cu ft
Weight: 20 lb

Individual Tactical
Load-Bearing Vest (ITLBV)

The Individual Tactical Load Bearing Vest (ITLBV) was commissioned by the USMC to improve the fighting load's distribution of weight for the individual marine. Made of an 8-ounce nylon fabric, the vest weighs 1.8 pounds empty and has permanently attached ammunition and grenade pockets designed to carry six 30-round magazines and two grenades. The vest is intended for use with the standard cartridge belt. The shoulder pads have two attachment points for the cover of the field pack.

General characteristics of the Individual Tactical Load Bearing Vest (ITLBV) include:

Length: 16 in
Width: 8 in
Height: 3.5 in
Weight: 1.8 lb
Color: woodland camouflage

Infantry Shelter

The USMC Infantry Shelter provides cover and protection from the elements for two marines and their equipment. It is made of 1.9-ounce ripstop nylon and is a tent with an integrated waterproof floor and a waterproof, opaque, free-standing fly with vestibule. The tent provides protection from wind and rain, weighs less than 8 pounds, and, using telescoping aluminum poles, can be erected and struck rapidly.

The new Infantry Shelter replaces the traditional shelter half, which was not only time-consuming to erect and strike, but afforded inadequate protection from wind and rain and weighed too much.

The general characteristics of the Infantry Shelter include:

Storage, length: 22 in
Storage, diameter: 7 in
Sheltered area: 34 sq ft
Height: 45 in at apex
Weight: 8 lb

Laser Rangefinder AN/GVS-5

The AN/GVS-5 is a handheld, binocular-style laser rangefinder used by marines for observation and target acquisition. It consists of a panel assembly, optical assembly, and laser transmitter module and can use either battery or vehicle power. The rangefinder allows accurate determination of range to targets and includes 7 × 15 sighting optics, a multiple target indicator, and minimum range adjustment. The rangefinder can take one reading per second, up to 100 rangings per battery. The rangefinder provides a means of verifying the location of targets to be engaged by air or ground fire. The instrument is also useful in determining the adjustment of rounds on the target.

General characteristics of the Laser Rangefinder AN/GVS-5 include:

Length: 9 in
Width: 8 in
Height: 4 in
Weight: 5 lb with battery
Emission wavelength: 1.06 microns
Beam divergence: 1 milliradian
Range measurement limits: 650–3,277 ft
Range error: + or –32.8 ft
Power requirements: 24 volts

Marine Assault Climbers Kit

The Marine Assault Climbers Kit was developed to enable marines to safely negotiate obstacles up to a vertical distance of 300 feet. Fielded to infantry regiments, special operations training groups and reconnaissance units, the kit consists of equipment certified by the Union of International Alpinists Association and is intended for use on obstacles common to built-up areas, to complete operations over rivers and gorges, and to complete assaults on oil platforms or bridges. Each kit is sufficient to allow a 200-man company to negotiate a 300-foot vertical obstacle. The advantage of the Marine Assault Climbers Kit is that it is much lighter and more portable than previous mountaineering equipment. Moreover, traditional equipment is limited in function, difficult or impossible to remove, and leaves a trail signature. In contrast, the equipment in this kit is recoverable, reusable, quiet, need leave no trail signature, and represents the state-of-the-art in alpine gear.

MC-5 Static Line/Free-Fall Ram Air Parachute System (SL/FF RAPS)

The USMC has developed a state-of-the-art parachute system for insertion of reconnaissance and special operations forces. The highly versatile MC-5 Static Line/Free-Fall Ram Air Parachute System can be configured for static line or free-fall, depending on mission requirements. It uses identical main and reserve canopies, which reduces the logistics involved with separate canopies and eliminates the need for separate training and maintenance of two different canopies.

Manufactured by the Paraflite Company, the main and reserve parachutes are each 370 square feet, seven-celled, and are manufactured from 1.1 ounce F-111 nylon ripstop fabric. The parachute may be used at altitudes from 3,000 feet to 30,000 feet and achieves a forward speed of 15 to 25 miles per hour and a rate of descent of 14 to 18 feet per second, maximum. At 50 percent brakes, descent is from 8 feet to 14 feet per second. The MC-5 SL/FF RAPS is thus especially well suited to the high-altitude, high-opening (HAHO) parachute operations the USMC typically uses for insertion missions.

Modular Sleeping Bag (MSB)

In the mid-1990s, the USMC acquired an advanced-design modular sleeping bag to replace the heavier, water-absorbing, intermediate cold weather and extreme cold weather bags then in use. Not only are the new bags more comfortable, affording greater protection of wet and cold, they are also 7 pounds lighter than the traditional bags. The modular concept allows greater flexibility in adapting to a range of climate and weather.

The Modular Sleeping Bag system consists of two bags: a lightweight outer patrol bag (rated to 30°F) and an intermediate inner bag (rated to −10°F). The bags can be used independently or together to create the extreme cold weather bag, which is rated to −30°F. The bags are made from lightweight polyester fibers, which provide a very high degree of insulation. The bag is described as "hydrophobic" (water hating)—that is, highly waterproof. It is ultralight at under 7 pounds and is readily carried in its own compression stuff sack. The USMC maintains a large inventory of the MSB: 129,324 units for the active forces, and 42,848 for the MARINE CORPS RESERVE.

General characteristics of the MSB include:

Manufacturer: Tennier Industries, Inc.
Storage volume: 1,991 cu in
Weight: 4.5 lb

Oxygen Transfer Pump System

The USMC reconnaissance underwater combat diver and airborne-qualified marine must be able to undertake missions that include extended closed-circuit underwater diving and high-altitude parachute operations. These difficult and demanding missions require state-of-the-art oxygen breathing devices, which, in turn, must be safely and efficiently maintained in a ready status. The Oxygen Transfer Pump System is designed to maintain the equipment needed to perform closed-circuit diving and high altitude jumps in an environment that is oxygen safe.

The system is composed of a variety of oxygen-transferring times within a Marine Corps Expeditionary Shelter System. This equipment allows personnel to maintain all of their closed-circuit diving and military free-fall equipment on or off deployments. The system is designed for use in a variety of mission scenarios, ranging from expeditionary to shipboard. It is also operable in a range of climates, from extreme cold to extreme heat. As of 2004, the USMC maintained 14 Oxygen Transfer Pump Systems for its active forces and three for the Marine Corps Reserve.

General characteristics of the Oxygen Transfer Pump System include:

Length: 20 ft
Width: 96 in
Height: 96 in
Weight: 4,500 lb
Power Requirements: 120/208 volt AC, 3 phase, 60 hertz, 60 amperes max

Parachutist Individual Equipment Kit (PIEK)

The USMC uses the Parachutist Individual Equipment Kit (PIEK) to provide its parachutists with comprehensive protection from the environment. Manufactured by a variety of vendors—Intimar, Pennsylvania; Cabellas, California; Steve Snyder Enterprises, New Jersey; North American Aeronutronics, North Carolina; REI, Washington; and Television Associates, Inc., New York—the kit consists of a Goretex jumpsuit, a Polartec jumpsuit liner, a cotton ripstop jumpsuit, flyer's gloves, Goretex cold-weather gloves, overboots, an MA2-30 altimeter, helmet, flyer's helmet bag, and flyer's kitbag. The principal purpose of the kit is to combat the extreme cold encountered during high-altitude parachute operations.

Reverse Osmosis Water Purification Unit

USMC forces must be self-sufficient under the most difficult of environmental conditions. The Reverse Osmosis Water Purification Unit is a system designed to treat water from any available source and to render it potable. The unit performs a purification process that removes all nuclear-biological-chemical (NBC) contaminants from water, that produces potable water from brackish, shallow, and deep-well sources, and that also effectively produces freshwater from seawater sources.

Used by all U.S. armed forces, the Reverse Osmosis Water Purification Unit has performed especially well for the USMC. It was extensively employed during Operations Desert Shield/Desert Storm (the PERSIAN GULF WAR) and was shown to increase the expeditionary capability that is at the heart of USMC operational doctrine.

General characteristics of the unit include:

Transportation: the unit is transported in an 8 foot by 8 foot by 10 foot rigid frame
Production rate, seawater source: 600 gal/hr
Production rate, freshwater source: 1,800 gal/hr
Weight: 7,300 lb
Length: 120 in
Width: 96 in
Height: 96 in
Power source: 30-kilowatt generator

Second-Generation Extended Cold Weather Clothing System (ECWCS)

The second-generation Extended Cold Weather Clothing System (ECWCS) has been especially developed for the USMC to provide protection from wind, rain, and snow. The system consists of outer garments, including a parka and trousers. The parka features two hand-warming/cargo pockets, two side-access breast pockets, two upper-sleeve pockets, and a roll-and-stow hood, which fits into the collar. The parka also features water-shedding slide fasteners and zippered armpit vents. The trousers have suspender attachments, belt loops, two side-leg cargo pockets, and knee-high zippers for easy donning and doffing while wearing boots. Both garments are made of a tri-laminate using a waterproof, vapor-permeable membrane laminated between two nylon knits, and both are produced in a woodland camouflage pattern. The USMC inventory is planned to include 174,000 units for active forces and 45,203 for reserves.

General characteristics of the second-generation Extended Cold Weather Clothing System (ECWCS) include:

Weight, parka: 1.3 lb
Weight, trousers: 1 lb
Color: woodland camouflage

Single-Action Release Personal Equipment Lowering System (SARPELS)

Among the specialized equipment developed for USMC parachutists is the Single-Action Release Personal Equipment Lowering System (SARPELS), which is an integrated system for safely lowering a parachutist's combat equipment. Usable in both static line and free-fall parachute operations, the SARPELS allows parachutists to carry a variety of configurations of combat equipment. The system enables the parachutist to land with his equipment in a way that avoids injury: by lowering the equipment below the parachutist. Conventionally, separate types of equipment-lowering systems were required for static line and free-fall operations. The USMC SARPELS accommodates both. Moreover, it provides ready access to weapons and equipment after landing. Its single-action release makes for rapid and safe deployment of equipment, and this versatile system can be front or rear mounted on the parachutist.

The system consists of the SARPELS Cargo Carrier, horizontal and vertical cargo carrier securing straps, the single-action release handle, military free-fall equipment attaching strap, a 15-foot static lowering line, and an 8-foot military free-fall lowering line.

Tandem Offset
Resupply Delivery System (TORDS)

The Tandem Offset Resupply Delivery System (TORDS) is a parachute delivery system that the USMC uses to provide reconnaissance personnel with a parachute delivery system for supply and resupply of combat equipment or personnel. The system has a payload capacity of more than 500 pounds and consists of square main and reserve canopies, each manufactured from 1.1-ounce F-111 ripstop nylon fabric. The TORDS has a six-foot drogue parachute, which is deployed to reduce the terminal velocity of the tandem master and load (passenger/combat equipment) to approximately 120 miles per hour at opening altitude. The drogue, deployed by ripcord, also acts as a pilot chute and in turn deploys the main canopy.

USMC force reconnaissance teams often use highly maneuverable square parachutes for High Altitude High Opening (HAHO) parachute insertion operations. The Tandem Offset Resupply Delivery System is used in these operations to deliver an increased payload of combat-essential equipment or personnel.

Manufactured by Relative Workshop of Florida, TORDS consists of a main canopy with a surface area of 421 square feet arranged in nine cells, and a nine-cell reserve canopy of 360 square feet. The system can be deployed from 8,000 feet to 25,000 feet. Forward speed is 15 to 25 miles per hour, and rate of descent at full flight is 16 to 20 feet per second. At 50 percent brakes, rate of descent is 10 to 16 feet per second.

Woolly-pully

In the USMC, an olive-green rib-knit pullover sweater with reinforced shoulders, elbows, and forearms worn optionally during fall and winter.

The name is derived from the manufacturer's trademarked name, Woolly-Pully.

Personnel Administration School

One of the USMC's COMBAT SERVICE SUPPORT SCHOOLS located at Camp Johnson, North Carolina, Personnel Administration School provides basic, intermediate, and advanced resident formal school instruction to USMC personnel administrators, with a special emphasis on combat service support. The Administrative Clerk Course and the Personnel Clerk Course are the entry-level offerings. Career-level courses are the Adjutant Course, Personnel Officer Course, Advanced Personnel Administration Course, Senior Clerk Course, and Reserve Administration Course.

Philippine Insurrection

Shortly after the SPANISH-AMERICAN WAR, the Filipino nationalist leader Emilio Aguinaldo, who had led guerrilla forces as an ally of the United States during the war with Spain, believed his nation had been betrayed because it won independence from Spain only to be annexed by the United States. Aguinaldo led an anti-U.S. insurrection, attacking Manila on February 4, 1899. Later in the year, two USMC battalions were sent to augment army efforts to pacify the rebels, but most were withdrawn in 1900 for service in China during the BOXER REBELLION. Returning later in the year, the marines operated mostly against the Moros, a Muslim people living on Samar and other southern Philippine islands. The Moros were adamant in their refusal to submit to U.S. control, and in October of 1900, a USMC battalion was placed under U.S. Army control to suppress Moro resistance. Within less than a month, most Moro resistance had been crushed, although no formal agreement to submit to U.S. authority was concluded.

platoon   See ORGANIZATION BY UNITS.

A Marine Corps drill instructor screams instructions to a poolee. *(U.S. Marine Corps)*

poolees
Unofficial but universally used name for USMC enlistees awaiting recruit training (boot camp). The time "in the pool" is typically three to 12 months.

private   See RANKS AND GRADES.

private first class   See RANKS AND GRADES.

promotion system
The modern USMC promotion system was instituted in 1915 and has been modified repeatedly since. The objective of the promotion system is to ensure that officers best suited are selected for advancement while those who are least well suited are repeatedly passed over and eventually retire at a relatively low rank.

Entry-level USMC officers are commissioned as second lieutenants. A second lieutenant becomes eligible for promotion to first lieutenant after 24 months of service in grade. Promotion from first lieutenant to captain, all the way up through the ranks to major general, is by selection (merit) rather than seniority. However, years in service generally figure as a prerequisite for selection for promotion. Promotion to captain generally requires four years in service; to major, 10 years (9–11); to lieutenant colonel, 16 years (15–17); and to colonel 22 years (21–23). Failure to be promoted within the usual time span does not preclude promotion, as long as the candidate remains on active duty.

A regularly constituted selection board receives the names and files of officers eligible for consideration for promotion. The board begins with the most senior officer of the grade under consideration who has not previously failed to be selected. From here, the board works its way down through seniority in considering each candidate for promotion. Officers who are in the promotion zone (for example, captains with nine to 11 years in service and who are therefore eligible for promotion to major) but who fail to be selected are said to have been passed over. USMC regulations prescribe certain limits for service within each grade, beyond which retirement is mandatory.

The constitution of the selection board is very important. Generally, USMC boards consist of nine active or MARINE CORPS RESERVE officers. The board is convened by the SECRETARY OF THE NAVY annually, The members of the board are committed to recommend the best-fitted officers for promotion. They give equal weight to line duty as well as to administrative duty. They are not to consider as prejudicial the fact that a candidate for promotion may have been passed over previously, provided the candidate is within the allowable time-in-grade. They must make their promotions within the numerical limits set by the secretary of the navy.

Selection for promotion does not automatically and immediately secure promotion. Selected officers are placed on a promotion list in order of seniority. As vacancies occur, the selected officers are promoted in order of seniority.

pugil stick

The pugil stick is a six-foot-long pole with padded ends used by the USMC in BASIC TRAINING to simulate bayonet combat.

Puller, Lewis B. "Chesty" (1898–1972)
Marine Corps general

Born in West Point, Virginia, Puller enlisted in the USMC during WORLD WAR I, in August 1918. He earned a reserve commission as second lieutenant in 1919, but was almost immediately inactivated when the USMC was reduced in size during the

Lieutenant General Lewis B. Puller (USMC)   *(U.S. Marine Corps)*

rush to demobilize following the Armistice. The very image of a GUNG-HO marine, Puller, undaunted, reenlisted as a noncommissioned officer. He served in HAITI with the ambiguous rank of USMC sergeant but as *captain* of the Haitian Gendarmerie. Puller served for five years in the turbulent island nation.

In 1924, Puller returned to the United States and received an officer's commission. After service at Norfolk and Marine Corps Base Quantico, Puller took flight training at Pensacola Naval Air Station in 1926. He shipped out to NICARAGUA in 1928 as an instructor assigned to train the U.S.-supported Nicaraguan Guardia Nacional in its fight against rebels led by Augusto Sandino. Puller fought in frequent engagements against the Sandinistas and was decorated with the Navy Cross.

After returning to the States in 1931, Puller attended a company officers' course, then returned to Nicaragua to continue leading the National Guard against the Sandinistas. During the course of this assignment, he won a second Navy Cross. From Nicaragua, Puller was assigned to the USMC legation detachment in Peking (Beijing) in 1933. After sea duty, Puller was made instructor at the basic school in Philadelphia (1936). Returning to sea duty in 1939, he was attached to the 4th Marines in 1940, and soon promoted to commanding officer of the unit.

At the outbreak of WORLD WAR II, Puller was given command of 1st Battalion, 7th Marines, which he led to Samoa and then in the assault on GUADALCANAL. Seriously wounded in this engagement, he refused evacuation until the defense of Henderson Field was complete. For this, he was given a third Navy Cross.

While recovering from his wounds, Puller toured U.S. posts, then rejoined the 7th Marines as executive officer of the division. He participated in the landings at Cape Gloucester and led a 1,000-man patrol on New Britain Island, earning his fourth Navy Cross. He led the marines in the invasion of PELELIU, his regiment sustaining 50 percent casualties.

Following World War II, Puller commanded the training regiment at Marine Corps Base Camp Lejeune, then was assigned as director of the 8th Reserve District. In 1950, he once again assumed command of the 1st Marines and led this regiment in the INCHON landing during the KOREAN WAR. His unit crossed the 38th parallel and advanced to the Yalu River, the border with Manchuria. When a massive Chinese counterattack drove Allied forces back, Puller was in charge of the covering operations that protected the vulnerable USMC flanks. Following this operation, Puller received a fifth Navy Cross, and in January 1951 was promoted to brigadier general and assigned as assistant division commander.

Back in the United States, Puller was given command of the 3rd Brigade and became assistant commander after the unit was upgraded to a division. Assigned to direct marine training at Coronado, California, Puller was promoted to major general in 1953 and was given command of the 2nd Division, headquartered at Camp Lejeune. He retired on November 1, 1955, with the rank of lieutenant general. "Chesty" Puller is celebrated as one of the great exemplary marines. His rise from enlisted man to general officer is regarded as the stuff of real-life legend.

Pusan, Defense of

As the biggest port in South Korea, Pusan was critically important to the defense of that nation. When the North Koreans invaded South Korea on June 25, 1950, starting the KOREAN WAR, the United Nations force, including elements of the U.S. Army, fell back on Pusan, forming a defensive perimeter with a radius of about 100 miles and centered on Pusan. The USMC's 1st Provisional Brigade, about 6,500 men, arrived at Pusan on August 2, 1950, and was put in at the extreme left of the Pusan perimeter, assigned to take the city of Sachon. This was accomplished on August 13. The brigade next moved 90 miles north to defend the Naktong Bridge, decisively repulsing the 4th North Korean Division and sending it into retreat across the Naktong River.

On September 3, the brigade supported the USA 2nd Division to blunt a major North Korean attack.

After the September action, the marines were withdrawn and held in reserve pending the arrival of the remainder of the 1st USMC Division. The entire division would play a key role in the daring INCHON landing.

Q

quad body

A marine qualified as a SCUBA diver and a paratrooper, and who has had Ranger training as well as exchange training with the British Royal Marines.

See also U.S. MARINE CORPS RECONNAISSANCE BATTALIONS.

R

R4D Skytrain   See AIRCRAFT, FIXED-WING.

ranks and grades

"Rank" refers to a person's official position within the military hierarchy. "Grade" is an alphanumeric symbol associated with rank, which is keyed to pay level (and is therefore often called "pay grade"). Officer grades range from O-1 to O-10 and enlisted grades from E-1 to E-9. Personnel of grades O-1 through O-3 are often termed "company grade officers."

USMC ranks and grades fall into two groups: commissioned officers and enlisted marines.

Commissioned Officers (in descending order)

General (O-10)

The highest-ranking officer in the USMC, the general wears a four-star insignia. There is no USMC equivalent to the army and air force's five-star generals, (general of the army and general of the air force). The equivalent USA and USAF rank is general, and the equivalent USN rank is admiral.

Lieutenant General (O-9)

The lieutenant general is, in the USMC, USA, and USAF, a general officer of grade O-9, outranking a major general and below a general. The insignia is three silver stars, and the U.S. Navy equivalent is vice admiral.

Major General (O-8)

In the USMC, USA, and USAF, the major general ranks below a lieutenant general and above a brigadier general. Two silver stars denote the rank of this officer, who typically commands a division. Equivalent navy rank is rear admiral.

Brigadier General (O-7)

The lowest-ranking general officer in the USMC, the brigadier ranks above a colonel and below a major general. Insignia is a single star in silver. The equivalent USA and USAF rank is brigadier general, and the equivalent USN rank is rear admiral, lower.

Colonel (O-6)

A field-grade officer in the USMC, USA, and USAF, colonel ranks above lieutenant colonel and below brigadier general. The equivalent USN rank is captain. Insignia is a silver eagle.

Lieutenant Colonel (O-5)

In the USMC, USA, and USAF, the lieutenant colonel ranks above a major and below a colonel. The insignia is a silver oak leaf, and the equivalent navy rank is commander.

Major (O-4)

This USMC, USA, or USAF officer ranks below a lieutenant colonel and above a captain. The insignia is a gold oak leaf, and the USN equivalent rank is lieutenant commander.

Captain (O-3)

In the USMC, as in the army and air force, a captain is a company-grade officer, ranking below a major and above a first lieutenant. This rank is equivalent to a navy lieutenant. The insignia of rank is two vertical silver bars.

First Lieutenant (O-2)

In the USMC, USA, and USAF, the first lieutenant is the second-lowest ranking commissioned officer, above a second lieutenant and below a captain. The insignia is a vertical single silver bar. Equivalent USN rank is lieutenant (j.g.).

Second Lieutenant (O-1)

The lowest-ranking commissioned officer in the USMC, USA, and USAF, the second lieutenant wears a single vertical gold bar and typically commands a platoon. Equivalent USN rank is ensign.

Enlisted Marines (in descending order)

Sergeant Major of the Marine Corps (E-9)

The SMMC is a noncommissioned officer of grade E-9, but outranks all other USMC noncommissioned officers. The appointment is unique and made directly by the COMMANDANT OF THE MARINE CORPS. The SMMC is the senior enlisted assistant and adviser to the commandant and is the USMC equivalent of the U.S. Army's sergeant major of the army, the U.S. Navy's master chief petty officer of the navy, and the U.S. Air Force's chief master sergeant of the air force.

Sergeant Major (E-9)

A senior noncommissioned officer, ranking below only the sergeant major of the Marine Corps, the sergeant major wears three chevrons above four rockers enclosing a star. Equivalent USA ranks are command sergeant major and staff sergeant major. USAF equivalent is chief master sergeant. Equivalent USN rank is master chief petty officer. The USMC sergeant major is the chief administrative assistant of a headquarters, with duties that are often of a support or technical nature.

First Sergeant (E-8)

In the USMC, this noncommissioned officer ranks above gunnery sergeant and below sergeant major.

A master sergeant is also an E-8, but, in the USMC, is junior to the first sergeant.

The first sergeant is the senior sergeant in a company and handles most administrative and personnel matters. Insignia is three chevrons over three rockers, enclosing a diamond device. The first sergeant is familiarly called a first shirt (or, if female, first skirt), first hog, first sleeve, first pig, top, topper, or top sergeant. Equivalent army rank is master sergeant; air force, senior master sergeant or first sergeant; navy, senior chief petty officer.

Master Sergeant (E-8)

A grade E-8 noncommissioned officer ranking above gunnery sergeant and below sergeant major and first sergeant, the master sergeant wears three chevrons above three rockers enclosing crossed rifles. The army equivalent rank is first sergeant. There are no exact air force or navy equivalents, although this rank is comparable to the air force master sergeant and navy senior chief petty officer.

Gunnery Sergeant (E-7)

The "gunny" typically functions as the senior NCO of a company or, in some cases, even a larger unit. Insignia is three chevrons over two "rockers" enclosing a crossed-rifles device. Gunnery sergeant is below first sergeant or master sergeant and above staff sergeant. The equivalent USAF rank is a first sergeant or master sergeant; USA rank, sergeant first class; USN, chief petty officer.

Staff Sergeant (E-6)

A USMC staff sergeant is equivalent to an army staff sergeant and an air force technical sergeant. The equivalent navy rank is petty officer first class.

Sergeant (E-5)

The USMC sergeant wears three chevrons above a crossed-rifle device and is equivalent in rank to the USA sergeant and the USAF staff sergeant. Equivalent USN rank is petty officer second class. In the USMC, sergeants are authorized to wear swords during ceremonies. In the other services, swords are reserved for commissioned officers exclusively.

Corporal (E-4)

In the USMC, the corporal is a noncommissioned officer ranking below a sergeant and above a lance corporal. Insignia is two chevrons, and the corporal usually functions as assistant squad leader. Equivalent USN rank is petty officer third class; USAF, airman first class or senior airman.

Lance Corporal (E-3)

An enlisted marine, the lance corporal ranks below a corporal and above a private first class. Insignia is a single chevron above a crossed-rifles device. This rank is equivalent to a private first class in the army, airman first class in the air force, and seaman in the navy. The lance corporal commands a fire team.

Private First Class (E-2)

Also called marine private first class, this marine ranks below lance corporal and above private. The rank is equivalent to a USA private and a USAF airman. The equivalent USN rank is seaman apprentice.

Private (E-1)

Private is the entry-level USMC rank and is equivalent to a USA private and a USAF airman basic. Equivalent USN rank is seaman recruit.

recruit

A newly enlisted marine, pay grade E-1, rank private.

recruiter

USMC recruiters are noncommissioned officers, from sergeant to gunnery sergeant (E-5 to E-7), responsible for recruiting personnel. The position is highly demanding, requiring great motivation and self-discipline. Moreover, recruiters generally live off base, among civilians. They are expected to meet a quota of acceptable recruits—generally three to four per month—and to manage POOLEES, enlistees who receive periodic training while awaiting boot camp. The recruiter's performance is evaluated not only on how well he or she meets a prescribed quota, but also on the retention rate among the recruits who actually enlist. The recruiter is therefore motivated to screen and evaluate candidates carefully.

regiment   See ORGANIZATION BY UNITS.

Reising Gun   See WEAPONS, INDIVIDUAL AND CREW-SERVED.

Reverse Osmosis Water Purification Unit
See PERSONAL AND MISCELLANEOUS EQUIPMENT.

revolver, .38-caliber   See WEAPONS, INDIVIDUAL AND CREW-SERVED.

rifle grenade   See WEAPONS, INDIVIDUAL AND CREW-SERVED.

Riverine Assault Craft (RAC)   See LANDING CRAFT.

Roi-Namur, Battle of

Twin islands in the Kwajalein atoll in the Marshall Islands, these were heavily fortified by the Japanese during WORLD WAR II. There was a garrison of 3,500 and, on Roi, an airfield with at least 150 planes.

In January 1944, Operation Flintlock targeted Roi-Namur. The campaign began on January 28 with bombing raids followed by naval bombardment. Next, three USMC battalions (25th Marines) occupied the small islands around Roi-Namur, set up howitzer positions on them, and shelled the main objective. Finally, on February 1, the 23rd and 24th Marines landed on Roi and Namur. Roi was lightly defended and fell within two hours of the landing. Namur, however, offered much more resistance, but the 24th Marines secured this island, too, by February 2. The Japanese garrison on both islands had been killed, virtually to a man.

Possession of Roi-Namur gave the U.S. forces a superb harbor and two airstrips, all positioned well forward and affording excellent staging areas for further penetration of Japan's defensive ring.

Russell, John H. (1872–1947) *Marine Corps commandant*

Sixteenth COMMANDANT OF THE MARINE CORPS, Russell was born on Mare Island, California, and graduated from the U.S. Naval Academy in 1892. After two years at sea as a midshipman, Russell was commissioned a second lieutenant in the USMC in 1894 and saw action during the SPANISH-AMERICAN WAR aboard the *Massachusetts* on blockade duty off Santiago, Cuba.

After the war, Russell was variously posted in the United States, Hawaii, and GUAM, then served on the faculty of the Naval War College. He led a battalion in the invasion of VERACRUZ in 1914 and, now as a lieutenant colonel, commanded 3rd Regiment in SANTO DOMINGO. Promoted to colonel, Russell commanded the 1st Marine Brigade in HAITI during 1919. Promoted to brigadier general in 1920, Russell served as U.S. high commissioner for Haiti, then returned to the States in 1930 as assistant commandant, becoming commandant in 1935 as a major general. Russell retired in 1937, having made two major operational contributions to the USMC: the transformation of the Expeditionary Force into the FLEET MARINE FORCE, and the creation of selection boards to govern the promotion of officers.

S

Saboted Light Armor Penetrator (SLAP) ammunition   See ANTIARMOR WEAPONS.

Saint-Mihiel

This French town in the department of the Meuse was the geographical focus of a German salient during WORLD WAR I, the reduction of which figured as a key Allied objective in the final months of the war. The American Expeditionary Force was given major responsibility for attacking the Saint-Mihiel salient, and the 4th, 5th, and 6th Marine Brigades commenced the attack early in September 1918. The operation was concluded successfully on September 15. The role of the USMC was less central at Saint-Mihiel than at BELLEAU WOOD, but all mission objectives were accomplished. USMC casualties were 703 killed and wounded.

Saipan

In the Pacific theater of WORLD WAR II, Saipan, a northerly island in the Marianas group, was a major Japanese base, manned by about 29,000 Japanese naval and air personnel. Twelve hundred miles from the Japanese home islands, Saipan was a key defensive point; moreover, possession of the island would give the Americans a base for B-29 bombing operations against Japan.

Operation Forager, as the invasion of the Marianas was called, began on June 15, 1944, with a USMC landing on Saipan, backed by the navy's Fifth Fleet in the largest assemblage of warships in the Pacific theater. Resistance was extremely heavy, and the 2nd and 4th Divisions suffered severe casualties, as did army reinforcing units. The Japanese defenders were dug into very well-prepared defenses, including natural caves.

The operation proceeded slowly, painfully, but successfully. A massive, last-ditch banzai charge on the night of July 7 inflicted severe casualties on Marine Corps and army units, but failed to dislodge them. Two days later, the island was declared secure, although mop-up operations during August killed almost 2,000 more Japanese soldiers. USMC casualties on Saipan totaled 3,119 killed and 10,992 wounded. As for the Japanese, the overwhelming number of Saipan's 29,000 defenders were killed; very few surrendered. Persuaded by Japanese propaganda that the American invaders would torture and rape them, large numbers of the island's civilian population committed suicide by leaping off the island's rocky cliffs.

Samar, USMC

One of the southern Philippines, Samar was a stronghold of the Moros, Philippine Muslims who fiercely resisted the U.S. occupation of the Philippine Islands during the PHILIPPINE INSURRECTION. In 1901, the USMC's 1st Regiment was deployed to Cavite to assist the U.S. Army in pacifying the

Moros. When, on September 16, Moros ambushed the army's 9th Infantry, the marines, 314 strong, retaliated with the terror tactics of total warfare, burning villages and summarily executing Moro prisoners. On November 15, the marines made a concerted strike against the village of Basey on Samar, wiping out the last of the organized resisters.

Following this action, on December 28, 1901, Major Littleton Waller (USMC) led 55 marines, native interpreters, and 30 Moro bearers on a mission to survey a telegraph route. The survey party was lost, and 10 marines died of disease and exposure. Waller assumed that his native interpreters and bearers had deliberately deceived him. He convened an ad hoc tribunal—a drumhead court—convicted 11 natives, and had them shot. When Waller returned to the naval base at Cavite, he was placed under arrest and tried for murder, but ultimately acquitted. The USMC and USA actions on Samar are a stain on the record of the U.S. administration of the islands.

Santo Domingo

When chronic political instability in this Caribbean nation (the eastern portion of the island of Hispaniola) rendered it vulnerable to European intervention at the start of the 20th century, the United States, invoking the Monroe Doctrine, assumed responsibility for Santo Domingo's finances. This did little to stabilize internal politics on a permanent basis, however, and on May 15, 1916, President Woodrow Wilson ordered two USMC companies (350 men) to the island. They were accompanied by 225 sailors. The marines and sailors occupied the capital city; two weeks later, additional marines were landed, bringing total USMC strength on Santo Domingo to 1,700, a regiment.

Under Colonel JOSEPH PENDLETON, the marines began a systematic campaign against rebel forces on all parts of the island, and, in July 1916, a U.S. military government was established. The USMC remained a presence on Santo Domingo for the next eight years, garrisoning towns and training the Guardia Nacional Dominicana, an indigenous police force.

In 1924, the USMC withdrew pursuant to a 1922 agreement with the nation, now renamed the Dominican Republic.

Saratoga Chemical Protective Overgarment

See NUCLEAR-BIOLOGICAL-CHEMICAL EQUIPMENT.

SB-3865 Automatic Telephone Switchboard   See COMMUNICATIONS EQUIPMENT.

School of Infantry

Located at Marine Corps Base Camp Lejeune, SOI provides infantry military occupational specialty (MOS) qualification to entry-level infantry marines, trains all noninfantry marines in the infantry skills essential to operate in a combat environment, and infantry NCOs and SNCOs with advanced infantry skills. Additionally, SOI supports "Marine Leader Training" courses. SOI is the next step after BASIC TRAINING.

Infantry marines are assigned to the Infantry Training Battalion, whose mission is to train and qualify trainees for MOS 0311 Rifleman, 0331 Machinegunner, 0341 Mortarman, 0351 Assaultman, or 0352 Anti-tank Guided Missileman. ITB consists of a 52-day training schedule. After completing ITB, marines are given their first duty assignment.

Noninfantry marines are assigned to Marine Combat Training Battalion, which provides training in the infantry skills essential to operate in a combat environment. After completing 22 days of MCTB, marines go on to specialized training at the appropriate MOS school.

Second-Generation Extended Cold Weather Clothing System (ECWCS)   See PERSONAL AND MISCELLANEOUS EQUIPMENT.

second lieutenant   See RANKS AND GRADES.

Second Seminole War

The Second Seminole War spanned 1835 to 1842 and was triggered by efforts of the government during the administration of Andrew Jackson to "remove" the Seminole and the closely related Creek (as well as other Indians east of the Mississippi) to "Indian Territory" (the region of modern Oklahoma and parts of neighboring states) pursuant to the Indian Removal Act of 1830. Two USMC battalions arrived in Georgia in June 1836 and quickly engaged the Creek, defeating them by early September. In Florida, ARCHIBALD HENDERSON led one of two brigades assigned to the area—although the men he commanded were a mixed unit of marines, army regulars, and volunteers. Henderson won a significant battle at Hatchee-Lustee in January 1837, which prompted a treaty in March.

Believing the war had ended, Henderson and most of the marines returned to Washington, leaving behind just two companies of marines. Despite the treaty, they were continually involved in combat with Seminole under the highly skilled war leader Osceola. Although that chief was captured in mid-1837, guerrilla action continued until the government withdrew the remaining marines and other troops in 1842. The war ended indecisively. Although some 4,000 Seminole and Creek had been "removed" to Indian Territory, many remained in the Everglades. It had become too costly, in men and money, to root them out.

secretary of the navy

Under Title 10 of the United States Code, SECNAV is responsible for the conduct of all the affairs of the Department of the Navy, including those of the department's two uniformed services, the U.S. Navy and the U.S. Marine Corps. Specific authority and responsibilities extend to the areas of recruiting, organizing, supplying, equipping, training, mobilizing, and demobilizing. SECNAV oversees the construction, outfitting, and repair of ships, equipment, and facilities and bears ultimate responsibility for the formulation and implementation of policies and programs consistent with the national security policies and objectives established by the president and the secretary of defense.

Semper Fidelis

Latin for "Always Faithful," Semper Fidelis has been the motto of the USMC since 1871, when it replaced "First to Fight." Marines, including retired veterans, may greet each other with a shortened version, "Semper Fi." "Semper Fidelis" is also the name of the march JOHN PHILIP SOUSA wrote for the USMC in 1888.

sergeant   See RANKS AND GRADES.

sergeant first class   See RANKS AND GRADES.

sergeant major   See RANKS AND GRADES.

sergeant major of the Marine Corps   See RANKS AND GRADES.

Sergeant Rock

The name of a comic book character, adopted by the USMC as a term for the ideal GUNG-HO marine, fearless and aggressive.

Shepherd, Lemuel C. (1896–1990) *Marine Corps commandant*

The 20th COMMANDANT OF THE MARINE CORPS, Shepherd was born in Norfolk, Virginia, attended Virginia Military Institute, and was commissioned a second lieutenant in the USMC in April 1917, shipping out for France during WORLD WAR I in June of that year. With the 5th Marines, he saw action at CHÂTEAU-THIERRY and at BELLEAU WOOD, where he was wounded twice. After recuperating, he participated in the SAINT-MIHIEL campaign and in the Argonne, where he was wounded for a third time. Shepherd was decorated with the Navy Cross, the Distinguished Service Cross, and the French Croix de Guerre.

Shepherd remained in Europe after the war as part of the army of occupation, then participated in mapping the areas of France in which the USMC fought. After this, he was appointed aide-de-camp to the commandant, served sea duty, then was assigned command of the Sea School, Norfolk. Shepherd served in China during 1927–29, then was posted to HAITI until 1934. In 1936, after graduating from the Naval War College, Shepherd, a lieutenant colonel, was assigned command of a FLEET MARINE FORCE, Atlantic battalion. After briefly serving as assistant commandant at Marine Corps Base Quantico, Shepherd was assigned in March 1942 to command of the 9th Marines. He led the unit to the Pacific under the 3rd Division. As brigadier general, he was assistant divisional commander during the Cape Gloucester campaign and was assigned command of the 1st Marine Provisional Brigade in May 1942. Shepherd led the brigade in operations on GUAM.

Early in 1945, Shepherd took command of the 6th Division and landed them in the assault against OKINAWA on April 1. By the end of the war, the 6th Division was occupying China at Tsingtao.

After WORLD WAR II, in December 1946, Shepherd was appointed assistant commandant. In 1950, now a lieutenant general, Shepherd participated in the INCHON landings during the KOREAN WAR. He became commandant on January 1, 1952, and introduced important organizational changes. He was also the first USMC commandant to enjoy coequal status with the Joint Chiefs whenever USMC-related matters were under consideration. Although he retired on January 1, 1956, Shepherd returned to duty for a time as chairman of the Inter-American Defense Board.

Shoulder-Launched Multipurpose Assault Weapon (SMAW)   See WEAPONS, INDIVIDUAL AND CREW-SERVED.

Shoup, David M. (1904–1983)   *Marine Corps commandant*

The 22nd COMMANDANT OF THE MARINE CORPS, Shoup was born in Battle Ground, Indiana, and graduated from Indiana's De Pauw University in 1926, having enrolled in the ROTC. After brief service as an army second lieutenant, Shoup was commissioned a USMC second lieutenant in July 1926 and saw service the following year at Tientsin, China. After completing basic school, he was posted variously in the United States, then served sea duty during 1929–31. During the 1930s, he served in various stateside posts, was an officer in the Civilian Conservation Corps, then shipped out to China, where he was posted at Shanghai and in Peking (Beijing). During the late 1930s, Shoup served as an instructor at Marine Corps Base Quantico.

In June 1940, Shoup was attached to the 6th Marines, with which he shipped out to Iceland in May 1941 and served as operations officer for the brigade. Early in WORLD WAR II, Shoup became operations officer for the 2nd Division, which he accompanied to New Zealand in October 1942. He was an observer with the 1st Division on GUADALCANAL and with the army's 43rd Division on NEW GEORGIA, suffering a wound during this campaign.

At TARAWA, Shoup, now a colonel, commanded the 2nd Marines. He was wounded at Tarawa and awarded the Medal of Honor. In December 1943, he was made chief of staff, 2nd Division, and took part in the invasions of SAIPAN and TINIAN before returning to the United States in October 1944. Shoup served at HEADQUARTERS MARINE CORPS in Washington, D.C., until 1947, when he was appointed commanding officer, Service Command, FLEET MARINE FORCE, Pacific. Two years after this, he was appointed chief of staff, 1st Division, then, in 1950, was assigned command of Basic School, Quantico.

Promoted to brigadier general, Shoup served as the USMC's first fiscal director. Promoted to major general, he commanded 1st Division in June 1957 and 3rd Division (on OKINAWA) in March 1958. Promoted to lieutenant general, he was assigned to headquarters in Washington and, on January 1, 1961, was appointed commandant by President Dwight D. Eisenhower in an action that jumped him over five seniors.

During Shoup's tour as commandant, the USMC took a leading position in the developing VIETNAM WAR; Shoup also built up the USMC presence at GUANTÁNAMO BAY to full regimental strength and oversaw deployment of the 5th Marine Expeditionary Brigade to the Caribbean in support of the quarantine imposed on Cuba during the Cuban missile crisis of October 1962. Shoup retired on December 31, 1964.

Single Action Release Personal Equipment Lowering System (SARPELS)   See PERSONAL AND MISCELLANEOUS EQUIPMENT.

Single Channel Ground and Airborne Radio System (SINCGARS)   See COMMUNICATIONS EQUIPMENT.

skinhead

USMC term for a recruit immediately after receiving the "high-and-tight" buzz-cut hairdo.

See also JARHEAD.

Smith, Oliver P. (1893–1977) *Marine Corps general*

A naive of Menard, Texas, Smith graduated from the University of California at Berkeley in 1916 and joined the USMC with a commission as second lieutenant in May 1917, the month after the United States entered WORLD WAR I. He served in Guam for the first two years of his USMC career, then, after sea duty and a posting in Washington, D.C., was dispatched to HAITI, where he served with the U.S.-controlled Gendarmerie on that troubled island.

Back in the United States, Smith attended the U.S. Army field officer's course at Fort Benning, Georgia, in 1931 and became an instructor and administrator at Marine Corps Base Quantico. Assigned to embassy duty in Paris in 1934, Smith attended the French Ecole de Guerre, then returned to the United States in 1936 as a Quantico instructor.

In 1939, Smith was transferred to the FLEET MARINE FORCE in San Diego and in 1940 was named to command a battalion of the 6th Marines. He served with this unit in Iceland in May 1941 during America's period of "armed neutrality" prior to its entry into WORLD WAR II.

Smith was working in the Division of Plans by May 1942, and in April 1943 took command of the 5th Marines, which he led in the NEW BRITAIN campaign. As assistant divisional commander of the 1st Division, Smith took part in the PELELIU campaign during September and October 1944. Next, Smith was appointed USMC deputy chief of staff of the Tenth Army and figured importantly in the OKINAWA campaign.

After the war, Smith commanded Quantico until he was named assistant COMMANDANT OF THE MARINE CORPS in April 1948. With the outbreak of the KOREAN WAR, Smith assumed command of the 1st Division in June 1950 and played a key role in the spectacular INCHON landing and the drive north. It was Smith who led the marines in their harrowing retreat from the CHOSIN RESERVOIR in November 1950 after the massive Communist Chinese incursion into Korea.

Smith was named commandant of Marine Corps Base Camp Pendleton in May 1951, then became commander of Fleet Marine Force, Atlantic in July 1953. He retired with the rank of general in September 1955.

sniper

A USMC specialist rifleman skilled at killing the enemy, from concealment and at great distance. The USMC trains not only marine snipers but also snipers in other agencies, including the FBI and CIA, and the Navy SEALs. Training takes place at Marine Corps Base Quantico, Virginia. Minimum sniper qualifications require an 80 percent on-target rate at 1,000 yards (stationary target) and 800 yards (moving target). Snipers must also demon-

Teamwork is an important part of being a scout sniper. While a sniper is firing, his partner, or spotter, tells him where his shots impact the target. *(U.S. Marine Corps)*

strate mastery of camouflage and concealment tactics and techniques.

sniper team

In the USMC and USA, a two-person firing team, one who fires (SNIPER) and the other who spots targets (spotter), using binoculars or a 20x sniper scope. USMC sniper teams are typically equipped with the M-40A1 rifle and a 10x Unertl scope.

Soldiers of the Sea

Self-adopted nickname for the USMC.

Solomon Islands Campaign

The Solomons, located northeast of Australia, were occupied by the Japanese early in WORLD WAR II and were intended by them to serve both as a jump-

ing-off point for an invasion of Australia and as a base from which they could interdict U.S. and Allied supply lines to the South Pacific. Recognizing the danger posed by the Japanese presence in the Solomons, U.S. planners authorized the first American offensive of the Pacific war, the invasion of GUADAL-CANAL by the USMC's 1st Division. The operation stepped off in August 1942 and, in conjunction with the Battle of MIDWAY, represented a major turning point of the war. The Japanese were not only forced to evacuate Guadalcanal, they were also compelled to assume the defensive. From this point forward, the initiative was transferred to the U.S. forces.

The next major USMC-USA advance came at NEW GEORGIA in mid-1943, followed by a landing at BOUGAINVILLE in November. Bougainville became a major base and staging area from which army and Marine Corps units attacked and destroyed the principal Japanese base at Rabaul in the NEW BRITAIN campaign.

Somalia

This nation in northeast Africa on the Red Sea and Indian Ocean had been for years without real government, subject to civil warfare among various warlords. As part of a United Nations relief effort, the U.S. government sent military personnel primarily to provide protection to relief workers and to ensure that UN relief provisions did not fall into the hands of the warlords. The USN, USAF, and USA were given primary responsibility for the mission, but the first ground troops were mostly marines of the I Marine Expeditionary Force. Soon, some 9,000 marines were deployed, most of them in the capital city of Mogadishu.

From the beginning, the marines were put in an impossible situation, constrained by UN rules of engagement from disarming the warring clans. When disarming operations finally began, the warlords had gained a powerful hold on the populace, which turned against the marines and other UN forces. Judging the situation hopeless, President Bill Clinton ordered the withdrawal of most U.S. forces in May 1993. The last personnel were withdrawn in March 1995.

The popular view of the Somalia operation was that it failed and was, in fact, a military humiliation for the United States. While it is true that the U.S. military was withdrawn without significant resolution of the situation in Somalia, USMC and other

USMC amphibious vehicles land in Somalia.
(*U.S. Marine Corps*)

U.S. operations in the country did succeed in distributing relief supplies. To a significant degree, albeit for a limited period, the mission was a humanitarian success.

Sousa, John Philip (1854–1932) *composer*

The "March King," Sousa composed the most famous of all American marches, including "Washington Post March," "Stars and Stripes Forever," and "Semper Fidelis." Although he earned his fame and fortune as a civilian bandleader and composer, his musical career began in the United States Marine Corps.

Born in Washington, D.C., Sousa was the son of Antonio Sousa, a carpenter who worked on the commandant's quarters at the MARINE BARRACKS and also played in the U.S. MARINE BAND. Wishing to instill discipline in his willful son, the elder Sousa persuaded the commandant to allow the 13-year-old boy to enroll as a band apprentice. Sousa served in the USMC from 1867 until 1875, playing in the band during much of that period. After his discharge, he became a civilian bandleader, then, in 1880, was appointed leader of the U.S. Marine Band.

Sousa was a dynamic leader who transformed the band into a world-class musical organization. In 1891, he secured permission from President Benjamin Harrison to take the band on a national tour, which has since become an annual tradition.

The 1891 tour was Sousa's first and last. He left the USMC in 1892 to organize his own peerless band and to embark on his extraordinary career as a composer of marches as well as operettas and songs. Sousa also found time to write several popular novels.

Intensely patriotic, Sousa attempted to return to the USMC at the outbreak of the SPANISH-AMERICAN WAR in 1898, but the Corps had no bandmaster positions available. Sousa joined the army, but a bout of illness kept him from serving. During WORLD WAR I, however, he did join the USN and was commissioned a lieutenant commander, assigned as musical director of the Great Lakes Training Center north of Chicago. His concerts

John Philip Sousa   *(U.S. Marine Corps)*

with the Great Lakes band promoted the purchase of Liberty Bonds.

Discharged from the navy in 1919, Sousa resumed his civilian musical career. He returned to lead the U.S. Marine Band in 1932 at a Washington, D.C., celebration. He died a few days later, at Reading, Pennsylvania, the day before a scheduled band concert. Sousa was honored by the USMC, which allowed his body to lie in state at the Marine Barracks before interment.

Spanish-American War

When, in April 1898, the United States embarked upon war with Spain, ostensibly over the issue of Cuban independence, the nation was poorly prepared to fight a land war. Invasion plans were hastily prepared, and by the end of April the 2nd Marine Battalion was en route to Florida to reinforce the USMC detachments serving with the U.S. Navy fleet blockading the harbor at Santiago,

Cuba. Admiral William Sampson used the marines to capture Guantánamo BAY on June 10, 1898, which Sampson wanted to secure as a coaling station for his fleet. Although the landing was almost unopposed, the marines had to contend with sporadic sniper fire.

On June 14, two USMC companies were assigned to capture Cuzco Well, a major water source for the Guantánamo area. The marines were subject to friendly fire from USN ships, but nevertheless succeeded in defeating some 500 Spanish defenders of Cuzco Well.

All USMC forces were relieved in Cuba by the arrival of U.S. Army troops under General William Shafter later in the month. They saw no further action on Cuba; however, they would maintain a presence in the Philippines during the rest of the war and the PHILIPPINE INSURRECTION that followed. The marines had first been used in the Philippines on May 1, 1898, by Commodore George Dewey, who sent a marine detachment to seize the Spanish naval station at Cavite. Although successful in this mission, there was an insufficient number of marines to expand the action on land. Dewey blockaded Manila Bay until the arrival of army forces under General Wesley Merritt.

Special Purpose Force (SPF)   See ORGANIZATION BY UNITS.

squad   See ORGANIZATION BY UNITS.

squadron   See ORGANIZATION BY UNITS.

Stinger Weapons System: RMP and Basic
See AIR DEFENSE ARTILLERY.

Streeter, Ruth Cheney (1895–1990) *Marine Corps administrator*
Ruth Cheney Streeter was the first director of the U.S. MARINE CORPS WOMEN'S RESERVE, which was

activated on February 13, 1943. Streeter served as director until her retirement on December 7, 1945.

Born in Brookline, Massachusetts, Streeter was educated abroad and at Bryn Mawr College (Bryn Mawr, Pennsylvania), from which she graduated in 1918. During the 1930s, Streeter worked in public health and welfare, unemployment relief, and old-age assistance in New Jersey. Simultaneously, she pursued her passionate interest in aviation, completing a course in aeronautics at New York University and serving as adjutant of Group 221 of the Civil Air Patrol. Learning to fly in 1940, she became the only woman member of the Committee on Aviation of the New Jersey Defense Council the following year, also serving as chairperson of the Citi-

Colonel Ruth Cheney Streeter (USMC)   *(U.S. Marine Corps)*

zen's Committee for Army and Navy, Inc., based at Fort Dix, New Jersey. Streeter received a commercial pilot's license in April 1942.

After General THOMAS HOLCOMB approved the creation of a Women's Reserve, Streeter was selected to head the program and was commissioned a USMC major on January 29, 1943, the first woman to hold that rank in the service. She was promoted to lieutenant colonel on November 22, 1943, and to colonel on February 1, 1944. By the end of WORLD WAR II, Streeter commanded a force of 18,460 women, and on February 4, 1946, was recognized with the award of the Legion of Merit.

Supply School
One of the USMC's COMBAT SERVICE SUPPORT SCHOOLS located at Camp Johnson, North Carolina, the Supply School designs, develops, conducts, and evaluates entry-level, intermediate, and advanced formal resident education and training for officers and enlisted personnel assigned to the USMC supply occupational field. The school offers the following courses of study:

◆ Ground Supply Officer Course
◆ Noncommissioned Officer Supply Course
◆ Ground Supply Chief Course
◆ Enlisted Supply Independent Duty Course
◆ Basic Preservation and Packaging Course
◆ Enlisted Supply Basic Course
◆ Enlisted Warehouse Basic Course
◆ Functional System Administrator Course
◆ Enlisted Supply Basic Course (Reserve)
◆ Ground Supply Officer Course (Reserve)

Suribachi
This mountain on the Pacific island of IWO JIMA was made famous by the flag raising there on February 23, 1945, by members of the 28th Marines, 5th Division.

See also IWO JIMA MEMORIAL.

T

T-34C Turbo Mentor
See AIRCRAFT, FIXED-WING.

T-44 Pegasus
See AIRCRAFT, FIXED-WING.

T-45A Goshawk
See AIRCRAFT, FIXED-WING.

TA-4J Skyhawk
See AIRCRAFT, FIXED-WING.

Tactical Bulk Fuel-Delivery System, CH-53E (TBFDS, CH-53E)
See AIRCRAFT, ROTARY-WING.

Tactical Petroleum Laboratory, Medium (TPLM)

The USMC has developed a Tactical Fuel System to support Marine Air/Ground Task Forces and Marine Expeditionary Forces in receiving, dispensing, and testing Class III (A) and III (W) fuel products. The Tactical Petroleum Laboratory, Medium (TPLM) provides an organic quality control capability for bulk fuel operations in the field by affording facilities to monitor critical physical and chemical characteristics of aviation and ground fuels. The laboratory can test suspect deliveries for acceptability and suitability and permits captured fuels to be tested for suitability as well.

The Tactical Petroleum Laboratory provides the essential testing components integrated into a standard USMC 8 foot by 8 foot by 20 foot International Standard Organization shelter. The laboratory is capable of monitoring the critical physical and chemical characteristics of aviation and ground fuels, including JP-4, JP-5, JP-8, diesel, and their commercial grade equivalents. The USMC maintains 14 such laboratories.

General characteristics of the Tactical Petroleum Laboratory, Medium (TPLM) include:

Manufacturer: Lexington-Bluegrass Army Depot (GOCO)
Length: 20 ft
Width: 8 ft
Height: 8 ft
Weight: 9,960 lb

Tandem Offset Resupply Delivery System (TORDS)
See PERSONAL AND MISCELLANEOUS EQUIPMENT.

Tarawa

The principal island of this Gilbert Islands atoll is a mere three miles long and 800 yards wide at its widest, but in mid-1943, during WORLD WAR II, the Japanese created a strong defensive position here, in effect a fortress garrisoned by 4,800

Marines assault a Japanese position on Tarawa.
(Arttoday)

Tinian

A nearly unpopulated Pacific island in the Marianas, three miles south of the large island of SAIPAN, Tinian was the objective of a superbly conducted USMC operation during WORLD WAR II. The 4th Division landed on the northwest coast on July 24, 1944, while the 2nd Division distracted the 6,000-man Japanese garrison near the island's only settlement, Tinian Town. The extremely efficient capture of the island was completed on August 1, 1944, with the loss of 317 marines.

Guarded by a USMC garrison (8th Marines), U.S. forces built a large airfield to accommodate B-29s, and Tinian became a key base from which the Japanese homeland was bombed. It was the base from which the two aircraft that released atomic bombs on Hiroshima and Nagasaki, *Enola Gay* and *Bock's Car,* were launched in August 1945.

tracked vehicles

The following tracked vehicles are either currently included in the marine inventory or are of historical importance in the service.

M-1A1 Main Battle Tank

The Marine Corp's M-1A1 Main Battle Tank is an improved version of the M-1 Main Battle Tank (MBT), which includes a 120-mm smoothbore main gun, an NBC (nuclear-biological-chemical) overpressure protection system, an improved armor package, a Deep Water Fording Kit (DWFK), a Position Location Reporting System (PLRS), enhanced ship tiedowns, a Digital Electronic Control Unit (DECU, which allows significant fuel savings), and Battlefield Override. The tank proved itself in battle during Operation Desert Storm (PERSIAN GULF WAR), when it successfully engaged enemy armor at ranges of nearly 13,000 feet.

The M-1A1 Main Battle Tank is fully compatible with all navy amphibious ships and craft, including navy Maritime Prepositioning Ships. The M-1A1 replaces the now obsolescent M-60A1 Rise/Passive tank, which cannot be expected to survive, let alone defeat, the threats of the modern

elite troops, and it was seen as necessary to capture the island and its small airfield. The 2nd Division was tasked with the mission on November 20, 1943.

The mission was made especially difficult by a restriction imposed on prelanding bombardment and air support. It was feared that such an attack would bring on an offensive from the Japanese navy. Although the USMC landings went reasonably well, the marines encountered severe resistance from well-defended positions. Betio, the principal island, was taken after 70 hours of combat, in which 980 marines and 29 sailors were killed. Japanese losses were almost total: 4,690 killed. Throughout the rest of the war, marines referred to the costly victory as "terrible Tarawa."

"Tell It to the Marines!"

A popular, somewhat dated expression used to indicate contemptuous disbelief. The phrase did not originate with the USMC, but with the British Royal Marines, probably during the 18th century. Sailors considered the marines gullible landlubbers who would believe anything told to them about ships and sea matters.

Marines of the 2nd Marine Division's 2nd Tank Battalion maneuver their M-1A1 main battle tanks during a combined arms exercise at the Marine Corps Air Ground Combat Center, Twentynine Palms, California. *(Department of Defense)*

battlefield. The marines collaborated with the army on the design of the M-1A1 (called the Abrams, in the army) to ensure mutual supportability as well as interoperability. As of 2004, the marines fielded 403 of the M-1A1 tanks. The tank was introduced into the marine inventory in 1990.

General characteristics of the M-1A1 Main Battle Tank include:

Manufacturer: General Dynamics (Land Systems Division)
Power plant: AGT-1500 turbine engine
Power train: hydrokinetic, fully automatic, with four forward and two reverse gear ratios
Propulsion: 1,500-horsepower gas (multifuel) turbine engine
Length, gun forward: 385 in
Width: 144 in
Height: 114 in
Weight, fully armed: 67.7 tons

Main gun: 120-mm M256
Commander's weapon: M-2 .50-caliber machine gun
Loader's Weapon: 7.62-mm M-240 machine gun
Coaxial Weapon: 7.62-mm M-240 machine gun
Cruising Range: 289 miles without NBC system; 279 miles with NBC system
Sight radius: 8 degrees at 8x power
Speed, maximum: 42 mph
Speed, cross-country: 30 mph
Ground clearance: 19 in
Obstacle crossing, vertical: 42 in
Obstacle crossing, trench: 9 ft wide
Slope: 60 degrees at 4.5 mph
Crew: four, including driver, loader, gunner, and tank commander
Warheads: capable of delivering both kinetic energy (sabot) and chemical energy (heat) rounds

Sensors: the 120-mm M256 main gun has a cant sensor, wind speed sensor, and automatic lead and ammunition temperature inputs to its ballistic fire control solution

M-1 Mine-Clearing Blade System

The M-1 Mine-Clearing Blade System is used on the M-1A1 Main Battle Tank to counteract and neutralize land mines. Electrically operated, the M-1 is capable of clearing surface or buried mines up to 6 feet in front of the path of the tank without additional equipment or the aid of supporting forces. (The M-1 was also used with the older Marine Corps M-60A1 Rise/Passive Tank, some of which are still maintained in the USMC inventory.) The Marine Corps has 71 M-1 systems in its inventory.

General characteristics of the M-1 Mine-Clearing Blade System include:

Manufacturer: Israel Military Industries
Weight: 4.5 tons
Length: 9.6 ft
Width: 14.9 ft
Height: 2.5 ft
Area: 143 sq ft
Volume: 346 cu ft

Four M-1 units are deployed per each USMC tank company.

M-9 Armored Combat Earthmover (ACE)

The M-9 Armored Combat Earthmover is a full-tracked, air transportable armored earthmover, which can be employed in a great many engineering tasks, including the clearing of obstacles, preparation of defilade and survivability positions, and myriad engineering construction tasks such as dozing, scraping, grading, hauling, towing, and winching. The M-9 ACE combines cross-country mobility with a high degree of armored protection. This versatility enables it to perform offensive as well as defensive operations in forward battle areas. The vehicle has a 200-mile range, is fully air transportable, and is amphibious. The M-9 ACE was first fielded with the USMC in 1995. As of 2004, the USMC inventory includes 87 of the vehicles.

General characteristics of the M-9 Armored Combat Earthmover (ACE) include:

Manufacturer: United Defense LP, York, Pennsylvania
Net weight: 36,000 lb
Ballasted weight: 54,000 lb
Length: 246 in
Height: 105 in
Width: 126 in
Speed, land: 30 mph
Speed, water: 3 mph
Cruising range: 200 mi

M-60A1 Armored Vehicle Launched Bridge (M-60A1 AVLB)

M-60A1 Armored Vehicle Launched Bridge is an armored vehicle modified to launch and retrieve a 60-foot scissors-type bridge. The vehicle consists of three major components: the launcher, the hull, and the bridge. The launcher is an integral part of the vehicle chassis, and the bridge, when emplaced, is capable of supporting tracked as well as wheeled vehicles with a military load bearing capacity up to Class 60. The roadway width is 12 feet, 6 inches. Once emplaced, the bridge can be retrieved from either end, so that the M-60A1 AVLB can emplace its bridge, cross it, then retrieve it and proceed to the next mission. Bridge emplacement normally takes no more than two to five minutes. Retrieval requires about 10 minutes and is generally performed under armor protection.

The vehicle was introduced in 1987, and, as of 2004, the USMC maintained an inventory of 55 bridges and 37 launchers. General characteristics of the M-60A1 Armored Vehicle Launched Bridge (M-60A1 AVLB) include:

Manufacturer: General Dynamics (Land Systems Division)
Contractor: Anniston Army Depot
Power plant: 12-cylinder diesel engine, AVOS-1790-20
Power train: CD-850-6A, 2 speed forward, 1 reverse

M-60A1 Tank Chassis—
Weight, combat loaded: 56.6 tons
Ground clearance: 18 in
Length: 31 ft
Width: 12 ft
Maximum speed (governed): 30 mph
Cross-country speed: 8–12 mph
Trench crossing: 8.5 ft wide
Range: 290 mi
Fuel capacity: 375 gal

Bridge—
Length, extended: 63 ft
Length, folded: 32 ft
Effective bridge span: 60 ft
Width, overall: 13.1 ft
Width, roadway: 12.5 ft
Width, treadway: 5.75 ft
Height, unfolded: 3.1 ft
Weight: 14.65 tons
Crew requirement: two

Mobile/Unit Conduct of Fire Trainer (M/U-COFT)

The Mobile/Unit Conduct of Fire Trainer (M/U-COFT) provides training in critical tasks performed by M-1A1 Main Battle Tank gunners and tank commanders in a simulated battlefield environment. The U-COFT gunnery trainer is housed at the unit level in transportable shelters mounted on concrete pads, whereas the mobile M-COFT is mounted on a trailer to be used by company-size elements of the MARINE CORPS RESERVE. Both configurations use the same basic hardware and software.

The COFT crew compartment replicates the turret interior of an M-1A1 tank, and the computer-generated scenes viewed through the fire control optics react to manipulation of the controls in a realistic fashion, thereby providing training in target acquisition, identification, and engagement with the main gun, coaxial machine gun, and the tank commander's weapons station. The COFT also includes an Instructor/Operator (I/O) Station, which provides the capability of monitoring both the gunner's and the commander's fire control

equipment; selects from several hundred increasingly difficult scenarios to test crew members' judgments and reactions; and provides an automatic scoring and feedback system for evaluating individual and crew performance.

As of 2004, the USMC has four U-COFT and two M-COFT units. Before these were developed, tank gunnery training was restricted to annual periods of main gun firing and qualification. Not only did this limit training, it also greatly increased training costs. The COFT units provide initial and subsequent gunnery sustainment training and significantly improve crew proficiency in all aspects of tank gunnery. However, the USMC has not abandoned live-fire training, which is still required for combat training and qualification.

General characteristics of the Mobile/Unit Conduct of Fire Trainer (M/U-COFT) include:

Mobile Conduct of Fire Trainer
Builder: Elbit Computers
Length: 45 ft
Width: 8 ft
Height: 13 ft
Volume: 4,680 cu ft

Unit Conduct of Fire Trainer
Builder: Elbit Computers
Length: 33.5 ft
Width: 24.75 ft

Training and Education Command

Part of the U.S. MARINE CORPS COMBAT DEVELOPMENT COMMAND, based at Marine Corps Base Quantico, the Training and Education Command develops, coordinates, resources, executes, and evaluates training and education concepts, policies, plans, and programs to prepare marines "to meet the challenges of present and future operational environments." The command consists of the following schools:

Combat Service Support School
Communication and Electronics School
Field Medical Service School–Lejeune
Field Medical Service School–Pendleton

Instructional Management School
Mountain Warfare Training Center
School of Infantry–Lejeune
School of Infantry–Pendleton
Weapons Training Battalion

triple threat
A marine qualified as a SCUBA diver and a para-trooper, and who has also had Ranger training.

See also U.S. MARINE CORPS RECONNAISSANCE BATTALIONS.

Tube-Launched, Optically Tracked, Wire-Guided (TOW) Missile Weapon System
See ANTIARMOR WEAPONS.

U

UH-34/VH-34 Seahorse See AIRCRAFT, ROTARY-WING.

unconventional warfare (UW)

Unconventional warfare is a general and somewhat imprecise term used to describe military operations conducted in enemy-controlled territory or in politically sensitive places. UW is typically clandestine and makes extensive use of local resources and local personnel. UW may include guerrilla warfare, sabotage, and escape and evasion. The USMC excels at UW. Its MARINE CORPS RECONNAISSANCE BATTALIONS are typically deployed on such missions, often in conjunction with Navy SEALs and/or U.S. Army Special Forces.

uniforms

The first marine uniform was authorized for the CONTINENTAL MARINES in September 1776 and consisted of white trousers and a white-faced green coat. Headgear was a round hat with an upturned brim featuring a cockade. Most distinctive was the leather collar, or neck stock, a measure intended to ward off sword blows, but always uncomfortable and much despised by marines until 1875, when it was finally dispensed with. The leather collar gave marines their most enduring nickname, LEATHERNECKS, which gained its greatest currency during WORLD WAR II, long after the collar had been eliminated.

The USMC was disbanded after the conclusion of the AMERICAN REVOLUTION, and when it was reconstituted in 1798, it was issued surplus uniforms from the army of General Anthony "Mad Anthony" Wayne. The coat was blue with red facings—the first "dress blues" of the service. As earlier, the hat was round with an upturned brim. In 1804, this uniform was updated in a lighter shade of blue with scarlet facings, and the round hat was replaced by a high shako featuring a brass eagle emblem.

In 1834, pursuant to orders of President Andrew Jackson, the USMC uniform was toned down. The coat was gray green with buff facings. Trousers were gray. When it was found that the gray green rapidly faded, a more reliable blue was reintroduced in 1841: a coat of dark blue and trousers of light blue. The undress uniform featured a dark blue cap with leather visor; the dress uniform retained the high shako with a new device, a brass anchor encircled by a wreath. In 1859, new headgear, modeled after the French kepi (also used by the U.S. Army), was adopted for fatigue wear.

After the Civil War, in 1869, the USMC adopted a blue-black jacket with standing "choke" collar and light blue trousers. Officers wore the MAMELUKE SWORD. This uniform became the dress blues still worn today; however, field uniforms continued to evolve more radically. During the 1890s, the coat was abandoned for field use and was replaced by a blue flannel shirt. Marines were issued tall leggings, and a broad-brimmed white hat replaced the kepi.

It bore the now-familiar USMC EMBLEM. For dress parades, a spiked helmet, like those worn by the Prussian army, was adopted.

The SPANISH-AMERICAN WAR demonstrated the need for a tropical-weight field uniform. Khaki became standard. More than a decade later, in 1912, a service uniform of forest green was adopted, which included the "carbonized" (dull) brass buttons that are still part of the Class A service uniform. The Prussian helmet was discarded in favor of a visored hat. In the field, the high-crowned campaign hat was worn—the same headgear that still distinguishes USMC DRILL INSTRUCTORS today.

The pressing demands of WORLD WAR I forced the USMC to adopt what was in essence the uniform of the U.S. Army for field service, and, for the first time, a steel helmet (the British "washbasin"-style used by the U.S. Army) was worn. Between the wars, marines were distinguished by a roll-collar coat and khaki shirt with a green tie for service uniforms. WORLD WAR II saw the introduction of a lightweight fatigue and combat uniform as well as the redesigned helmet also worn by the U.S. Army. The combat uniform changed little until the era of the VIETNAM WAR, when combat uniforms were made even lighter in weight and in camouflage color schemes. After Vietnam, the most significant changes have been those made in the combat uniform, which include an array of new camouflage schemes and the adoption of a lightweight but very durable Kevlar helmet. Body armor, also based on Kevlar, is also often worn.

unmanned aerial vehicle (UAV)

Unmanned aerial vehicles are remotely piloted aircraft typically used for reconnaissance, but sometimes used as weapons platforms. The USMC uses close-range UAVs, aircraft that are small and lightweight, typically about 200 pounds, with a minimum flight radius of 18 miles. The purpose of these aircraft is strictly tactical, to provide an "over-the-hill" view of enemy disposition and activity.

For missions requiring somewhat longer range, the USMC uses short-range UAVs, which are heavier than the close-range aircraft, weighing in at about 1,000 pounds. Range is up to 186 miles, and flight endurance is an impressive 8 to 12 hours, so that these aircraft can be flown over a target and made to "loiter" for an extended period.

unmanned ground vehicle (UGV)

Unmanned ground vehicles are robot vehicles used to perform remote reconnaissance with a wide variety of sensors. In addition to assessing enemy disposition and activity, UGVs can be used to detect and even to clear obstacles and to detect chemical and biological warfare agents. UGVs can also be used to disarm unexploded ordinance, booby traps, and mines.

urban warfare

Urban warfare is any combat within urban areas. Traditionally, military battles have been fought in the open, usually on rural battlefields. Recently,

A marine from Charlie Company rushes to his objective at the Military Operations in Urban Terrain facility at Camp Lejeune, North Carolina. *(Department of Defense)*

wars and conflicts have been fought increasingly in the streets. Marine training now includes extensive experience with urban warfare scenarios.

U.S.-French Quasi-War

Shortly after the conclusion of the AMERICAN REVO-LUTION, the Franco-American alliance that had prevailed during that war broke down. Subsequently, as the French government perceived that U.S. policy increasingly favored British interests over those of France, relations deteriorated further. When President John Adams authorized the U.S. minister to France, Charles Cotesworthy Pinckney, to call on the French Directory (successor government after the Reign of Terror) in an effort to repair relations, the Directory refused to receive the American minister. At this, Adams dispatched a commission consisting of Pinckney, John Marshall, and Elbridge Gerry to Paris in 1797. Three agents greeted the commissioners, conveying to them the startling message that before a new Franco-American treaty could be discussed, the United States would have to "loan" France $12,000,000 and pay Prime Minister Talleyrand a personal bribe of $250,000. Exposure of this diplomatic outrage resulted in the XYZ Affair (the French agents were designated not by name, but as X, Y, and Z), and, with French naval operations against the British in the West Indies already disrupting U.S. shipping, Congress launched an undeclared war in the spring of 1798.

In May 1799, a USMC detachment was put aboard the newly completed frigate *Constitution* and sailed with it for operations in the Caribbean. Ninety marines were put aboard a captured French sloop early in 1800 and sailed into Puerto Plata, Santo Domingo. There they captured a 14-gun French ship, after which they took the harbor fort, whose cannon they spiked.

This, the first USMC amphibious operation, was a modest but complete success. When Napoleon began his general withdrawal from the Caribbean, in order to concentrate on his European wars, harassment of U.S. shipping ceased, as did the Quasi-War.

U.S. Marine Band

Nicknamed the "President's Own," the Marine Band currently consists of 143 musicians led by five officers; their sole mission is to provide music for the president of the United States. The band's musicians are the only marines exempted from boot camp; however, they do receive a course in military etiquette and in marching, both administered at the MARINE BARRACKS in Washington, D.C., which is also where the band is quartered. Musicians hold the rank of staff sergeant.

The U.S. Marine Band was the first symphonic military band established in the United States, created by act of Congress on July 11, 1798. Although the band can march, it is primarily a concert orchestra. The schedule for the President's Own is crowded—about 600 engagements each year, including, every four years, the inauguration ceremonies.

The uniforms of the President's Own feature a scarlet blouse. The drum major sports a bearskin busby, wears a baldric sash listing the USMC's battle honors, and, although an enlisted man, wears an officer's belt buckle, emblazoned with the USMC emblem; he or she carries a mace surmounted by the U.S. Capitol dome and embellished with the seal of the president, battle honors, the USMC emblem, and a likeness of JOHN PHILIP SOUSA, the 17th and by far the most famous director of the U.S. Marine Band.

U.S. Marine Corps Air-Ground Task Force Expeditionary Training Center

Located at the U.S. Marine Corps Air-Ground Combat Center in Twentynine Palms, California, the training center was created on October 1, 1993, to oversee and integrate the resources of the Air-Ground Combat Center, the U.S. MARINE CORPS MOUNTAIN WARFARE TRAINING CENTER, and MARINE AVIATION WEAPONS AND TACTICS SQUADRON ONE.

U.S. Marine Corps Code

"Unit, Corps, God, Country." This is known in the USMC simply as "The Code," and it constitutes the individual marine's creed.

U.S. Marine Corps Color Guard

The Color Guard performs for parades, ceremonies, and official functions in the United States and elsewhere. The unit is assigned to Company A, MARINE BARRACKS, Washington, D.C., and consists of 13 members. In any given ceremony, the color guard consists of four members, two color bearers flanked by two riflemen. The USMC Color Guard is under the command of the color sergeant of the U.S. Marine Corps.

U.S. Marine Corps Combat Development Command (MCCDC)

MCCDC, based at Marine Corps Base Quantico, is the USMC agency responsible for education and development. The command's mission is to develop USMC warfighting concepts and to determine associated required capabilities in the areas of doctrine, organization, training and education, equipment, and support facilities to enable the USMC to field combat-ready forces.

U.S. Marine Corps Development Center

Built in 1994, the center is a 100,000-square-foot building at Marine Corps Base Quantico, which houses the Warfighting Development Integration Division, Requirements Division, Doctrine Division, Concepts and Plans Division, Studies and Analysis Division, Coalition and Special Warfare Division, and the MARINE CORPS INTELLIGENCE Center. The incorporation of these units and functions in a single facility is intended to facilitate the USMC's ability to assess its capabilities and resources in order to provide optimum support for FLEET MARINE FORCES.

U.S. Marine Corps Mountain Warfare Training Center (MWTC)

MWTC, nicknamed Pickle Meadows, is located at Bridgeport, California, and was established as part of the U.S. commitment to NATO to train marines in mountain and cold-weather combat. In this

A U.S. Marine on snowshoes patrols up a snowy slope with his squad from Kilo company at the Mountain Warfare Training Center, Bridgeport, California. *(Department of Defense)*

Sierra-based camp, marines are taught winter warfare and mountain warfare tactics, including fighting on skis. High-altitude climbing is taught during the summer months, both by day and by night.

U.S. Marine Corps Reconnaissance Battalions

"Scoop 'n Poop" teams are USMC units specially trained to infiltrate behind enemy lines, gather intelligence, and return or conduct clandestine search-and-destroy missions. The battalions specialize in infiltration and exfiltration without detection. The first recon battalions were trained in

WORLD WAR II, and the concept of commando training was brought into the USMC during the 1950s, inspired by units of Britain's Royal Marines. The first teams were formally established in 1961 and were widely deployed in the VIETNAM WAR.

Currently, the USMC has two recon battalions, one stationed at Marine Corps Base Camp Pendleton, California, and the other at Marine Corps Base Camp Lejeune, North Carolina. Membership in the battalions is voluntary and subject to stringent and demanding training.

See also DOUBLE TROUBLE; QUAD BODY; TRIPLE THREAT.

U.S. Marine Corps Research Center (MCRC)

The MCRC was put into operation at Marine Corps Base Quantico on May 6, 1993, and is the USMC's principal research facility, housing three libraries, the Marine Corps University archives, and conference facilities. The center is an adjunct and complement to the U.S. MARINE CORPS COMBAT DEVELOPMENT COMMAND.

U.S. Marine Corps Security Force (MCSF)

The MCSF is tasked with providing security force detachments for service on board U.S. Navy vessels, including aircraft carriers, submarine tenders, and guided missile cruisers, and at ammunition storage depots and other key military sites. Specially trained marines safeguard the security of nuclear weaponry, classified documents, and other sensitive material. On board ship, MCSF personnel also serve as a landing force and operate certain gun systems. In this, the MCSF performs the historical marine function, combining shipboard security with landing force and gun duty.

All MCSF detachments are under the control of a headquarters at Norfolk, Virginia. In 1993, this central command replaced the Atlantic Battalion (Norfolk) and the Pacific Battalion (Mare Island, California).

The Fleet Anti-Terrorism Security Team (FAST) is a contingent of the MCSF trained and equipped to respond worldwide to crisis situations that threaten military bases, nuclear ammunition or fuel facilities, and so on. FAST companies consist of 200 marines. Regular shipboard MCSF detachments are smaller; for instance, the detachment onboard an aircraft carrier consists of 64 enlisted marines and two officers.

U.S. Marine Corps Security Guard Battalion

Pursuant to the Foreign Service Act of 1946, marines of this battalion are responsible for providing security for U.S. embassies, consulates, and legations in foreign countries. Marine Embassy Guards were put into place beginning in 1949, replacing civilian guards in these installations.

The Security Guard Battalion currently consists of 140 State Department security detachments, ranging in size from six-marine units to 36-marine units. Each detachment is under the command of a noncommissioned officer—the only U.S. Marine Corps instance in which an NCO has independent command of a unit; however, with each diplomatic mission, the marine detachment is under operational command of an Embassy Security Officer and the ambassador. The guard detachment is responsible for safeguarding classified material and protecting embassy staff. Outside of the embassy proper, security is the responsibility of the host nation.

The Security Guard Battalion is staffed by more than 1,000 marines, carefully selected volunteers who are given six weeks of specialized training at the Marine Security Guard School (Department of State), located at Marine Base Quantico.

U.S. Marine Corps Women's Reserve

The USMC, with some reluctance, established the Women's Reserve during WORLD WAR II pursuant to a plan approved in November 1942. It was the last of the services to create a women's force.

Initial authorized strength was 1,000 officers and 18,000 enlisted women. The Reserve was commanded by Major RUTH STREETER. The first recruits were trained at Hunter College, New York City, and officers were trained at Mount Holyoke College (South Hadley, Massachusetts). Within months, however, all training was transferred to facilities at Marine Corps Base Camp Lejeune. The Women Reservists were not combat marines, but were assigned as clerks and stenographers. By the beginning of 1944, 85 percent of enlisted personnel at MARINE HEADQUARTERS in Washington were Women Reservists.

The organization had been formed on the understanding that it would be disbanded after the war and all personnel discharged; however, a small cadre of Women Reservists were retained, and in June 1948, the SECRETARY OF THE NAVY ordered the integration of women into the regular USMC.

Shortly after being commissioned at Mount Holyoke in South Hadley, Massachusetts, the new lieutenants pin on their bars.   *(Mount Holyoke War Archives)*

U.S. Marine Drum and Bugle Corps

Known as the "Commandant's Own," the Drum and Bugle Corps was created in 1934 and is stationed at the MARINE BARRACKS, Washington D.C., with field units in Georgia and California. The main unit, at the Marine Barracks, consists of 75 musicians. In contrast to the U.S. MARINE BAND, Drum and Bugle Corps musicians are trained like other marines. After completing BASIC TRAINING, they are trained at the Navy School of Music (U.S. Naval Base Little Creek, Virginia).

The Drum and Bugle Corps performs 11 months out of the year, touring the United States and abroad.

U.S.-Mexican War

Texas had won independence from Mexico in 1836 and existed as a republic until the U.S. Congress voted to annex it in 1845, even though Mexico warned that to do so would mean war. On April 25, 1846, Mexican forces crossed the Rio Grande and attacked U.S. dragoons. The army fought two major battles, at Palo Alto on May 8 and at Resaca de la Palma on May 9, emerging victorious from both. Initially, the USMC presence was restricted to the complements aboard the navy's Gulf Squadron. However, these detachments were formed into a battalion and staged raids on Frontera and Tampico, playing a key role in the capture of Tampico in November 1846.

During March 1847, marines were involved in the troop landings at VERACRUZ. The principal USMC role was to secure gulf ports that remained under Mexican control after the Veracruz operation.

Marines also participated in General Winfield Scott's (USA) assault on Mexico City. An advance battalion of a newly formed marine regiment joined Scott's army at Puebla in August 1847, as the general prepared the final assault. While the army advanced on the gates of Mexico City, the marines were assigned to guard baggage trains; however, marines did participate in the taking of Chapultepec Castle in September. After this operation, marines were part of the force that stormed

San Cosme Gate on September 13, and it was a U.S. marine who cut down the Mexican flag and ran up the U.S. flag over the Palacio Nacional after Mexican commander Santa Anna evacuated the city.

In addition to participating in the invasion of Mexico proper, marines were also involved in the Bear Flag Rebellion, which quickly became the California theater of the U.S.-Mexican War. A USMC "California Battalion" was formed and participated in battles at San Diego and San Pascual, as well as the occupation of Los Angeles in January 1847.

USMC amphibious forces attacked Mexican west coast ports during 1847, occupying Guaymas, San Blas, and San Jose. Mazatlán fell to a combined USMC-USN force of some 700 on November 10, 1847. Captain Jacob Zeilin (USMC) served as military governor at Mazatlán until the Treaty of Guadalupe Hidalgo, ending the war, was concluded on February 2, 1848.

V

V-22 Osprey   See AIRCRAFT, ROTARY-WING.

Vandegrift, Alexander (1887–1973) *Marine Corps commandant*

Born in Charlottesville, Virginia, Vandegrift became the 18th COMMANDANT OF THE MARINE CORPS. He attended the University of Virginia for two years before entering the USMC as a second lieutenant in 1909. During 1912–23, he served in the Caribbean and Central America and took part in action in NICARAGUA, in the invasion and occupation of VERACRUZ, Mexico, in 1914, and, in 1915, the pacification of HAITI.

As a major, Vandegrift commanded a USMC battalion at Marine Corps Base Quantico, Virginia, from 1923 to 1926. In 1926, he was appointed assistant chief of staff at Marine Corps Base San Diego, then shipped out to China in 1927–28. He then served in Washington, D.C., and again at Quantico. Promoted to lieutenant colonel in 1934, Vandegrift returned to China the following year and was promoted to colonel in 1936. He was stationed at HEADQUARTERS MARINE CORPS during 1937–41, was promoted to brigadier general in 1940 and became assistant commander of 1st Marine Division in 1941. Early in 1942, he was made commanding general of the division.

Major General Vandegrift led the division to the South Pacific in May 1942 and commanded it during the GUADALCANAL campaign (August–December 1942), for which he received the Medal of Honor. Promoted to lieutenant general, Vandegrift commanded the First Marine Amphibious Corps during the opening of the BOUGAINVILLE campaign, returning to the United States late in 1943 to become commandant of the Marine Corps (January 1, 1944).

As commandant, Vandegrift presided over the continued wartime expansion of the USMC, then directed its orderly contraction after the war, fighting a strenuous battle to prevent its complete dissolution. Promoted to general in March 1945, Vandegrift was the first USMC officer to attain that rank while on active duty. Vandegrift stepped down as commandant on January 1, 1948, and retired from the USMC the following year.

Veracruz

A major Mexican seaport on the Bay of Campeche, Veracruz figured in two USMC operations. The first, during the U.S.-MEXICAN WAR, was a landing by the 1st Marine Battalion in August 1847, which followed landings by the U.S. Army. The second came in 1914, when President Woodrow Wilson ordered the seizure of the city following a diplomatic incident. The Wilson administration refused to recognize the government of General Victoriano Huerta, and, amid bad feelings between the dictatorial Huerta regime and the United States, some U.S. sailors were imprisoned briefly. The admiral commanding the U.S. Gulf Squadron demanded an apology and a 21-gun salute to the U.S. flag. The incident might have stopped with that had not the Wilson administration discovered that a German ship was bound for Veracruz with arms for Huerta. Following this discovery, the 2nd Marine Regiment landed on April 21, 1914. Light resistance met the landing, but the city itself was more heavily defended. The 2nd Marine Regiment was accordingly reinforced by the USMC's Panama Battalion and a brigade of sailors to a strength of 7,000 (3,100 were marines). After street fighting, the Mexican garrison surrendered on April 24.

The Veracruz operation proved highly effective. With the city in U.S. hands and the port blockaded, Huerta stepped down as head of state on July 15, 1914.

VH-3D Sea King   See AIRCRAFT, ROTARY-WING.

VH-60A Black Hawk   See AIRCRAFT, ROTARY-WING.

VH-60N Seahawk   See AIRCRAFT, ROTARY-WING.

Vietnam War

During the administrations of Harry S. Truman and Dwight D. Eisenhower, the United States began sending increasing amounts of military aid, mainly in the form of financing, to the French, who were struggling to maintain their hold on French Indochina, or Vietnam. In 1954, however, following an ignominious defeat at Dien Bien Phu at the hands of the Viet Minh, the communist nationalists of Vietnam, the French agreed to leave. Vietnam was then partitioned along the 17th parallel, the communists to the north, the democratic Republic of Vietnam to the south.

Pursuant to the U.S. cold war policy of "containing" communism to prevent its spread without provoking a third world war, the United States supported the government of Ngo Dinh Diem in the south until he proved corrupt and incapable of holding his embattled nation together. With the covert cooperation of the CIA, Diem was overthrown and ultimately murdered by the South Vietnamese military. The U.S. desperately sought to bolster a succession of leaders and, under President John F. Kennedy, sent increasing numbers of military "advisers" to assist the South Vietnamese forces in prosecuting the war against the communists. On August 7, 1964, after North Vietnamese ships allegedly attacked two American destroyers (this "Tonkin Gulf incident" was later revealed to have been partially fabricated), the U.S. Congress passed the "Gulf of Tonkin Resolution," giving President Lyndon B. Johnson extensive war-making authority. From this point on, U.S. involvement in the Vietnam War escalated steadily. By 1969, more than a half-million American military personnel would be engaged in combat operations.

The USMC made its first appearance in Vietnam in April 1962, when a helicopter squadron arrived in the delta south of Saigon and was subsequently headquartered at Da Nang, second largest city in Vietnam. USMC helicopter pilots transported South Vietnamese Army (ARVN) troops into battle. By 1965, half of the USMC's helicopter squadrons were serving in Vietnam.

The first USMC advisers arrived in Vietnam in 1964, and in 1965, after an attack on the American outpost at Pleiku in early February, the 9th Expeditionary Brigade was landed at Da Nang. It was the first major U.S. ground combat force in country. The marines were assigned to protect the Da Nang airfield. By the end of summer 1965, the USMC had four ground regiments in Vietnam, plus four air groups.

The first major ground operation was Operation Starlight, which cleared Vietcong troops operating on the Von Tuong Peninsula south of Chu Lai. In another operation, the 9th Marines cleared the coastal areas as far as Hoi An. The objective of such operations was "pacification," flushing the Vietcong out of villages, then providing security and other benefits for the villagers, so that they would not be tempted to support the Vietcong again. Pacification—winning the "hearts and minds" of the people—was strongly advocated by the USMC, but higher military command increasingly adopted a strategy of search-and-destroy, abandoning the campaign to win the loyalty of the people. Throughout the war, this became a subject of bitter controversy between the USMC and the U.S. Army. Indeed, the USMC became largely subordinated to the USA, and its special skills as an expeditionary force were underutilized.

By June 1966, the rest of the 1st Division arrived in Vietnam and was deployed to Chu Lai. The III Marine Amphibious Force, under the command of Lieutenant General Lewis Walt, would consist of two divisions and would fight in Vietnam for nearly six years. In 1966, the USMC mission focused principally on defending three bases in the area of I Corps: Chu Lai, Phu Bai (near the ancient city of Hue), and Da Nang. Additionally, the USMC was assigned to guard the Demilitarized Zone (DMZ) in Quang Tri Province, effectively the buffer zone between North and South. Additionally, the USMC coordinated with the ARVN in several offensives. Near the DMZ, the marines enjoyed considerable success with combined arms assaults, the close coordination of ground troops, helicopter units, and close support from fixed-wing attack aircraft. However, because U.S. policy was to fight a strictly limited war, the marines were not permitted to penetrate into North Vietnam, so, even when defeated, the communist forces could retreat to safe haven.

The year 1967 brought 14 major battles, prosecuted mainly by the army, with the USMC providing support on the DMZ and along major transportation routes. In April, the 3rd Marines were successful in clearing the enemy from Khe Sanh, which became a key USMC outpost.

The Vietcong made two massive attacks on the 26th Marines at Khe Sanh as part of the Tet Offensive, an all-out communist push on virtually all fronts. Supported by tactical and strategic air strikes, the marines survived a 77-day siege at Khe Sanh and defeated the North Vietnamese, who had hoped to achieve against the United States what they had achieved against the French in 1954 at Dien Bien Phu.

By far the heaviest fighting during the Tet offensive occurred in the ancient capital of Hue, which involved marines (and the ARVN) in difficult house-to-house combat during February. The city was declared secure on March 2.

Marine, U.S. Army, and ARVN forces had scored a major tactical victory in repelling, on all fronts, the Tet Offensive. However, the rules of engagement precluded exploiting this triumph by pursuing a general offensive with the object of final victory. Indeed, in the United States, amid burgeoning popular opposition to the war, Tet was grossly misperceived as a communist victory. It was nevertheless true that Tet demonstrated the incredible resolve of the communist forces, which showed themselves willing to absorb catastrophic losses and keep fighting.

Tet signaled a new direction in the war. U.S. operations were greatly reduced in scale as American political leaders desperately groped for an exit strategy. The USMC was called on less to conduct offensive operations and instead focused on the ongoing defense of Da Nang and the region near the Laotian border, through which the communists often infiltrated the South. In November 1968, six marine battalions destroyed more than 1,200 North Vietnamese troops along the border region, and early in 1969, parts of the 1st Division operated in the hill country west of Da Nang, while, to the north, the 3rd Division, operating in Quang Tri Province, cleaned out enemy bases in the Da Krong Valley (Operation Dewey Canyon).

When President Richard M. Nixon entered the White House in 1969, he began a program to withdraw U.S. ground forces in Vietnam and turn over more responsibility for the war to the South Vietnamese. The 9th Marines and elements of the 1st Air Wing were relieved in 1969; the 1st Division was sent late in the year to the Que Son Valley to replace army units, which had been withdrawn.

In September 1969, the 3rd Division was withdrawn and stationed in OKINAWA and at Marine

Corps Base Camp Pendleton, and in March 1970, the army took over the defense of Da Nang, while III Marine Amphibious Force—reduced essentially to the 1st Division—defended Quang Nam Province. Small-scale offensives were conducted, even during the period of withdrawal, with the marines acting mainly to support ARVN forces, which were expected to shoulder most of the burden. By February 1971, the 1st Marines was the only USMC presence left in Vietnam. Soon even this was reduced to a single amphibious brigade. Before the year was over, only some 500 marines remained in Vietnam, serving as legation guards and as advisers to ARVN forces. However, the North Vietnamese Easter offensive of 1972, in which some 120,000 communists invaded the northern provinces of South Vietnam brought additional USMC air units into the country on a short-term basis.

When the final North Vietnamese offensive began in March 1975, the 9th Amphibious Brigade, during April, effected the evacuation of U.S. citizens. USMC legation guards, reinforced by elements of the 9th Marines, guarded the U.S. Embassy in Saigon as helicopters evacuated remaining U.S. personnel and certain Vietnamese and foreign citizens. The last marines were themselves airlifted from the embassy on the morning of April 30, 1975.

The largest USMC complement to serve in Vietnam was nearly 86,000 men. USMC casualties were 12,926 men killed in action and 88,582 wounded.

W

Wake Island

Despite its name in the singular, Wake Island is a group of three remote coral islets in the Pacific 2,300 miles west of Hawaii. Claimed by the United States after the SPANISH-AMERICAN WAR, Wake Island was defended by 449 marines of the 1st Defense Battalion at the outbreak of WORLD WAR II. There were also a dozen F4F Wildcat fighter aircraft based on Wake.

The Japanese first attacked the island on December 11, 1941, but were repulsed by the small USMC garrison. Firing five-inch guns, marines sank two destroyers, damaged a third, and also damaged two Japanese cruisers. On December 22, the Japanese returned in force and, with 2,000 men, overwhelmed the USMC garrison. In addition to the cost in warships, the Japanese suffered 1,500 infantry killed in the taking of this outpost.

War of 1812

The War of 1812, between the United States and Britain, involved substantial action at sea. Most of the USMC, which numbered fewer than 500 men in 1812, served aboard U.S. Navy ships and participated in such celebrated naval battles as that between USS *Constitution* and HMS *Guerrière*, USS *Wasp* versus HMS *Frolic*, *Constitution* versus *Java*, and *United States* versus *Macedonian*. In contrast to most of the land battles, which U.S. federal and militia forces often lost to the British, the fledgling navy and Marine Corps performed with extraordinary skill and success against the Royal Navy, most powerful seagoing force in the world.

In addition to oceangoing service, marines served with Commodore Oliver Hazard Perry (USN) in the spectacular U.S. triumph on Lake Erie.

On land, marines participated in the disastrously failed defense of Washington, D.C., against the advance of British general Robert Ross. On August 24, 1813, Ross defeated U.S. Army and militia forces, augmented by 400 sailors and 103 marines, at Bladensburg, Maryland, just five miles outside of Washington, D.C. After crossing the Anacostia River, Ross quickly routed the remaining militia. The sailors and marines, however, held a line across the main road, using five naval guns to repulse several British attacks. However, with overwhelming strength, the British were able to flank this force and send it into retreat. Once the USN-USMC line had collapsed, Ross marched into Washington and burned most of the public buildings.

The Battle of New Orleans, fought at the end of 1814 and beginning of 1815, had a much happier outcome. Three hundred marines participated in the battle and played a key role in the very center of General Andrew Jackson's defenses. The main British attack was launched on January 8, 1815, and was repulsed within 20 minutes. Of 3,500 British troops involved, 2,300 were killed or wounded. Edward Pakenham, the British commander, was among the dead. That the battle was fought some two weeks after the Treaty of Ghent had formally ended the War of 1812 (neither Jackson nor Pakenham had received word of this) did not diminish the positive impact of the victory on the American public. It made a costly war, which gained the United States virtually nothing, seem like a brilliant triumph.

weapons, individual and crew-served

The following individual and crew-served weapons and auxiliary equipment are either currently included in the USMC inventory or are of historical importance in the service.

AN/PAQ-3 Modular Universal Laser Equipment (MULE)

The AN/PAQ-3 Modular Universal Laser Equipment, or MULE, is a man-portable, tripod-mounted or shoulder-fired unit that incorporates a laser rangefinder/target designator compatible with all laser-guided weapons now under development. This target locator and guide for laser-guided projectiles can track moving targets and can combine range, azimuth, and elevation into a digital message that is sent to the tactical fire control center. The MULE consists of the Laser Designator/Rangefinder Module and the Stabilized Tracking Tripod Module. Additionally, the North Finding Module assists in orientation of the equipment. The system can be run on 24-volt rechargeable batteries or from 24-volt vehicle-supplied power. The MULE effectively ranges a moving target to almost 10,000 feet and a stationary target to 16,400 feet. Drawbacks to the MULE include its weight and bulk (108 pounds when configured with the night sight) and technical limitations of its sight. Nevertheless, the MULE has enjoyed a significant degree of acceptance by marines in the field.

General characteristics of the AN/PAQ-3 Modular Universal Laser Equipment (MULE) include:

Manufacturer: Hughes Aircraft
Weight, daylight operations: 42 lb

Weight, night operations: 108 lb
Weight in shipping cases: 220 lb
Laser designator/rangefinder module field of view: 4 degrees
Laser designator/rangefinder module magnification: 10x
Stabilized tracking tripod module field of rotation: 360 degrees
Stabilized tracking tripod module elevation: up 16.9 degrees, down 22.5 degrees
Terrain capability: 0–15 degrees
Power requirements, rechargeable batteries: 24 volts, nickel-cadmium
Run time: 10 min for each 7-hour recharge

Unit may also be run on vehicle-supplied power.

AN/PAQ-4A/4C Infrared Aiming Light

The AN/PAQ-4A Infrared Aiming Light is a lightweight, battery-powered, pulsating, infrared-emitting target-marking beam. Invisible to the unaided eye, the AN/PAQ-4A's beam allows the user to engage targets at night while wearing night-vision goggles. The aiming light is adapted for use with the M-16A2 rifle and can also be adapted for use on the M-60 Machine Gun, the M2-HB Browning Machine Gun, and the M-249 SAW.

The AN/PAQ-4A uses a Class I laser (helium-neon) to generate the aiming point, marking targets out to a minimum of 325 feet and a maximum of 650 to nearly 1,000 feet, depending on the ambient light available. The system can be powered by one standard lithium battery, which will operate the aiming light for about 40 hours continuously. If necessary, two standard AA batteries can also be used. Once the beam is boresighted to the weapon, the firer simply places the pulsating beam on the target and shoots. The AN/PAQ-4A is intended for use in conjunction with AN/PVS-7B Night Vision Goggles. The AN/PAQ-4C is an improved version of the AN/PAQ-4A. General characteristics of both versions include:

Manufacturer: Insight Technology, Manchester, New Hampshire

Length: 6.1 in
Width: 1.7 in (4.32 cm)
Weight, with batteries: 9 oz
Range: 325 ft min
Beam divergence: less than 2 milliradians
Power source: 1 BA-5567 or 2 AA batteries (BA-3058)

AN/PVS-4 Individual Weapon Night Sight

The USMC employs the AN/PVS-4 Individual Weapon Night Sight as a night vision device for passive night vision and aiming fire of individual weapons using ambient light—moonlight, starlight, or skyglow—for illumination. This advanced instrument, portable and battery operated, amplifies reflected light to enhance night vision. The device is entirely passive and does not emit visible or infrared light, which can be detected by the enemy.

The AN/PVS-4 Individual Weapon Night Sight can be used with the M-16 Rifle, M-249 Machine Gun, and M-60 Machine Gun, as well as the 83 mm Mk-183 Mod 1 (SMAW) Rocket. The AN/PVS-4 comes furnished with mounting brackets for the M-16 and M-60; reticules and mounting brackets for use with other weapons are separately requisitioned.

General characteristics of the night sight include:

Manufacturer: IMO Industries, Garland, Texas
Length: 12 in
Width: 4 in
Height: 4.5 in
Weight: 4 lb
Magnification: 3.6x
Range (man-sized target), starlight: 400 yd
Range (man-sized target), moonlight: 600 yd
Field of view: 14.5 degrees, circular
Power source: 2.7-volt mercury battery

AN/PVS-5 Night Vision Goggles (NVG)

The AN/PVS-5 Night Vision Goggles (NVG) are a self-contained, passive, image intensifying, night-vision viewing system worn on the head either with or without the standard battle helmet or aviator helmet. They are a second-generation binocular system that magnifies starlight or moonlight for enhanced night vision. Although the system is passive, it incorporates a built-in infrared light source for added illumination to aid in performing such close-up tasks as map reading. The goggles are equipped with a headstrap for "hands-free" operation and demist shields to prevent fogging of the eyepiece. The USMC has some 8,200 AN/PVS-5s in its inventory.

The AN/PVS-5 Night Vision Goggles (NVG) were first acquired by the USMC in the early 1980s and, since that time, have been used by vehicle drivers, riflemen, and unit leaders.

General characteristics of the AN/PVS-5 Night Vision Goggles (NVG) include:

Manufacturer: IMO Industries, Garland, Texas; ITT, Roanoke, Virginia; Litton, Tempe, Arizona
Length: 6.5 in
Width: 6.8 in
Height: 4.7 in
Weight: 30 oz
Magnification: 1x
Range (man-sized target), starlight: 164 ft
Range (man-sized target), moonlight: 500 ft
Field of view: 40 degrees (circular)
Power source: 2.7-volt mercury battery

AN/PVS-7B Night Vision Goggle (NVG)

The AN/PVS-7B is a single-tube night vision goggle system, which employs a Generation III image intensifier using prisms and lenses to provide the user with simulated binocular vision. The device incorporates a high light-level protection circuit in a passive, self-contained image intensifier device, which amplifies existing ambient light—starlight, moonlight, skyglow—to enhance night vision for night operations. A demist shield prevents fogging of the eyepiece.

The AN/PVS-7B augments the earlier AN/PVS-5 Night Vision Goggles (NVG) and will eventually replace it entirely. It is a state-of-the-art instrument.

General characteristics of the AN/PVS-7B Night Vision Goggle (NVG) include:

Manufacturer: ITT, Roanoke, Virginia; Litton, Tempe, Arizona
Length: 5.9 in
Width: 6.1 in
Height: 3.9 in
Weight: 24 oz
Magnification: 1x
Range, starlight, man-sized target: 325 ft
Range, starlight, vehicle-sized target: 1,640 ft
Range, moonlight, man-sized target: 1,000 ft
Field of view: 40 degrees (circular)
Power source: mercury, nickel-cadmium, or lithium battery
Operation time: 12 hours on one 2.7-volt battery

AN/TVS-5 Crew-Served Weapon Night Sight

The AN/TVS-5 Night Sight is a portable, battery operated, electro-optical instrument used for observation and aimed fire of weapons at night. Entirely passive, it emits no light of its own, but works by amplifying reflected ambient light from such sources as moonlight, starlight, and sky glow. An eye guard ensures that no visible and/or infrared light will escape from the eyepiece to alert enemy forces.

The AN/TVS-5 is currently the standard USMC night sight for the M-2 50-caliber machine gun and the 40-mm Mk-19 machine gun; however, the sight can also be used as a stand-alone instrument, mounted on a tripod or even hand-held for surveillance.

The AN/TVS-5 was designed in the 1970s and was acquired by the USMC in the 1980s. Its general characteristics include:

Manufacturer: IMO Industries, Garland, Texas, and various other vendors
Length: 15 in
Width: 6 in
Height: 6 in
Weight: 8 lb
Magnification: 6.5x
Range (vehicle-sized target), starlight: 1,000 yd

Range (vehicle-sized target), moonlight: 1,200 yd
Field of view: 9 degrees (circular)
Power source: 2.7-volt mercury battery

Flamethrower

A weapon that may be mounted on a tank or carried by an individual marine and that propels a burning stream of gelled gasoline. Marines made extensive use of flamethrowers during the Pacific Campaign in WORLD WAR II, in which Japanese troops were often hunkered down in extremely inaccessible positions, especially in caves on coral islands.

Joint Service Combat Shotgun

The USMC, like other services, plans to adopt a semiautomatic, repeating 12-gauge shotgun to replace the 12-gauge shotgun models in current use. The Joint Service Combat Shotgun is planned as a compact, lightweight, semiautomatic weapon configured with a standard magazine with a minimum capacity of six 2.75-inch cartridges. It will be capable of firing 12-gauge 3.0-inch magnum ammunition and will be interoperable with standard 2.75-inch ammunition without adjustment to the operating system. Construction will be of lightweight polymer materials and corrosion-resistant metal components. It will be equipped with such modular components as modular stocks in various configurations and modular barrels of various lengths. The new weapon is intended for use by USMC units in the execution of security and selected Special Operations missions.

General characteristics of the weapon include:

Length: 41.75 in or less
Weight: 6–8.5 lb
Bore diameter: 12 gauge
Maximum effective range: 130–165 ft with "00" buckshot load

Krag-Jorgenson Rifle

This .30-caliber rifle was adopted by the USA and USMC in 1894, modified from a Danish-made bolt-action design. The side-mounted magazine gate of this rifle held five cartridges packed with 40 grains of smokeless powder, which produced a muzzle velocity far superior to the black powder cartridges used in earlier rifles. The Krag-Jorgenson was replaced in 1903 by the Springfield 1903 model.

M-1 .30-caliber Carbine

This Winchester weapon was adopted early in World War II by all the services to replace both submachine guns and the .45-caliber automatic pistol. Although the USMC used the weapon, preference was given to the heavier M-1 Garand, which had heftier striking power. Nevertheless, the weapon was used by USMC forces through the KOREAN WAR and well into the 1950s.

M-2-HB Browning Machine Gun

This weapon was issued during World War II to the USMC and other services and was a heavy—.50-caliber—air-cooled machine gun weighing 125 pounds. It could be mounted in a four-gun configuration (the "quad 50"), which made it highly effective against nonarmored vehicles. Range was 1,000 yards. The weapon was defensive in nature, and its effect against attacking personnel was devastating.

M-9 Personal Defense Weapon

A Beretta 9-mm semiautomatic, double-action pistol that is used in the USMC and throughout the Department of Defense. The weapon was first fielded in 1985 and replaced the M-1911A1 .45-caliber pistol and the .38-caliber revolver formerly used by officers. However, the M-1911A1 is still used by USMC Maritime Special Purpose Forces (MSPF).

M-14 7.62-mm Rifle

The M-14 7.62-mm magazine-fed, gas-operated rifle is designed primarily for semiautomatic fire and was the standard USMC service rifle until it was replaced in the late 1960s by the 5.56-mm M-16A1 rifle, which, in turn, has been replaced by the M-16A2 rifle. Although the M-14 is no longer standard issue for the USMC, it is still used in the Competition in Arms program and for drill and ceremonial purposes.

General characteristics of the M-14 7.62-mm rifle include:

Length: 44.14 in
Length of barrel: 22 in
Weight, empty magazine: 8.7 lb
Weight, full magazine and sling: 11.0 lb
Bore diameter: 7.62 mm
Maximum effective range: 1,509.26 ft
Muzzle velocity: 2,800 ft/sec
Cyclic rate of fire: 750 rounds/min
Magazine capacity: 20 rounds

M-16A2 Rifle

The standard 5.56-mm semiautomatic combat rifle issued to marines and U.S. Army troops. Air cooled and gas operated, the M-16A2 is a low-impulse rifle weighing less than 9 pounds and carrying a 20- to 30-round magazine. The shooter can select three-burst or semiautomatic mode, firing at the rate of 90 rounds per minute in three-burst mode and 45 rounds per minute in semiautomatic mode. The standard M-16A2 load is a steel penetrator inside a lead and copper jacket, which pierces lightly armored vehicles and body armor. Muzzle velocity is 3,250 feet per second.

The M-16A2 represents a substantial improvement on accuracy over the M-16A1, thanks to redesigned rifling. The M-16A1 was never a favorite with the USMC.

M-40A1 Sniper Rifle

This modification of the Remington 700 bolt-action rifle is used by the USMC as its principal scout and sniper rifle. Weighing 14.5 pounds, the 7.62-mm rifle is equipped with a 10x sight and has an effective range of 3,250 feet. The integral magazine holds five rounds.

M-60 Machine Gun

Based on World War II German designs, the M-60 replaced the M-1919A4 Browning Machine Gun during the VIETNAM WAR. It was widely adopted by the army and Marine Corps and is gas operated, bipod equipped, and can fire 550 rounds per minute or can be used as a single-shot weapon.

M-82 Special Application Scope Rifle (SASR)

The SASR is a semiautomatic .50-caliber rifle used by marine (and army and navy) snipers. The weapon is manufactured by Barrett, is 5 feet long, and weighs almost 30 pounds. It delivers a muzzle velocity of 2,732 feet per second and has a great range, in excess of a mile. Two M-82 SASRs are assigned to USMC surveillance and target-acquisition (STA) platoons.

M-203 40-mm Grenade Launcher

The USMC employs the M-203 40-mm Grenade Launcher as an attachment to the M-16A2 Rifle to create a lightweight, compact, breech-loading, pump-action, single-shot launcher. Basic components of the launcher include a hand guard and sight assembly with a folding, adjustable, short-range blade sight assembly and an aluminum receiver assembly, which houses the barrel latch, barrel stop, and firing mechanism. The launcher also has a quadrant sight, which may be attached to the M-16A2 carrying handle. This sight is used to increase precision out to the maximum effective range of the weapon. The launcher fires a variety of low-velocity 40-mm ammunition and was designed as a replacement for the M-79 grenade launcher of the Vietnam War era. The USMC inventory holds 10,500 of the weapons as of 2004.

General characteristics of the M-203 40-mm Grenade Launcher include:

Weight, launcher: 3 lb (1.36 kgs)
Weight, M-16A2 rifle: 8.79 lb
Weight, total (including 30 rounds): 11.79 lb
Bore diameter: 40 mm
Maximum effective range, area target: 1,148.35 ft
Maximum effective range, point target: 492.15 ft
Maximum range: 1,312.4 ft
Minimum safe range, training: 426.53 ft
Minimum safe range, combat: 101.71 ft

M-240G Machine Gun

A gas-operated, air-cooled, belt-fed 7.62-mm machine gun with cyclical rate of fire of 600 rounds per minute and a sustained rate of 100 rounds per minute. The weapon is typically mounted on a LAV-25 vehicle.

M-249 SAW

"SAW" stands for Squad Automatic Weapon. The M-249 is a gas-operated, air-cooled weapon with a cyclical rate of fire of 750 rounds per minute and a sustained 85-round-per-minute rate. The weapon is highly portable at a little over 16 pounds and has an effective range of more than 3,000 feet. Nine SAWs are assigned to each USMC platoon.

M-1911A1 .45-caliber Pistol

The .45-caliber semiautomatic pistol M-1911A1 was the standard handgun of the USMC for many years. A magazine-fed semiautomatic weapon, it fires one round each time the trigger is squeezed once the hammer is cocked by prior action of the slide or thumb. The thumb safety may be activated only after the pistol is cocked, and the hammer remains in the fully cocked position once the safety is activated. This is the old "single-action only" design; modern pistols are "double action" designs, which allow the hammer to move forward to an uncocked position when the thumb safety is activated.

The longevity of the M-1911A1 was in large part due to its reliability and lethality. However, its single-action design proved a significant liability in that it required the user to be highly trained and experienced when carrying the pistol in the ready-to-fire mode. Because of the potential hazard, M-1911A1s were often ordered to be carried without a round in the chamber, which, of course, compromised their usefulness as a ready weapon. Moreover, even with this restriction, the pistol was involved in many unintentional discharges. By the 1980s, it was replaced by the modern M-9 Personal Defense Weapon; however, a modified version of the weapon, the MEU (SOC) Pistol, is still used as a backup weapon for USMC units armed with the MP-5N Heckler and Koch 9-mm Submachine Gun.

General characteristics of the venerable M-1911A1 .45-caliber Pistol include:

Length: 8.625 in
Length of barrel: 5.03 in
Weight, magazine empty: 2.5 lb
Weight, magazine loaded: 3.0 lb
Bore diameter: .45 cal
Maximum effective range: 82.02 ft
Muzzle velocity: 830 ft/sec
Magazine capacity: 7 rounds

M-1917A1 Browning Machine Gun

This heavy (93 pounds) .30-caliber water-cooled machine gun was introduced in WORLD WAR I and saw use throughout World War II and even in the Korean War. During World War I and at the beginning of World War II, it was fed by a 250-round fabric belt, which, later in World War II, was replaced by a disintegrating link belt. The weapon could fire 450 to 600 rounds per minute. Its weight ensured that the M-1917A1 would function in a defense rather than assault role.

M-1918 Browning Automatic Rifle (BAR)

The BAR was a relatively lightweight weapon (16 pounds), capable of firing in semiautomatic and automatic mode and firing a 30.06 cartridge at the (automatic) rate of 500 pounds per minute. It was used in World War I, World War II, and, modified as the M-1918A2, in the Korean War and Vietnam War. It was replaced by the M-60 Machine Gun and the M-249 SAW.

M-1919A4 Browning Machine Gun

This .30-caliber air-cooled machine gun was designed during World War I, but was not adopted by the USMC until after the war. Its great advantage was its light weight of 31 pounds, compared to 93 pounds for the M-1917A1 Browning Machine Gun. The M-1919A4 saw extensive service in World War II as a marine weapon and continued to be used throughout the Korean War until it was replaced by the M-60 Machine Gun.

M-1919A6 Browning Machine Gun

This was an improvement on the M-1919A4 Browning Machine Gun. Its redesigned mount and butt rest made it faster to set up. Moreover, unlike the A4, it required no tripod, but had a detachable shoulder stock and a self-contained folding bipod. More than 43,000 of these weapons were produced during World War II, and many A4 models were converted to A6s. The USMC used the weapon in the Korean War as well as in the early stages of the Vietnam War.

M-1921 and M-1928A1 Thompson Submachine Gun

This weapon was made famous—or infamous—by its widespread use among American gangsters during the late 1920s and 1930s. As a military weapon, it was invented by a retired USA colonel, John Thompson, and proved highly valuable in raider-type operations. The weapon fired .45-caliber ball ammunition from a 50-round drum or a 20-round magazine at the very high rate of 800 rounds per minute.

The weapon was not officially adopted by the USMC before World War II, but was nevertheless used in marine action in NICARAGUA. The M-1928 models were produced and purchased in quantity during World War II. Even after it was officially replaced by the M-1 Carbine during the war, USMC raider units continued to favor the Thompson. The weapon continued to see limited use by the USMC after World War II, both in the Korean War and in the Vietnam War.

M-1941 Johnson Light Machine Gun

The USMC adopted this weapon in World War II when it could not obtain sufficient numbers of the older and more desirable M-1918 Browning Automatic Rifle (BAR). At 12.3 pounds, the Johnson was lighter than the BAR, making it ideal for use by raiders and other forward troops. It could fire between 300 and 900 30.06 mm rounds per minute. The Johnson became popular with marines during the war, but it was not an adequate replacement for the BAR.

MEU (SOC) Pistol

This weapon is a modification of the M-1911A1 .45-caliber Pistol that was long-standard USMC issue before it was replaced by the M-9 Personal Defense Weapon. The MEU (SOC) Pistol is a "near match" or "combat accurazited" version of the M-1911A1 and is the designated backup weapon of USMC units armed with the MP-5N Heckler and Koch 9 mm Submachine Gun. These units chose the M-1911A1 because of its reliability and lethality. The MEU (SOC) modifications make the venerable design safer and generally more user friendly. These modifications include the incorporation of a commercial/competition-grade ambidextrous safety, a precision barrel, precise trigger, rubber-coated grips, rounded hammer spur, high-profile combat sights, and an extra-wide grip safety for increased comfort and controllability—aiding in a quick follow-up second shot. The standard-issue magazines are replaced with stainless-steel competition-grade magazines that include a rounded plastic follower and extended floor plate. The USMC maintains an inventory of 500 of the modified weapons.

Designed in 1986, the modifications that produced the MEU (SOC) Pistol are hand crafted by specially trained armorers at the USMC's Rifle Team Equipment (RTE) shop in Quantico, Virginia.

General characteristics of the MEU (SOC) Pistol include:

Length: 8.625 in
Length of barrel: 5.03 in
Weight, magazine empty: 2.5 lb
Weight, magazine loaded: 3.0 lb
Bore diameter: .45-caliber
Maximum effective range: 164 ft
Muzzle velocity: 830 ft/sec
Magazine capacity: 7 rounds

Mk-19 40-mm Machine Gun, MOD 3

The Mk-19 40-mm machine gun, MOD 3 is a fully automatic weapon, air-cooled, fed by disintegrating metallic link-belt ammunition, and blowback operated. With limited amounts of ammunition, the weapon is crew transportable over short distances.

The Mk-19 can fire a variety of 40-mm grenades, including the M-430 HEDP 40 mm grenade, which will pierce armor up to 2 inches thick and will produce fragments lethally effective against personnel within 16 feet of the point of impact and will wound personnel within 50 feet of the point of impact.

The machine gun is usually mounted on the Mk-64 Cradle Mount, MOD 5, or the M-3 Tripod Mount. It may also be mounted in the up-gunned weapons station of the LVTP-7A1.

Originally developed for the USN as a riverine patrol weapon in the Vietnam War, the weapon was subject to a product improvement program in the late 1970s, which produced the Mk-19 Mod 3 that was subsequently adopted by the USMC. General characteristics include:

Manufacturer: Saco Defense Industries
Length: 43.1 in
Weight, gun: 72.5 lb
Weight, cradle (Mk-64 Mod 5): 21.0 lb
Weight, tripod: 44.0 lb
Weight, total: 137.5 lb
Muzzle velocity: 790 ft/sec
Bore diameter: 40 mm
Maximum range: 7,200 ft
Maximum effective range: 5,250 ft
Rate of fire, cyclic: 325–375 rounds/min
Rate of fire, rapid: 60 rounds/min
Rate of fire, sustained: 40 rounds/min

MP-5N Heckler and Koch 9-mm Submachine Gun

The USMC employs the MP-5N Heckler and Koch 9-mm Submachine Gun as its main weapon in the close-quarters battle (CQB) environment. The weapon fires from a closed and locked bolt in either the automatic or semiautomatic modes. Recoil operated, the weapon incorporates a unique, delayed roller, locked bolt system, a retractable butt stock, a removable suppressor, and an illuminating flashlight that is integral to the forward handguard. The flashlight is operated by a pressure switch fitted to the pistol grip. The USMC inventory includes both suppressed and nonsuppressed versions of the

MP-5 weapon, which is the same basic weapon used by the FBI's Hostage Rescue Team and other counterterrorist organizations. Force Reconnaissance companies and Marine Security Force battalions are the principal USMC users of the weapon.

General characteristics of the MP-5N Heckler and Koch 9 mm Submachine Gun include:

> **Manufacturer:** Heckler and Koch, Sterling, Virginia
> **Length, collapsed stock:** 19.29 in
> **Length, extended stock:** 25.98 in
> **Weight (with 30-round magazine):** 7.44 lb
> **Bore diameter:** 9 mm
> **Maximum effective range:** 328.1 ft
> **Rate of fire:** 800 rounds/min

Reising Gun

A submachine gun developed in 1940 on the eve of World War II by Eugen Reising, the gun was produced in a Model 50 and a Model 55. Model 50 had a wooden stock and was intended for standard infantry use; weighing just 6 pounds, it fired .45-caliber ammunition. It had a muzzle-mounted compensator to reduce climbing during fire. Model 55 was equipped with a folding metal stock, a shorter barrel, and lacked the compensator. This more compact, lighter weapon was intended for paratroop use.

The Reising Gun was, at best, an expedient used by the USMC early in the war, through 1942. The weapon tended to malfunction in humid conditions—precisely the conditions found in the Pacific, where it was most extensively used. It jammed frequently, and it had a dangerously faulty safety mechanism.

Revolver, .38-caliber

The USMC has used .38-caliber revolvers, manufactured by Colt and by Smith & Wesson, since World War II. During the 1970s, Ruger-made weapons entered USMC service; however, during the mid-1980s, the revolvers were largely replaced by the M-9 Personal Defense Weapon.

The .38-caliber revolver is a pistol with a rotating cylinder that presents six loaded chambers to

the barrel for discharge in succession. The USMC has used several models with 2-inch and 4-inch barrels, manufactured variously by Colt, Ruger, and Smith & Wesson. Criminal Investigation Division and counterintelligence personnel still sometimes use the 2-inch barrel revolvers, while USMC aviators formerly used the 4-inch barrel weapons, which have been more common in the USMC.

All revolvers are cylinder-loaded, exposed-hammer, selective double-action hand weapons. The action of cocking the hammer causes the cylinder to rotate and align the next chamber with the barrel. At the full cocked position, the revolver is ready to fire in the single action mode by a relatively light squeeze on the trigger. If the hammer is not in the full cocked position, the revolver may still be fired, but in "double action," requiring a longer and heavier squeeze on the trigger.

General characteristics of the 4-inch-barrel weapon include:

> **Length:** 9.25 in
> **Barrel length:** 4 in
> **Weight:** 1.9 lb
> **Bore diameter:** .38-caliber
> **Maximum effective range:** 82.02 ft
> **Rate of fire:** 12–18 rounds/min

Rifle Grenade

A grenade designed to be fired from a rifle instead of thrown by hand. Rifle grenades may be fired using an M-203 Grenade Launcher, an attachment designed for the M-16A1 rifle; however, the standard weapon currently in use is the Mk-19-3 40-mm Automatic Grenade Launcher, a machine-gunlike weapon that fires 325 to 375 grenades per minute.

Shoulder-Launched Multipurpose Assault Weapon (SMAW)

The Shoulder-Launched Multipurpose Assault Weapon (SMAW) is primarily a portable antiarmor rocket launcher capable of using a dual-mode rocket to destroy bunkers and other fortifications during assault operations. With an HEAA rocket, the SMAW can be used against main battle tanks.

As its name suggests, the Shoulder-Launched Multipurpose Assault Weapon is man-portable. It is an 83 mm weapon system consisting of the Mk-153 Mod 0 launcher, the Mk-3 Mod 0-encased HEDP rocket, the Mk-6 Mod 0-encased HEAA rocket, and the Mk-217 Mod 0 spotting rifle cartridge. The launcher component consists of a fiberglass launch tube, a 9 mm spotting rifle, an electro-mechanical firing mechanism, open battle sights, and a mount for the Mk-42 Mod 0 optical sight and the AN/PVS-4 night sight.

For use against bunkers, masonry and concrete walls, and light armor, the High Explosive, Dual Purpose (HEDP) rocket is employed. The High Explosive Antiarmor (HEAA) rocket is used against modern tanks and is effective, provided that they do not have additional armor. The 9 mm spotting rounds are ballistically matched to the rockets and significantly increase the gunner's first-round hit probability.

The SMAW Mk-153 Mod 0 launcher is based on an Israeli design, the B-300, and consists of the launch tube, the spotting rifle, the firing mechanism, and mounting brackets. The launch tube is constructed of fiberglass/epoxy with a gel coat on the bore. The spotting rifle is a British design and is mounted on the right side of the launch tube. The firing mechanism mechanically fires the spotting rifle and uses a magneto to fire the rocket. The encased rockets are loaded at the rear of the launcher.

The complete SMAW system was initially fielded in 1984 and was unique to the USMC. The Mk-6 Mod 0 encased HEAA rocket is a relatively new addition to the system. During Operation Desert Storm (PERSIAN GULF WAR), the USMC provided 150 launchers and 5,000 rockets to the U.S. Army, which has adopted it in limited use.

General characteristics of the Shoulder-Launched Multipurpose Assault Weapon (SMAW) include:

Length, carrying: 29.9 in
Length, ready-to-fire: 54 in
Weight, carrying: 16.6 lb
Weight, ready-to-fire (with HEDP missile): 29.5 lb

Weight, ready-to-fire (with HEAA missile): 30.5 lb
Bore diameter: 83 mm
Maximum effective range, 1 × 2 m target: 820 ft
Maximum effective range, tank-sized target: 1,650 ft

12-gauge Shotgun

The 12-gauge shotgun is a manually operated (pump) repeating shotgun, with a seven-round tubular magazine, a modified choke barrel, and ghost ring sights. The USMC version is equipped with a bayonet attachment, sling swivels, and a standard-length military stock. Some models have folding stocks. USMC infantry units use the 12-gauge as a special-purpose individual weapon for such missions as guard duty, prisoner supervision, local security, riot control, and any other situation requiring the use of armed personnel with limited range and ammunition penetration.

The USMC has used shotguns since 1901 and currently has four different 12-gauge models in its inventory: the Remington 870, Winchester 1200, Mossberg 500, and Mossberg 590. Maximum effective range of all of these weapons is about 50 yards using a "00" buckshot load.

Wharton, Franklin (1767–1818) Marine Corps commandant

The third COMMANDANT OF THE MARINE CORPS, Wharton was born in Philadelphia and commissioned a USMC captain on August 3, 1798. He served during the U.S.-FRENCH QUASI-WAR aboard the frigate *United States* until 1801, then was assigned to command the Philadelphia garrison until March 7, 1804, when, as a lieutenant colonel, he was named commandant.

Wharton oversaw development of the MARINE BARRACKS at 8th and I Streets in Washington, D.C., and was in command of the Corps during the war with the BARBARY PIRATES and the WAR OF 1812. With 400 sailors, his 103 marines were the only U.S. military personnel to resist the British march to Washington after the invaders dispersed the U.S. militia at the Battle of Bladensburg, Maryland, on

August 24, 1814. Wharton, however, was court-martialed in 1817 for having failed to attempt a defense of the capital (he fled with President James Madison and others). The court-martial exonerated him, and Wharton continued to serve as commandant until his death.

wheeled vehicles

The following wheeled vehicles are either currently included in the marine inventory or are of historical importance in the service.

High-Mobility Multipurpose Wheeled Vehicle

The HMMWV—or Humvee—has generally replaced the Jeep as the USMC's principal light, four-wheel-drive tactical vehicle. Diesel powered, the HMMWV is used variously as a light personnel transport, an ambulance, a light cargo transport, and as a vehicle to tow light artillery and missile systems. The HMMWV is manufactured by Hummer, a General Motors company.

Infantry Fighting Vehicle

The IFV is a lightly armored combat vehicle for transporting marines and for conducting mounted warfare. The marine IFV is the LAV-25, an eight-wheeled Light Assault Vehicle, also used as a personnel carrier.

See also AMPHIBIOUS VEHICLES.

M-113 Armored Personnel Carrier

The "Battle Taxi" is a lightly armored vehicle designed to carry marines into combat. At 16 feet long and almost 9 feet wide, the M-113 carries a crew of two and 11 combat marines. Its six-cylinder turbocharged engine propels the 24,000-pound

A Humvee from the Combined Antiarmor Team of the 1st Battalion, 6th Marines   *(U.S. Marine Corps)*

vehicle to a top speed of 42 miles per hour on land and 3.6 miles per hour in water. Range is 300 miles. The vehicle's thin aluminum armor is supplemented by bolt-on exterior armor panels and interior Kevlar liners.

The M-113 is a venerable vehicle, having been introduced in 1964. The LAV-25 vehicle has replaced it in many combat roles, but it is still used in such roles as maintenance support, engineer squad transport, and as an armored ambulance. It is also suitable for use as a command vehicle.

KLR 250-D8 Marine Corps Motorcycle

The marines use motorcycles as an alternate means of transporting messages, documents, and light cargo, and also for conducting some reconnaissance. The KLR 250-D8 Marine Corps Motorcycle is a lightweight and rugged cross-country motorcycle modified from commercial production for military use. In addition to transporting messages, documents, and light cargo between units, the motorcycle is also used to transport forward observers, military police, and reconnaissance personnel. The motorcycle is equipped with a pair of detachable document carrying cases. The 1991 model KLR 250-D8 replaces the 1984 KLR 250 and is the second generation of marine motorcycles. Field commanders have learned to rely on it as a backup and alternate means of communication, and its commercial design ensures the ready availability of repair parts and ordinary commercial service facilities.

General characteristics of the KLR 250-D8 Marine Corps Motorcycle include:

Length: 7 ft
Weight: 258 lb
Estimated range: 210 mi (highway)

Mk-48 Power Unit and Mk-14 Container Transporter Rear Body Unit

The marines introduced this heavy tactical vehicle system during the mid-1980s. The key component of the system is the Logistics Vehicle System (LVS), a modular system that consists of an Mk-48 front power unit and interchangeable rear body units

(RBU). The front power unit and rear body units are joined by a hydraulically powered articulated joint, which assists in steering the vehicle and allows a significant degree of independent movement between the front and rear units for enhanced mobility. The articulated joint transfers automotive power to the rear body unit axles and also provides hydraulic power for any hydraulically operated equipment in the RBU.

Complete LVS units are 8 × 8 vehicles, four powered wheels in front and four in the rear, with two front steering axles. Each LVS has an off-road payload of 12.5 tons and an on-road payload of 22.5 tons.

The Mk-48 Front Power Unit incorporates an enclosed cab, a diesel engine, and an automatic transmission. By itself, it is a 4 × 4 vehicle, which provides all automotive and hydraulic power for the various LVS combinations.

The Mk-14 Container Transporter Rear Body Unit is a flatbed trailer designed for transporting bulk cargo as well as standardized cargo containers. It is equipped with ISO (International Standards Organization) lock points for securing 20-foot standard containers, as well as Marine Corps Field Logistics System (FLS) bulk liquid tanks and pump units (SIXCONS). The Mk-14 is also capable of transporting the entire standard Marine Corps Expeditionary Shelter System (MCESS).

The Mk-14 Container Transporter Rear Body Unit can be equipped with a tow bar adapter kit, which allows it to be tandem towed as an un-powered trailer behind another Mk-48/Mk-14 combination. However, the tandem tow is limited to the 12.5 ton off-road payload in all environments.

Mk-48 Power Unit and Mk-15, Recovery/Wrecker Rear Body Unit

For Logistics Vehicle System (LVS) background and a description of the Mk-48 Power Unit, see Mk-48 Power Unit and Mk-14 Container Transporter Rear Body Unit.

The Mk-15 Recovery/Wrecker Rear Body Unit is a component of the USMC's Logistics Vehicle System (LVS) and provides a lift and tow capability and an ability to recover disabled heavy vehicles.

Mk-48 Power Unit and Mk-16, Fifth-Wheel Semi-trailer Adapter Rear Body Unit

The Mk-16 Fifth-Wheel Semi-trailer Adapter Rear Body Unit is designed for use in the USMC's Logistics Vehicle System (LVS) to move semi-trailers with loads up to 70 tons.

Mk-48 Power Unit and Mk-18 Self-loading Container and Ribbon Bridge Transporter

The Mk-18 Self-loading Container and Ribbon Bridge Transporter is intended for use as a component of the USMC's Logistics Vehicle System (LVS). The USMC inventory includes 325 Mk-18 Self-loading Container and Ribbon Bridge Transporters. These units are capable of self-loading and off-loading fully loaded 20-foot standard containers as well as the ribbon bridge interior and ramp bays and the standard bridge boat.

In addition to the Mk-18, the USMC has developed 164 Mk-18A1 units, which feature an improved loading and off-loading mechanism.

Mk-155 Mine Clearance Launcher

The function of the USMC's Mk-155 Mine Clearance Launcher is to clear a lane through a minefield during breaching operations. The Mk-155 is part of the Mark 2 Mine Clearance System, which also includes one M58A3/A4 Linear Demolition Charge (LDC) and one Mk-22 Mod 3/4 Rocket. Mounted on an M353 Trailer Chassis, the Mk-155 is towed by an assault amphibious vehicle. The LDC is fired, clearing a lane 328 feet long by 52 feet wide. This is normally the initial minefield breaching asset employed; however, because the LDC is effective only against single impulse, non-blast-resistant, pressure fused mines, its use must be supplemented by a mechanical proofing device, which is used in the lane that has been breached explosively.

The Mk-155 is a hydraulic system, with all of the hydraulics self-contained. A hand pump is operated to store hydraulic pressure in an accumulator. A lanyard, running from the accumulator to inside the towing vehicle, is pulled, thereby raising the launch rail to firing position. A power cable is fed from the launcher to the towing vehicle, from which the launch equipment for the Mk-22 rocket is operated.

As of 2004, the USMC had 271 Mk-155 LMC kits, most of which were deployed with combat engineer battalions and engineer support battalions. The Mk-155 was developed during the 1960s and was used in the VIETNAM WAR.

General characteristics of the Mk-155 Mine Clearance Launcher include:

> **Host vehicle:** M353 General Purpose, 3.5-ton, 2-wheeled, Trailer Chassis
> **Weight (including trailer and launch rail):** 3,775 lb
> **Weight, fully loaded (including one Linear Demolition Charge and one rocket):** 6,405 lb
> **Shipping height:** 74 in

Wilson, Louis H., Jr. (1920–   ) *Marine Corps commandant*

The 26th COMMANDANT OF THE MARINE CORPS, Wilson was born in Brandon, Mississippi, and enlisted in the MARINE CORPS RESERVE in May 1941. He was tapped for active duty in June. After attending Officer Candidate School, he was commissioned a second lieutenant in November and assigned to Marine Corps Base San Diego with the 2nd Division. He was commissioned in the regular USMC in April 1942 and in February 1943 served at GUADALCANAL with the 9th Marines, 3rd Division.

Promoted to captain, Wilson landed on BOUGAINVILLE and GUAM, where he was wounded while resisting one of numerous banzai attacks on the 9th Marines. For his leadership during a 10-hour defense of his unit's position, Wilson received the Medal of Honor.

The wounded Wilson was evacuated to the United States, where he served in Washington for the rest of WORLD WAR II. After the war, he served as aide-de-camp to the commander of FLEET MARINE FORCE, Pacific, then returned to the United States in 1949 as officer in charge of the

New York USMC recruiting station. After serving at Marine Corps Base Quantico from 1951 to 1954, Wilson was assigned to the 1st Division in Korea and, the following year, was given command of a battalion of the 5th Marines. Back in the States in 1958, he commanded the Basic School at Quantico, then, in 1962, was assigned to the Plans and Programs section of HEADQUARTERS MARINE CORPS, Washington.

In the 1960s Wilson served a tour in Vietnam during the VIETNAM WAR and was promoted to major general. He served as commander of Fleet Marine Force, Pacific, before becoming commandant on July 1, 1975. He served in that post until July 1, 1979, a period of great pressure on the USMC in the aftermath of the Vietnam War.

women in the Marines   See U.S. MARINE CORPS WOMEN'S RESERVE.

woolly-pully   See PERSONAL AND MISCELLANEOUS EQUIPMENT.

World War I

For the nations of Europe, World War I was triggered by the assassination, on June 28, 1914, of the heir to the thrones of Austria-Hungary, Archduke Francis Ferdinand and his wife, the Grand Duchess Sophie, in Sarajevo, Bosnia-Herzegovina. By the end of July, a tangle of treaties and alliances, some of them secret, had doomed virtually all of Europe to a war of unparalleled devastation. President Woodrow Wilson navigated a course of strict neutrality for the United States, but the actions of Germany made this increasingly difficult. That nation's policy of unrestricted submarine warfare resulted in the sinking of the British liner *Lusitania* on May 7, 1915, with the loss of American lives. Although Wilson negotiated the suspension of unrestricted submarine warfare, other vessels were subsequently lost, and, on January 31, 1917, Germany resumed unrestricted submarine war-

fare. On February 3, 1917, the United States severed diplomatic relations with Germany. Then, on March 1, in this climate of crisis, the American government published the infamous Zimmerman Telegram, a German proposal of an alliance with Mexico against the United States. On April 6, the Congress voted a declaration of war against Germany.

The United States entered the war with a military that was minuscule by comparison with the massive armies of the European belligerents. Nevertheless, the National Defense Act of 1916 authorized the expansion of the USMC from 10,000 to 15,500 men, and by May 1917, voluntary enlistment raised this number to 31,000. (The strength of the U.S. Army was raised far more precipitously by means of conscription.) Military planners had never given much consideration to deploying U.S. land forces to a European war. It was generally assumed that the USMC would serve, as usual, aboard ships and in defense of bases at home, with occasional small-force forays abroad. But USMC commanders instantly lobbied for a role in the American Expeditionary Force (AEF), and in June 1917 the 5th Regiment embarked for France, where it was assigned to guard duty at Saint-Nazaire, an Atlantic port city. Early in 1918, a new regiment, the 6th, was formed, along with a machine gun battalion. Together, these units constituted the 4th Brigade, which joined with the U.S. Army's 3rd Brigade to make up the 2nd Division. The first major action the 2nd Division—and the marines—saw was at BELLEAU WOOD during June 4–July 10, 1918. On June 6, with the 4th Brigade in the lead, the 2nd Division attacked German positions, beginning a brutal 20-day battle for the sector. The 4th Brigade suffered 55 percent casualties, the highest casualty rate any U.S. brigade would incur during the war. However, the Germans were repulsed, and their last-ditch drive into Paris was halted. The performance of the USMC was celebrated by the French, who renamed Belleau Wood "Bois de la Brigade de Marine." And the Germans paid perhaps an even higher compliment, cursing the marines as "Devil Dogs."

Marines in France, on their way to the front   *(Arttoday)*

Driven by the conviction that American numbers would soon increase along the front, Erich Ludendorff, the principal German commander, swallowed the defeat and mounted yet another offensive on July 15, hoping to score a victory before additional U.S. forces were in place. He hurled at the Allies no fewer than 52 divisions. The U.S. 2nd Division was moved up to the Forêt de Retz, where it coordinated a counterattack with the French XX Corps near Soissons. On July 18, the marines attacked, overrunning the German front-line positions before being withdrawn to rest at Nancy.

At this point, Brigadier General JOHN LEJEUNE assumed command of the 2nd Division, and, on September 12, USMC forces coordinated with the army's 3rd Brigade in an assault on the Saint-Mihiel salient, long a key enemy incursion into the Allies' front. Defeat at Saint-Mihiel spelled the end of the final Ludendorff offensive, and the Allies

began a major advance on all fronts. The 2nd Division was attached to the French Fourth Army, with which it coordinated action in the Meuse-Argonne offensive. When the French advance was arrested at the end of September in the Champagne sector, the 2nd Division was assigned to take the key German strong point at Blanc Mont, a position the enemy had held since 1914.

On October 2, the USMC brigade attacked Blanc Mont head-on, while the army's 3rd Infantry hit the right flank and the French attacked another position, the so-called Essen Hook. The 6th Marines secured Blanc Mont, but the French drive stalled, and the 5th Marines simply passed through the French lines to achieve what the French could not. After driving the Germans from the Essen Hook, the marines pressed on with the attack, repulsed German counterattacks, and secured Saint-Etienne on October 6. After this action, 2nd Division was reassigned to the American V Corps, and France awarded the two USMC regiments the Croix de Guerre streamer.

As reassigned, 2nd Division was deployed along a narrow front in the center of the First U.S. Army line. The division advanced on November 1 and broke through the German defenses, forcing the Germans to withdraw across the Meuse. Stubbornly, however, the Germans continued to hold in the Argonne, and on November 10, the 5th Marines crossed the Meuse and attacked here. A battle was in progress when the Armistice was announced at 11 A.M. on November 11, 1918.

More than 32,000 marines served in France. Of this number, 2,459 were killed in action and 8,900 wounded. USMC performance was uniformly outstanding. Marines received 12 Medals of Honor, 34 Distinguished Service Medals, and 393 Navy Crosses. The brigade remained in Europe as part of the army of occupation until the fall of 1919.

World War II

World War II began in Europe when Germany invaded Poland on September 1, 1939. Within a year, Britain was the last remaining, major Western European democracy, fighting a desperate battle for survival. Although President Franklin D. Roosevelt clearly sided with Britain in the West and, after it was invaded by Hitler, the Soviet Union in the East, the United States ostensibly maintained a state of "armed neutrality," although it supplied Britain with arms. It was not until Germany's Pacific ally, Japan, attacked Pearl Harbor on December 7, 1941, that the United States entered the war as a combatant. For the United States, it would be chiefly a two-theater war, fought in Europe (after the Allied reconquest of North Africa) and the Pacific. For the USMC, it was overwhelmingly a one-theater war: Marines fought almost exclusively in the Pacific.

For the first six months of the Pacific war, the Japanese made stunning advances, taking Malaya, Singapore, Burma, the East Indies, and the Philippines. From the beginning, USMC garrisons confronted the onslaught. The 4th Marines surren-dered with U.S. Army and Filipino forces at Corregidor, Philippines, in May 1942. A marine garrison, overwhelmed, surrendered at GUAM and, after a remarkable defense, surrendered at WAKE ISLAND as well. However, the naval battles of the Coral Sea (May 1942) and Midway (June 1942) began to turn the tide of the Pacific War.

The Midway engagement was critical. The island served the United States as a forward air base. If the Japanese took it, the Americans would relinquish a major staging area for attacks on Hawaii and the West Coast. While a small USMC defense battalion held the island—suffering the loss of most of its obsolescent fighters—the U.S. Navy, at great cost, won the naval battle, sinking four Japanese aircraft carriers and destroying many Japanese aircraft. The Imperial Navy never recovered from these losses and, from Midway on, was unable to resume the offensive in the Pacific.

After Midway, it was the Americans' turn to seize the initiative. A strategy of "island hopping" was formulated, the object being to attack and occupy key Japanese-held islands, while hopping over others, which would, in effect, be cut off by the conquest of the targeted islands. In this way, relatively rapid progress could be made in the Pacific. The marines played the lead role in the extensive amphibious island hopping campaign, almost always making the initial landings and, in many cases, taking sole responsibility for the conquest of a particular island.

GUADALCANAL was the first objective. It was the site of a Japanese base and airfield that threatened the shipping lanes to Australia and New Zealand. In August 1942, the 1st Marine Division was landed and managed to hold off a sustained Japanese counterattack through December. Finally reinforced by the 2nd Division and U.S. Army units, the island was taken on February 8, 1943. Along with Midway, victory at Guadalcanal definitively changed the course of the war.

Beginning in mid-1943, the Allies advanced up the north coast of New Guinea, a strategy that culminated in the invasion of the Philippines late in 1944. In this southwestern Pacific campaign, the

1st Division coordinated with army forces. The marines played a more important role in the South Pacific, invading and securing the central and northern Solomon Islands. In November 1943, the 3rd Division invaded BOUGAINVILLE, which aided in neutralizing the major Japanese air and supply base at Rabaul. In the Central Pacific, the 2nd Division coordinated with the army in taking the TARAWA atoll in November 1943, after which the V Amphibious Corps, composed of the USMC 4th Division and the USA 7th Division, took the islands of ROI-NAMUR and KWAJALEIN in the Marshall chain during January 1944. Next to fall were the islands of Engebi and Parry, to a regiment of the 4th Division early in 1944.

Marines were next landed in the Marianas. The most important of these islands was SAIPAN, just 1,500 miles from Tokyo. Secure this, and the Americans would have a base from which B-29 bombing operations could be launched against the Japanese homeland on a continuous basis. The 2nd and 4th Divisions were landed on Saipan on June 15, 1944, and, supported by the army's 27th Division, advanced across the island in an extremely hard-fought and costly campaign. By July 9, Japanese forces were confined to the northern corner of Saipan. While virtually all 30,000 men of the Japanese garrison had been killed, USMC casualties, killed and wounded, amounted to a staggering 13,000.

After Saipan had been secured, the 2nd and 4th Divisions invaded TINIAN, taking it within two weeks, thereby securing another island from which B-29s could bomb Japan, and from which two aircraft in particular, *Enola Gay* and *Bock's Car,* would drop the atomic bombs that ended the Pacific war.

The campaign to retake Guam, lost in the first great Japanese onslaught of the war, commenced on July 21, 1944, as the 3rd Division and 1st Brigade, supported by the army's 77th Division, landed on the eastern shore of the island. Guam was retaken by August 10.

If American planners had been eager to retake Guam, they were even more committed to the reconquest of the Philippines. Army forces landed on Leyte in October 1944, provoking desperate action from the Japanese fleet, including the widespread deployment of kamikaze suicide attacks. To protect the eastern flank of Leyte operations, USMC ground and air forces attacked the Palau group of islands. The 1st Division landed on PELELIU on September 15 and encountered resistance extraordinary even for the Japanese. The division suffered nearly 50 percent casualties. The island did not fall until November 27.

Early in 1945, the Allied offensive in the southwest Pacific converged with that in the Central Pacific, as the Philippines became the major Pacific campaign focus. Here would be established the Allied bases from which the final invasion of Japan itself would be launched. However, an important tactical objective was to provide emergency landing bases for B-29s damaged in raids over Japan. Moreover, establishing air bases close to Japan would enable relatively short-range fighters to accompany the B-29s all the way into Japan. Thus IWO JIMA, a minuscule island strategically located, was targeted for the next USMC operation. The Japanese garrison, more than 23,000 strong, was housed in virtually impregnable caves and blockhouses. Taking Iwo Jima would prove the costliest USMC action of the war. The V Amphibious Corps, composed of the 4th and 5th Divisions, landed on February 19, 1945, and took the high ground, Mt. Suribachi, on February 23 (see IWO JIMA MEMORIAL). The fighting, however, was hardly over, and the island was not declared secure until March 26. USMC casualties topped 26,000.

In addition to major invasion bases in the Philippines, Allied commanders chose OKINAWA, a mere 850 miles from Tokyo, as the necessary forward base of operations. Some 100,000 Japanese troops garrisoned the island. Although U.S. Army forces were given primary responsibility for the campaign to take Okinawa, three USMC divisions participated as well—81,000 of the 182,000-man force that executed the campaign. Landings began on April 1, 1945, but the principal Japanese resistance was not encountered until USA and USMC forces had moved well inland. On June 18, when General Simon Buckner, commander of Tenth Army, was killed, overall command was temporarily assumed by Lieutenant General ROY GEIGER (USMC), who became the only marine ever to command an army. The island was secured by June 21.

Now, along with USA and USN forces, the USMC girded for the invasion of Japan itself, which, they knew, would be the costliest action of the entire war. But the invasion proved unneces-sary. Atomic attacks were launched against Hiroshima and Nagasaki on August 6 and 9, 1945, and, on August 10, Emperor Hirohito announced his acceptance of the Allies' Potsdam Declaration, a call for unconditional surrender. The surrender was formalized on September 2, 1945, in a ceremony on board the battleship *Missouri* in Tokyo Bay. USMC World War II casualties were 86,940 killed and wounded.

Z

Zeilin, Jacob (1806–1880) *Marine Corps commandant*

The sixth COMMANDANT OF THE MARINE CORPS, Zeilin was born in Philadelphia and commissioned a second lieutenant in the USMC on October 1, 1831. He served at sea until the U.S.-MEXICAN WAR, when he commanded a detachment that captured San Pedro, California, then served with the legendary Kit Carson as part of a reinforcement column for Stephen Kearny at San Bernardino in December 1846. Zeilin, promoted to captain, led a USMC landing at Mazatlán, Mexico, on November 10, 1847, and served there as military governor until June 1848.

In 1853, Major Zeilin commanded the 200-man USMC contingent attached to Commodore Matthew Perry's momentous diplomatic mission to Japan and China, and at the outbreak of the Civil War Zeilin commanded a company at the First Battle of Bull Run. He was wounded in the engagement and did not return to active service until August 1863, when he led 300 marines in reinforcing army and USMC forces attempting to take Charleston, South Carolina. He was appointed commandant on June 9, 1864, and promoted to colonel. He served in this post for a dozen years.

U.S. Marine Corps Abbreviations and Acronyms

AAV   Assault Amphibious Vehicle

APC   Armored Personnel Carrier

BAR   Browning Automatic Rifle

COMMARFOREUR   Commander, Marine Forces Europe

CP   Command Post

DMZ   Demilitarized Zone

FMF   Fleet Marine Force

HMX-1   Marine Helicopter Squadron One

KIA   Killed in Action

LCP   Landing Craft, Personnel

LCT   Landing Craft, Tank

LCVP   Landing Craft, Vehicle Personnel

LST   Landing Ship, Tank

LVT   Landing Vehicle, Tracked

LVTP   Landing Vehicle, Tracked Personnel

MACV   Marine Amphibious Corps Vietnam

MAF   Marine Amphibious Force

MAG   Marine Air Group

MAGTF   Marine Air-Ground Task Force

MarDiv   Marine Division

MARFORLANT   Marine Forces Atlantic

MARFORPAC   Marine Forces Pacific

MARFORSOUTH   Marine Forces South

MARFORUNITAS   Marine Forces Unitas. Cooperative program with several South American armed forces.

MARINE (as acronym)   "My Ass Rides In Navy Equipment." Denotes the USMC's position within the Department of the Navy.

MAWTS-1   Marine Aviation Weapons and Tactics Squadron One

MBT   Main Battle Tank

MCRD   Marine Corps Recruit Depot

MEB   Marine Expeditionary Brigade

MEF   Marine Expeditionary Force

MEU   Marine Expeditionary Unit

MFR   Marine Forces Reserve

MIA   Missing in Action

MPF   Marine Prepositioning Force

MPS   Maritime Prepositioning Squadron

RAP   Rocket-Assisted Projectile

RCT   Regimental Combat Team

SOP   Standing Operating Procedure

SPF   Special Purpose Force

SWTU   Special Weapons Training Unit

USMARFORK   U.S. Marine Forces Korea

USMCR   United States Marine Corps Reserve

VMA   USMC unit designation for an attack squadron. A VMA flies the AV-8B Harrier "jump jet," of which the typical VMA squadron carries 20.

See also VMA(AW); VMFA; VMFA (AW).

VMA (AW)   USMC unit designation for an Attack (All Weather) squadron. These units flew the A-6E Intruder. With the phaseout of this aircraft and the transition to the F/A-18D Hornet, the units are being redesignated VMFA(AW).

VMAQ   USMC unit designation for an Electronic Warfare Squadron. These squadrons fly the EA-6B Prowler. Each VMAQ squadron flies five Prowlers.

VMFA   USMC unit designation for Fighter Attack Squadron. Currently, these squadrons fly the F/A-18 Hornet strike fighter. Each VMFA flies 12 F/A-18s. See also VMFA (AW).

VMFA (AW)   USMC unit designation for a Fighter Attack (All Weather) Squadron. These squadrons fly the F/A-18D Hornet in a reconnaissance role.

VMGR   USMC unit designation for a Refueler-Transport Squadron. These squadrons fly the KC-130/F/R/Hercules tanker. One VMGR squadron is tasked to support the U.S. Navy's famed Blue Angels Flight Demonstration Squadron, which tours widely.

VMO   USMC unit designation for an Observation Squadron. These squadrons formerly flew the OV-10A/D Bronco, an STOL aircraft used for counterinsurgency, reconnaissance, and escort until it was removed from operational service in 1994. The last active VMO was disestablished on July 31, 1993.

V/STOL (Vertical/Short Takeoff and Landing)   Aircraft capable of vertical takeoff and landing (without requiring runway movement) and of short takeoff and landing (requiring very limited runway movement). The most common USMC V/STOL examples are the AV-8 Harrier "jump jet" and the V-22 Osprey. See also VTOL.

VTOL (Vertical Takeoff and Landing)   Designation applied to aircraft capable of vertical takeoff and landing, without requiring movement on a runway. The most common USMC VTOL aircraft is the helicopter; however, the AV-8 Harrier "jump jet" and the V-22 Osprey are also VTOL-capable aircraft, which may also be classified as V/STOL (Vertical/Short Takeoff and Landing) aircraft.

WIA   Wounded in Action

Bibliography
UNITED STATES MARINE CORPS

★ ━━━━━━━━━━━━━━━━━━━━━━━━━━━━━━━━━━━━━━

GENERAL WORKS

Adkin, Mark. *Urgent Fury: The Battle for Grenada.* Lanham, Md.: Lexington Books, 1989.

Alexander, Joseph H. *The Battle History of the U.S. Marines.* New York: HarperPerennial, 1999.

Asprey, Robert B. *At Belleau Wood.* Denton: University of North Texas Press, 1996.

Ballard, John R., and John J. Sheehan, *Upholding Democracy: The United States Military Campaign in Haiti, 1994–1997.* New York: Praeger, 1998.

Bartlett, Merrill L. *Lejeune: A Marine's Life, 1867–1942.* Annapolis, Md.: Naval Institute Press, 1996.

Belknap, Michael R., ed. *Civil Rights, the White House, and the Justice Department, 1945–1968: Integration of the Armed Forces.* New York: Garland, 1991.

Bierley, Paul E. *John Philip Sousa: American Phenomenon.* New York: Warner Books, 2001.

Bradley, James. *Flags of Our Fathers.* New York: Bantam, 2000.

Butler, Smedley D. *War Is a Racket.* New York: Round Table, 1935.

Clark, Eugene Franklin. *The Secrets of Inchon: The Untold Story of the Most Daring Covert Mission of the Korean War.* New York: Putnam, 2002.

Estes, Kenneth W. *The Marine Officer's Guide,* 6th ed. Annapolis, Md.: Naval Institute Press, 1996.

Foster, John. *Guadalcanal General: The Story of A. A. Vandegrift, USMC.* New York: William Morrow, 1966.

Frank, Richard B. *Guadalcanal: The Definitive Account of the Landmark Battle.* New York: Penguin USA, 1992.

Gailey, Harry A. *Historical Dictionary of the United States Marine Corps.* Lanham, Md.: Scarecrow, 1998.

Gamble, Bruce. *Black Sheep One: The Life of Gregory Pappy Boyington.* San Francisco: Presidio Press, 2000.

Glenn, John. *John Glenn: A Memoir.* New York: Bantam, 1999.

Hammel, Eric M. *The Root: The Marines in Beirut, August 1982–February 1984.* Pacifica, Calif.: Pacifica Press, 1993.

·Hickey, Donald R. *The War of 1812: A Forgotten Conflict.* Urbana and Chicago: University of Illinois Press, 1990.

Hoffman, Jon T. *Chesty: The Story of Lieutenant General Lewis B. Puller, USMC.* New York: Random House, 2001.

Iacampo, Martin. *"Sir, Yes Sir": U.S. Marine Corps Boot Camp, Parris Island.* New York: Vantage Press, 1994.

Kawano, Kenji. *Warriors: The Navajo Code Talkers.* Flagstaff, Ariz.: Northland Publishing Company, 1990.

Lenahan, Rod. *Confrontation Zone: The Story of the 1989 U.S. Intervention into Panama: Operation Just Cause.* Charleston, S.C.: Narwhal Press, 2002.

Moran, Jim. *Peleliu 1944.* London: Osprey, 2002.

Mason, Theodore K. *Across the Cactus Curtain: The Story of Guantanamo Bay.* New York: Putnam, 1984.

Millett, Allan R. *Semper Fidelis: The History of the United States Marine Corps.* New York: Free Press, 1991.

O'Brien, Cyril J. *Liberation: Marines in the Recapture of Guam.* Collingdale, Pa.: DIANE Publishing, 1994.

Owen, Joseph R. *Colder Than Hell: A Marine Rifle Company at Chosin Reservoir.* Annapolis, Md.: Naval Institute Press, 1996.

Pisor, Robert. *The End of the Line: The Siege of Khe Sanh.* New York: Norton, 2002.

Schmidt, Hans. *Maverick Marine: General Smedley D. Butler and the Contradictions of American Military History.* Lexington: University Press of Kentucky, 1998.

Soderbergh, Peter A. *Women Marines: The World War II Era.* New York: Praeger, 1992.

Thomas, Lowell J. *Old Gimlet Eye: The Adventures of Smedley D. Butler.* New York: Farrar & Rinehart, 1933.

Tomajczyk, S. F. *Dictionary of the Modern United States Military.* Jefferson, N.C., and London: McFarland, 1996.

Turner Publishing Company Staff. *History of the Defenders of the Philippines, Guam and Wake Islands 1941–1945.* Paducah, Ky.: Turner Publishing Company, 1991.

Walsh, John E. *The Philippine Insurrection, 1899–1902: America's Only Try for an Overseas Empire.* New York: Franklin Watts, 1973.

Wright, Derek. *Tarawa 1943.* London: Osprey, 2001.

WEAPONS AND HARDWARE

AIRCRAFT, FIXED-WING

Aviation Enthusiast Corner. Available online: URL: http://www.aero-web.org.

The Aviation History Online Museum. Available online: URL: http://www.aviation-history.com

Bowers, Peter M. *Curtiss Aircraft, 1907–1947.* Annapolis, Md.: Naval Institute Press, 1979.

Glines, Carroll V. *The Amazing Gooney Bird: The Saga of the Legendary DC-3/C-47.* Atglen, Pa.: Schiffer Publishing, 2000.

Hukee, Byron E. *The A-1 Skyraider Combat Journal.* Available online: URL: http://skyraider.org/hook/index.htm

Naval Historical Center. "U.S. Navy Aircraft, 1922–1962 Designation System." Available online: URL: http://www.history.navy.mil/photos/ac-usn22/ac-usn22.htm

Redding, Robert, and Bill Yenne. *Boeing: Planemaker to the World.* San Diego, Calif.: Thunder Bay Press, 1997.

Squadron 235 web site. "The F8U-Crusader." Available online: URL: http://www.vmf235.com/crusader.html

Tillman, Barrett. *The Dauntless Dive Bomber of World War Two.* Annapolis, Md.: Naval Institute Press, 1976.

U.S. Air Force Museum. "Northrop P-61C 'Black Widow.'" Available online: URL: http://www.wpafb.af.mil/museum/air_power/ap25.htm

U.S. Marine Corps. "Aircraft, Fixed Wing." Available online: URL: http://www.hqmc.usmc.mil/factfile.nsf/AVE?OpenView&Start=1&Count=1000&Expand=1#1

Warbird Alley. Information on various historical aircraft. Available online: URL: http://www.warbirdalley.com/index.htm

AIRCRAFT, ROTARY-WING

Aviation Enthusiast Corner. Information on various historical and current aircraft. Available online: URL: http://www.aero-web.org

Bell Helicopter-Textron. "AH-lJ SeaCobra." Available online: URL: http://www.paxmuseum.com/ah1/AH1.htm

FAS Military Analysis Network. "V-22 Osprey." Available online: URL: http://www.fas.org/man/dod-101/sys/ac/v-22.htm

GlobalSecurity.Org. "VH-60 Marine-1." Available online: URL: http://www.globalsecurity.org/military/systems/aircraft/vh-60.htm

The Rotorhead. "HH-1H Iroquois." Available online: URL: http://www.rotorhead.org/military/usiroquois.asp

U.S. Marine Corps. "USMC Fact File: CH-53E Super Stallion Helicopter." Available online: URL: http://www.hqmc.usmc.mil/factfile.nsf/7e931335d515626a85525628100676e0c/8a583a9bef2c6f8d8525626e0048f5fc

U.S. Marine Corps. "USMC Fact File: Tactical Bulk Fuel Delivery System, CH-53E (TBFDS, CH-53E)." Available online: URL: http//:www.hqmc.usmc.mil/factfile.nsf/7e931335d515626a852562

8100676e0c/1ce24aa4f7e1ad7485256289005a0d
d8?OpenDocument

U.S. Navy. "Fact File: CH-46D/E Sea Knight." Available online: URL: http://www.chinfo.navy.mil/navpalib/factfile/aircraft/air-ch46.html

U.S. Navy. "Fact File: CH-53D Sea Stallion." Available online: URL: http://www.chinfo.navy.mil/navpalib/factfile/aircraft/air-ch53d.html

U.S. Navy. "Fact File: VH-3D Sea King." Available online: URL: http://www.chinfo.navy.mil/navpalib/factfile/aircraft/air-vh3d.html

AIR DEFENSE ARTILLERY

FAS Military Analysis Network. "FIM-92A Stinger Weapons System: RMP & Basic." Available online: URL: http//:www.fas.org/man/dod-101/sys/land/stinger.htm

FAS Military Analysis Network. "HAWK: FAS Special Weapons Monitor." Available online: URL: http://www.fas.org/spp/starwars/program/hawk.htm

U.S. Army. "Avenger Low-Level Air Defense System, USA." Available online: URL: http://www.army-technology.com/projects/avenger/

U.S. Marine Corps. "USMC Factfile: Stinger Weapons System: RMP and Basic." Available online: URL: http://www.hqmc.usmc.mil/factfile.nsf/7e93133 5d515626a8525628100676e0c/526d081005e561f 58525626e00495937?OpenDocument

AIR-LAUNCHED WEAPONS

FAS Military Analysis Network. "AGM 114." Available online: URL: http://www.fas.org/man/dod-101/sys/missile/agm-114.htm

FAS Military Analysis Network. "AGM 122." Available online: URL: http://www.fas.org/man/dod-101/sys/missile/agm-122.htm

FAS Military Analysis Network. "AGM 123." Available online: URL: http://www.fas.org/man/dod-101/sys/smart/agm-123.htm

U.S. Air Force. "USAF Fact Sheet: AIM-7 Sparrow." Available online: URL: http://www.af.mil/factsheets/factsheet.asp?fsID=77

U.S. Marine Corps. "USMC Factfile: AGM-65E Maverick Missile." Available online: URL: www.hqmc.usmc.mil/factfile.nsf/7e931335d515626a8 525628100676e0c/65173baa6a6abb6d852 5626d00776f15?OpenDocument

U.S. Marine Corps. "USMC Factfile: AIM-9 Sidewinder Missile." Available online: URL: www.hqmc.usmc.mil/factfile.nsf/7e931335d515626a8 525628100676e0c/75b0842883e0798f852 5626e0048ad88?OpenDocument

U.S. Marine Corps. "USMC Factfile: AGM-45 Shrike." Available online: URL: www.hqmc.usmc.mil/factfile.nsf/7e931335d515626a8525628100676e0 c/fdce85522304f1328525626d00774d9d?OpenDocument

AMPHIBIOUS VEHICLES

Friedman, Norman. *U.S. Amphibious Ships and Craft: An Illustrated Design History.* Annapolis, Md.: Naval Institute Press, 2002.

Kutta, Tim. *DUKW in Action.* Carrollton, Tex.: Squadron/Signal Publications, 1997.

U.S. Marine Corps. "Refurbished Amtrack Makes Debut at AAS Battalion," in *Marine Corps News* (July 17, 1999), www.fas.org/man/dod-101/sys/land/docs/990717-aav7.htm

U.S. Marine Corps. "USMC Factfile: Assault Amphibian Vehicle Command Model 7A1 (AAVC7A1)." Available online: URL: www.hqmc.usmc.mil/factfile.nsf/7e931335d515626a8525628100676e0 c/523659798f90c04f852562cf00555fb5?OpenDocument

U.S. Marine Corps. "USMC Factfile: Assault Amphibian Vehicle Recovery Model 7A1 (AAVR7A1)." Available online: URL: www.hqmc.usmc.mil/factfile.nsf/7e931335d515626a8525628100676e0 c/faeb17a7dedc9541852562cf005117b4?OpenDocument

U.S. Marine Corps. "USMC Factfile: Light Armored Vehicle-Recovery (LAV-R)." Available online: URL: www.hqmc.usmc.mil/factfile.nsf/7e931335 d515626a8525628100676e0c/1cd7d76d126168ca 852 562830059f59f?OpenDocument

U.S. Marine Corps. "USMC Factfile: Light Armored Vehicle-Command and Control (LAV-C2)." Available online: URL: www.hqmc.usmc.mil/factfile.nsf/7e931335d515626a8525628100676e0 c/e84e5e3ba0614f318525628300594bda?OpenDocument

U.S. Marine Corps. "USMC Factfile: Light Armored Vehicle-Logistics (LAV-L)." Available online: URL: http://www.hqmc.usmc.mil/factfile.nsf/

7e931335d515626a8525628100676e0c/e40973a9
5e34cc1 58525628300589234?OpenDocument

U.S. Marine Corps. "USMC Factfile: Light Armored Vehicle-Mortar (LAV-M)." Available online: URL: www.hqmc.usmc.mil/factfile.nsf/7e93133 5d515626a8525628100676e0c/d988382d9ecb3ff d8525 62830059c0e0?OpenDocument

Zaloga, Steven. *Amtracs: U.S. Amphibious Assault Vehicles.* London: Osprey, 1999.

ANTIARMOR WEAPONS

Chamberlain, Peter. *Anti-Tank Weapons.* New York: Arco, 1975.

FAS Military Analysis Network. "M-47 DRAGON Anti-Tank Guided Missile." Available online: URL: www.fas.org/man/dod-101/sys/land/m47-dragon.htm

Redstone Arsenal. "TOW." Available online: URL: www.redstone.army.mil/history/systems/TOW.html

U.S. Army. "Javelin Anti-Armour Missile, USA." Available online: URL: http://www.armytechnology.com/projects/javelin/

U.S. Marine Corps. "USMC Factfile: AT-4 Light Antiarmor Weapon." Available online: URL: www.hqmc.usmc.mil/factfile.nsf/7e931335d515626a8 525628100676e0c/5fa1f5a45c4e0ebe8525627a00 7227ef?OpenDocument

U.S. Marine Corps. "USMC Factfile: Dragon Weapon System." Available online: URL: www.hqmc.usmc.mil/factfile.nsf/7e931335d515626a852562 8100676e0c/8d198eb6ac07b33b8525627b00567 d5e?OpenDocument

U.S. Marine Corps. "USMC Factfile: Saboted Light Armor Penetrator (SLAP) Ammunition." Available online: URL: www.hqmc.usmc.mil/factfile.nsf/ 7e931335d515626a8525628100676e0c/63aadbd3f 593b0378525628100774353?Open Document

U.S. Marine Corps. "USMC Factfile: Tube Launched, Optically Tracked, Wire Guided (TOW) Missile Weapon System." Available online: URL: www.hqmc.usmc.mil/factfile.nsf/7e931335d515626a8 525628100676e0c/4ba8f1e3958ca16d852 5628100789abb?OpenDocument

COMMUNICATIONS EQUIPMENT

U.S. Marine Corps. "USMC Factfile: AN/TTC-42 (V) Automatic Telephone Central Office." Available online: URL: http://www.hqmc.usmc.mil/factfile.

nsf/7e931335d515626a8525628100676e0c/ d195194b9ab01fbb8525626e0048bc24?Open Document

U.S. Marine Corps. "USMC Factfile: SB-3865 Automatic Telephone Switchboard." Available online: URL: www.hqmc.usmc.mil/factfile.nsf/7e931335 d515626a8525628100676e0c/cd1ea3ce7b847efc8 525 626e00494c2c?OpenDocument

U.S. Marine Corps. "USMC Factfile: Single Channel Ground and Airborne Radio System (SINCGARS)." Available online: URL: www.hqmc. usmc.mil/factfile.nsf/7e931335d515626a852562 8100676e0c/06c6b4fed8a1e97a8525627a0069a60 5?OpenDocument

DECORATIONS AND MEDALS

Aldebol, Anthony. *Army Air Force and United States Air Force: Decorations, Medals, Ribbons, Badges and Insignia.* Fountain Inn, S.C.: Medals of America Press, 1999.

Emering, Edward J. *U.S. Navy and Marine Corps Campaign and Commemorative Medals.* Atglen, Pa.: Schiffer, 1998.

Foster, Frank C. *The Decorations, Medals, Ribbons, Badges and Insignia of the United States Army: World War II to Present.* Fountain Inn, S.C.: Medals of America Press, 2000.

Thompson, James. *Decorations, Medals, Ribbons, Badges and Insignia of the United States Marine Corps: World War II to Present.* Fountain Inn, S.C.: Medals of America Press, 1998.

INDIRECT FIRE SYSTEMS

Hogg, Ian V. *British and American Artillery of World War II.* London: Greenhill Books, 2002.

Raytheon, Inc. "Advanced Field Artillery Tactical Data System." Available online: URL: www.raytheon.com/c3i/c3iproducts/c3i060/c3i060.htm

U.S. Marine Corps. "USMC Factfile: AN/TPQ-36 Firefinder Radar." Available online: URL: www.hqmc.usmc.mil/factfile.nsf/7e931335d515626a8 525628100676e0c/9904f05d636d7a91852 5627a006fd82b?OpenDocument

"USMC Factfile: AN/USQ-70 Position Azimuth Determining System." Available online: URL: www.hqmc.usmc.mil/factfile.nsf/7e931335d515 626a8525628100676e0c/19487d2e7e24303a8525 627a0071af0a?OpenDocument

U.S. Marine Corps. "USMC Factfile: M49 Telescope." Available online: URL: www.hqmc.usmc.mil/factfile.nsf/7e931335d515626a852562810067 6e0c/095a68c9bdaa831c8525627b006d56b4? OpenDocument

U.S. Marine Corps. "USMC Factfile: M101A1 105mm Light Howitzer, Towed." Available online: URL: www.hqmc.usmc.mil/factfile.nsf/7e931335d515 626a8525628100676e0c/58188e8bf0819ae4852 5627b006250dc?OpenDocument

U.S. Marine Corps. "USMC Factfile: M198 155mm Medium Howitzer, Towed." Available online: URL: www.hqmc.usmc.mil/factfile.nsf/7e931335 d515626a8525628100676e0c/d9d52bbe851eee6c 852 5627b006595b2?OpenDocument

U.S. Marine Corps. "USMC Factfile: M224 60mm Lightweight Mortar." Available online: URL: www.hqmc.usmc.mil/factfile.nsf/7e931335d515 626a8525628100676e0c/a072707cfe330d3b852 5627b006b6e36?OpenDocument

U.S. Marine Corps. "USMC Factfile: M252 81mm Medium Extended Range Mortar." Available online: URL: www.hqmc.usmc.mil/factfile.nsf/ 7e931335d515626a8525628100676e0c/969a278b 663f5cbc852 5627b006c5d03?OpenDocument

U.S. Marine Corps. "USMC Factfile: M94 Muzzle Velocity System (MVS)." Available online: URL: www.hqmc.usmc.mil/factfile.nsf/7e931335d515 626a8525628100676e0c/d681328f75b18de9852 5627b0077e113?OpenDocument

U.S. Marine Corps. "USMC Factfile: M90 Radar Chronograph." Available online: URL: www. hqmc.usmc.mil/factfile.nsf/7e931335d515626a8 525628100676e0c/b25ec569febe8ee58525 627b007685de?OpenDocument

LANDING CRAFT

U.S. Marine Corps. "U.S. Marine Corps Factfile: Riverine Assault Craft (RAC)." Available online: URL: www.hqmc.usmc.mil/factfile.nsf/7e931335 d515626a8525628100676e0c/d4cbb0016e10fe5e 852 562810074c922?OpenDocument

Alaska Hovercraft, Inc. "LACV-30." Available online: URL: http://www.ahv.lynden.com/ahv/lacv-30. html

FAS Military Analysis Network. "Landing Craft, Air Cushion (LCAC)." Available online: URL: www. fas.org/man/dod-101/sys/ship/lcac.htm

Friedman, Norman. *U.S. Amphibious Ships and Craft: An Illustrated Design History.* Annapolis, Md.: Naval Institute Press, 2002.

PERSONAL AND MISCELLANEOUS EQUIPMENT

U.S. Marine Corps. "USMC Factfile: AN/PSN-11 Precision Lightweight GPS Receiver (PLGR)." Available online: URL: www.hqmc.usmc.mil/factfile. nsf/7e931335d515626a8525628100676e0c/7c932 96961c94c378525627a006b173a?OpenDocument

U.S. Marine Corps. "USMC Factfile: AN/PSS-12 Metallic Mine Detector." Available online: URL: www.hqmc.usmc.mil/factfile.nsf/7e931335d515 626a8525628100676e0c/3bf67a6e2a110538525 62830054d19c?OpenDocument

U.S. Marine Corps. "USMC Factfile: Diver Propulsion Device (DPD)." Available online: URL: www. hqmc.usmc.mil/factfile.nsf/7e931335d515626a8 525628100676e0c/e35f778d99c25556852 5627b0052bf09?OpenDocument

U.S. Marine Corps. "USMC Factfile: Extreme Cold Weather Tent (ECWT)." Available online: URL: www.hqmc.usmc.mil/factfile.nsf/7e931335d515 626a8525628100676e0c/c7ee72d573aa709f852 5627a006751f5?OpenDocument

U.S. Marine Corps. "USMC Factfile: Field Pack, Large, with Internal Frame (FPLIF)." Available online: URL: www.hqmc.usmc.mil/factfile.nsf/7e931335 d515626a8525628100676e0c/1745728ff3abbd33 852 5627a00634955?OpenDocument

U.S. Marine Corps. "USMC Factfile: Improved ECWCS Fiberpile Shirt and Trousers." Available online: URL: www.hqmc.usmc.mil/factfile.nsf/ 7e931335d515626a8525628100676e0c/7dc31a7b b22666af852 5627a00647730?OpenDocument

U.S. Marine Corps. "USMC Factfile: Individual Tactical Load Bearing Vest (ITLBV)." Available online: URL: www.hqmc.usmc.mil/factfile.nsf/7e931335 d515626a8525628100676e0c/1ca315bbf3c1d761 852 5627a0068fd32?OpenDocument

U.S. Marine Corps. "USMC Factfile: Infantry Shelter." Available online: URL: www.hqmc.usmc. mil/factfile.nsf/7e931335d515626a85256281006 76e0c/7235b654d0c2e0b88525627a005e4599? OpenDocument

U.S. Marine Corps. "USMC Factfile: MC-5 Static Line/Free-Fall Ram Air Parachute System (SL/FF RAPS)." Available online: URL: www.hqmc.

usmc.mil/factfile.nsf/7e931335d515626a852562
8100676e0c/2b633bc0dcbcc88d852
5627c0064d965?OpenDocument

U.S. Marine Corps. "USMC Factfile: Modular Sleeping Bag (MSB)." Available online: URL: www.
hqmc.usmc.mil/factfile.nsf/7e931335d515626a8
525628100676e0c/3b45959ec48b4327852
5627a0058c062?OpenDocument

U.S. Marine Corps. "USMC Factfile: Oxygen Transfer
Pump System." Available online: URL: www.
hqmc.usmc.mil/factfile.nsf/7e931335d515626a8
525628100676e0c/f33ae91af995b0018525
6281005bede9?OpenDocument

TRACKED VEHICLES

U.S. Marine Corps. "USMC Factfile: M1A1 Main Battle Tank." Available online: URL: www.hqmc.
usmc.mil/factfile.nsf/7e931335d515626a852562
8100676e0c/9e6cdb7ba648f1388525627b0065de
66?OpenDocument

U.S. Marine Corps. "USMC Factfile: M1 Mine Clearing Blade System." Available online: URL: www.
hqmc.usmc.mil/factfile.nsf/7e931335d515626a8
525628100676e0c/84c7f670fca3dc0e8525627b00
61fa5d?OpenDocument

U.S. Marine Corps. "USMC Factfile: M-9 Armored
Combat Earthmover (ACE)." Available online:
URL: www.hqmc.usmc.mil/factfile.nsf/7e931335
d515626a8525628100676e0c/5dda17f09fae8b18
8525 6289005a2c7c?OpenDocument

U.S. Marine Corps. "USMC Factfile: M60A1 Armored
Vehicle Launched Bridge (M60A1 AVLB)." Available online: URL: www.hqmc.usmc.mil/fact-
file.nsf/7e931335d515626a8525628100676e0c/
ecc79c2c4fee4df08525627b006d8c75?Open
Document

U.S. Marine Corps. "USMC Factfile: Mobile/Unit Conduct of Fire Trainer (M/U-COFT)." Available
online: URL: www.hqmc.usmc.mil/factfile.nsf/
7e931335d515626a8525628100676e0c/f826275c0
6a5a228525 6281005b79ae?OpenDoc ument

WEAPONS, INDIVIDUAL AND CREW-SERVED

FAS Military Analysis Network. "Browning Automatic
Rifle (BAR)." Available online: URL: www.fas.
org/man/dod-101/sys/land/m1918.htm

FAS Military Analysis Network. "Machine Gun, Cal.
.30, M1919A4/M1919A6." Available online: URL:

www.fas.org/man/dod-101/sys/land/m1919.
htm

FAS Military Analysis Network. "Machine Gun, Cal.
.30, M1941, Johnson." Available online: URL:
www.fas.org/man/dod-101/sys/land/m1941.htm

FAS Military Analysis Network. "M82A1A .50 Caliber
Special Application Scoped Rifle." Available online: URL: www.fas.org/man/dod-101/sys/land/
m82.htm

FAS Military Analysis Network. "Submachine Gun,
Cal. .45, M1928A1, Thompson Submachine
Gun, Cal. .45, M1/M1A1 Thompson." Available
online: URL: www.fas.org/man/dod-101/sys/
land/m1928.htm

Global Security.Org. "M60 7.62mm Machine Gun."
Available online: URL: www.globalsecurity.org/
military/systems/ground/m60e3.htm

Kortegaard Engineering. "M1917A1 .30 Caliber Water-
Cooled Machine Gun." Available online: URL:
www.rt66.com/~korteng/SmallArms/30calhv.htm

Long, Duncan. *Complete AR-15/M16 Sourcebook:
What Every Shooter Needs to Know.* Boulder,
Colo.: Paladin Press, 2002.

U.S. Marine Corps. "USMC Factfile: M1911A1 .45
Caliber Pistol." Available online: URL: www.
hqmc.usmc.mil/factfile.nsf/7e931335d515626a8
525628100676e0c/7322d78f08368e19852
5627b00654175?OpenDocument

U.S. Marine Corps. "USMC Factfile: AN/TVS-5 Crew
Served Weapon Night Sight." Available online:
URL: www.hqmc.usmc.mil/factfile.nsf/7e931335
d515626a8525628100676e0c/5d5f801a85a1bc68
525 627a0070e5a0?OpenDocument

U.S. Marine Corps. "USMC Factfile: M203 40mm
Grenade Launcher." Available online: URL:
www.hqmc.usmc.mil/factfile.nsf/7e931335d515
626a8525628100676e0c/d50a120f00de543d852
5627b006b1fec?OpenDocument

U.S. Marine Corps. "USMC Factfile: AN/PAQ-3 Modular Universal Laser Equipment (MULE)." Available online: URL:www.hqmc.usmc.mil/factfile.
nsf/7e931335d515626a8525628100676e0c/3e647
6bafdce8a068525627a006c7d23?OpenDocument

U.S. Marine Corps. "USMC Factfile: Joint Service
Combat Shotgun." Available online: URL: www.
hqmc.usmc.mil/factfile.nsf/7e931335d515626a8
525628100676e0c/5ee9a6e9c96be5658525627b0
060500c?OpenDocument

U.S. Marine Corps. "USMC Factfile: M14 7.62mm Rifle." Available online: URL: www.hqmc.usmc.mil/factfile.nsf/7e931335d515626a85256281006 76e0c/6563e355ce34af538525627b0062a577? OpenDocument

U.S. Marine Corps. "USMC Factfile: AN/PVS-7B Night Vision Goggles (NVG)." Available online: URL: www.hqmc.usmc.mil/factfile.nsf/7e931335 d515626a8525628100676e0c/dd0d434bc4d6f3c8 525 627a006de64a?OpenDocument

U.S. Marine Corps. "USMC Factfile: AN/PVS-5 Night Vision Goggles (NVG)." Available online: URL: www.hqmc.usmc.mil/factfile.nsf/7e931335d515 626a8525628100676e0c/94d7168bba349f00852 5627a006d9c30?OpenDocument

U.S. Marine Corps. "USMC Factfile: AN/PVS-4 Individual Weapon Night Sight." Available online: URL: www.hqmc.usmc.mil/factfile.nsf/ 0/28a82b359e9bf7858525627a006d6992?Open Document

U.S. Marine Corps. "USMC Factfile: AN/PAQ-4A/4C Infrared Aiming Light." Available online: URL: www.hqmc.usmc.mil/factfile.nsf/7e931335d515 626a8525628100676e0c/2ae6b3135944b7bc852 5627a006d06da?OpenDocument

U.S. Marine Corps. "USMC Factfile: Laser Rangefinder AN/GVS-5." Available online: URL: www.hqmc.usmc.mil/factfile.nsf/7e931335d515626a8 525628100676e0c/1c2a810cbff00ef68525627b00 610852?OpenDocument

U.S. Marine Corps. "USMC Factfile: MK19 40mm Machine Gun, MOD 3." Available online: URL: www.hqmc.usmc.mil/factfile.nsf/7e931335d515 626a8525628100676e0c/9867a7c6f72a0ad0852 5627c006cb4ef?OpenDocument

U.S. Marine Corps. "USMC Factfile: MEU (SOC) Pistol." Available online: URL: www.hqmc.usmc.mil/ factfile.nsf/7e931335d515626a8525628100676e 0c/d6a3fc7de02523fe8525627c006c5814?Open Document

U.S. Marine Corps. "USMC Factfile: MP-5N Heckler and Koch 9mm Submachine Gun." Available online: URL: www.hqmc.usmc.mil/factfile.nsf/ 7e931335d515626a8525628100676e0c/20324744 eaf1aba3852 56281005b3593?OpenDocument

U.S. Marine Corps. "USMC Factfile: Revolver, .38 Caliber." Available online: URL: www.hqmc.usmc. mil/factfile.nsf/7e931335d515626a85256281006

76e0c/1b3878907cb0168b852562810073ceb0? OpenDocument

U.S. Marine Corps. "USMC Factfile: Shoulder-Launched Multipurpose Assault Weapon (SMAW)." Available online: URL: www.hqmc. usmc.mil/factfile.nsf/7e931335d515626a852562 8100676e0c/57c7ea3d1a309a1d8525628100779b 0c?OpenDocument

U.S. Marine Corps. "USMC Factfile: 12-Gauge Shotgun." Available online: URL: www.hqmc. usmc.mil/factfile.nsf/7e931335d515626a852562 8100676e0c/047150249be0bf6c8525627a006c3e 30?OpenDocument

WHEELED VEHICLES

U.S. Marine Corps. "USMC Factfile: KLR 250-D8 Marine Corps Motorcycle." Available online: URL: http://usmilitary.about.com/library/milinfo/mar inefacts/blmotorcycle.htm

U.S. Marine Corps. "USMC Factfile: MK48-14 and Container Transporter Rear Body Unit." Available online: URL: http://usmilitary.about.com/ library/milinfo/marinefacts/blmk48-14.htm

U.S. Marine Corps. "USMC Factfile: MK48 Power Unit and MK15, Recovery/Wrecker Rear Body Unit." Available online: URL: http://usmilitary. about.com/library/milinfo/marinefacts/blmk 48-15.htm

U.S. Marine Corps. "USMC Factfile: "MK48 Power Unit and MK16, Fifth-Wheel Semi-trailer Adapter Rear Body Unit." Available online: URL: http://usmilitary.about.com/library/milinfo/mar inefacts/blmk48-16.htm

U.S. Marine Corps. "USMC Factfile: MK155 Mine Clearance Launcher." Available online: URL: www.hqmc.usmc.mil/factfile.nsf/7e931335d515 626a8525628100676e0c/6b234caa30de31c1852 5627a004df31a?OpenDocument

U.S. Marine Corps. "USMC Factfile: MK48 Power Unit and MK18 Self-loading Container and Ribbon Bridge Transporter." Available online: URL: www.usmilitary.about.com/library/milinfo/ marinefacts/blmk48-18.htm

MISCELLANEOUS

United States Marine Corps History and Museums Division. "Lieutenant Colonel William Ward Burrows, USMC (Deceased)." Available online: URL:

http://hqinet001.hqmc.usmc.mil/HD/Historical/Whos_Who/Burrows_WW.htm

U.S. Marine Corps. "U.S. Marine Corps Factfile: Close Quarters Battle/Direct Action Program." Available online: URL: www.hqmc.usmc.mil/factfile.nsf/7e931335d515626a8525628100676e0c/d33e604ca949c175852 5627a00726280?OpenDocument

U.S. Marine Corps. "Marine Corps Combat Service Support Schools." Available online: URL: www.lejeune.usmc.mil/mccsss/schools.htm

United States Marine Corps. History and Museums Division. "General Robert E. Cushman, Jr., USMC (Deceased)." Available online: URL: http://hqinet001.hqmc.usmc.mil/HD/Historical/Whos_Who/Cushman_RE.htm

United States Marine Corps. History and Museums Division. "Sergeant Major Daniel ('Dan') Daly, USMC (Deceased)." Available online: URL: http://hqinet001.hqmc.usmc.mil/HD/Historical/Whos_Who/Daly_DJ.htm

U.S. Marine Corps. "U.S. Marine Corps Factfile: Diver Propulsion Device (DPD)." Available online: URL: www.hqmc.usmc.mil/factfile.nsf/7e931335d515626a8525628100676e0c/e35f778d99c2555852 5627b0052bf09?OpenDocument

United States Marine Corps. History and Museums Division, "General Wallace M. Greene, Jr., USMC (Deceased)." Available online: URL: http://hqinet001.hqmc.usmc.mil/HD/Historical/Whos_Who/Greene_WM.htm

U.S. Marine Corps. "United States Marine Corps (Ret.) Lieutenant General Victor H. Krulak." Available online: URL: www.usmc.mil/genbios2.nsf/0/e504ddb58bac48d685256a4000718813

U.S. Marine Corps. "Marine Aviation Weapons and Tactics Squadron One." Available online: URL: www.tecom.usmc.mil/mawts1/

U.S. Marine Corps. "U.S. Marine Corps Factfile: Marine Corps Combat Identification Program (MCBIP)." Available online: URL: www.hqmc.usmc.mil/factfile.nsf/7e931335d515626a85256288100676e0c/5d819ccea84e560d8525627c006861d8?OpenDocument

U.S. Marine Corps. "U.S. Marine Corps Factfile: Tactical Petroleum Laboratory, Medium (TPLM)." Available online: URL: www.hqmc.usmc.mil/factfile.nsf/7e931335d515626a8525628100676e0c/4f9646f0cbc30af6852562830055e7fb?OpenDocument

U.S. Marine Corps. "U.S. Marine Band." Available online: URL: www.marineband.usmc.mil/

U.S. Marine Corps. "Mountain Warfare Training Center." Available online: URL: www.mwtc.usmc.mil/

Spec War Net. "United States Marine Corps Reconnaissance Battalions." Available online: URL: www.specwarnet.com/americas/recon.htm

Index

Page numbers in **boldface** indicate primary discussions. Page numbers in *italic* indicate illustrations.

A

A-3 Falcon 3
A-4 Skyhawk 3–4, *4*
A-6 Intruder 4
A-12 Avenger 4
A-25/SB2C Helldiver 4
AAVC-7A1 Assault Amphibian
    Vehicle Command Model
    7A1 18
AAVP-7 19–20
AAVR-7A1 Assault Amphibian
    Vehicle Recovery Model
    7A1 18–19
abolitionism 67
ACE (M-9 Armored Combat
    Earthmover) 147
acronyms 180–181
Act of July 11, 1798 **1**
Act of June 30, 1834 **1–2**
AD-1 through AD-7 Skyraider
    4–5
Adams, John 37, 48, 152
Advanced Field Artillery
    Tactical Data System 76
advanced guard **2**
advanced party **2**
AEF. *See* American
    Expeditionary Force
Afghanistan 28, 64, 74
African Americans in the
    USMC **2**, **2–3**
AGM-45 Shrike 16
AGM-65E Maverick Missile 16
AGM-114 Hellfire *16*, 16–17
AGM-122 Sidearm 17
AGM-123 Skipper II 17
Aguinaldo, Emilio 126
AH-1G Huey Cobra 11
AH-1J SeaCobra 11
aiguillette **3**
AIM-7 Sparrow 17
AIM-9 Sidewinder Missile 17
aircraft, fixed-wing **3–11**, *4*, *9*,
    10

aircraft, rotary wing *11*,
    11–14, *12*, *16*, *70*. *See also*
    specific aircraft
air-cushion vehicles 90
air defense artillery **14–15**
    Avenger 14–15
    FIM-92A Stinger 15
    HAWK 15
    Stinger Weapons System:
        RMP and Basic 15
air-launched weapons *16*,
    16–17
    AGM-45 Shrike 16
    AGM-65E Maverick
        Missile 16
    AGM-114 Hellfire *16*,
        16–17
    AGM-122 Sidearm 17
    AGM-123 Skipper II 17
    AIM-7 Sparrow 17
    AIM-9 Sidewinder
        Missile 17
Air War College (AWC) 86
Alliant Techsystems 23
American Expeditionary Force
    (AEF) 135, 174
American Revolution **17–18**
    William Ward Burrows
        37
    history of USMC 70
    Samuel Nicholas 110
    Penobscot Bay Fiasco
        119–120
    uniforms 150
amphibious assault **18**
    beachhead 33
    history of USMC 72
    Quasi War 152
amphibious operation **18**, 72
amphibious vehicles **18–22**, *19*
amphibious warfare 92–93
amphibious warfare ships **22**
AN/PAQ-3 Modular Universal
    Laser Equipment (MULE)
    162

AN/PAQ-4A/4C Infrared
    Aiming Light 162–163
AN/PSN-11 Precision
    Lightweight GPS Receiver
    (PLGR) 121
AN/PSS-12 Metallic Mine
    Detector 121
AN/PVS-4 Individual Weapon
    Night Sight 163
AN/PVS-5 Night Vision
    Goggles 163
AN/PVS-7B Night Vision
    Goggle (NVG) 163–164
Anthony, William 71
antiarmor weapons *23*, **23–25**,
    26
AN/TPQ-36 Firefinder Radar
    76–77
AN/TTC-42 (V) Automatic
    Telephone Central Office
    46
AN/TVS-5 Crew Served
    Weapon Night Sight 164
AN/USQ-70 Position Azimuth
    Determining System 77
Argonne 40
Aristide, Jean-Bertrand 67
Arlington, Virginia 83
Army of the Republic of Viet
    Nam (ARVN) 75, 158–160
ARVN. *See* Army of the
    Republic of Viet Nam
astronaut 60, 61
AT-4 Light Anti-armor
    Weapon 23
Austin, Hudson 62
AV-8B Harrier II 5
Avenger 14–15
aviation 71
AWC (Air War College) 86

B

B-29 Superfortress
    Guam 64
    Iwo Jima 81

Okinawa 115
Saipan 135
Tinian 145
World War II 177
Bahamas 17, 48, 110
Baille, HMS 48
Barbary pirates **27**
    William Ward Burrows
        37
    history of USMC 70
    Presley O'Bannon 114
    Franklin Wharton 171
BAR (M-1918 Browning
    Automatic Rifle) 167
Barnett, George **27**
bases, camps, and other
    installations **27–32**
basic training *32*, **32–33**
    drill instructor 53
    Marine Corps Recruit
        Depot Parris Island
        32
    Navajo code talkers
        107
    U.S. Marine Drum and
        Bugle Corps 155
Basilone, John **33**
battalion 116
beachhead **33**
Bear Flag Rebellion 156
Beechcraft 10
Beirut USMC headquarters
    bombing 73, 93
Belleau Wood **33–34**
    Clifton B. Cates 41
    Château-Thierry 42
    Daniel Daly 50, *51*
    history of USMC 71
    Wendell C. Neville 108
    Lemuel C. Shepherd 137
    World War I 174
Bell Helicopter 11, 14
bellhop **34**
Betio Island 60

Biddle, William P. 27, **34**
bin Laden, Osama 74
biological warfare. *See* nuclear-
    biological-chemical
    equipment
Bishop, Maurice 62
"Black Sheep" Squadron 36
Bladensburg, Battle of **34**
    history of USMC 70
    War of 1812 161
    Franklin Wharton
        171–172
Block, Harlon H. *82,* 83
Bock's Car 145, 177
Boeing 5, 8, 14
Bonhomme Richard 48
Boomer, Walter E. *34,* **34–35**
boot camp 32
Bosnia-Herzegovina 73, 85,
    174
Bougainville, Battle of **35**
    Choiseul Raid 43
    Robert E. Cushman, Jr.
        49
    Solomon Islands cam-
        paign 140
    Alexander Vandergrift
        157
    Louis H. Wilson, Jr.
        173
    World War II 177
Boxer Rebellion **35–36,** *36*
    William P. Biddle 34
    Smedley D. Butler 38
    Daniel Daly 50
    Ben H. Fuller 57
    history of USMC 71
    Wendell C. Neville 108
    Philippine Insurrection
        126
Boyington, Gregory "Pappy"
    36, *37*
Bradley, John H. *82,* 83
Brewster Aeronautical 6
brig **36**
brigade 116
brigadier general (rank and
    grade) 131
British Royal Marines 66, 86,
    145
Brown, John 67, 68, 71
Buckner, Simon B. 60, 178
Bull Run, First Battle of 71,
    179
Burrows, William Ward **37**
Bush, George H. W. *103,* 118,
    120
Butler, Smedley D. **37–39,** *38,*
    50

C

C-12 Huron 5
C-47 Skytrain. *See* R4D
    Skytrain

Cacos 66–67
California 156
Cambodia 98, 104
camp **40**
"Camp X-Ray" 64
CAP (Civil Air Patrol) 143
captain (rank and grade) 132
Caribbean Sea 136, 152
Carlson, Evans F. *40,* **40–41,**
    96
Carmick, Daniel 109
Carranza, Venustiano 93
Carson, Kit 179
Carter, Jimmy 81
CAS (close air support) 71
Castro, Fidel 64
Cates, Clifton B. **41**
Cavite 54, 71, 142
Central Intelligence Agency
    (CIA) 49, 158
Cessna 9
CH-37 11
CH-46 Sea Knight 11, *11*
CH-53D Sea Stallion 12
CH-53E Super Stallion 12, *70*
Chance Vaught 7
Chapman, Leonard F., Jr. **42**
Chapultepec, Battle of **42,** 104
Charleston, South Carolina
    179
Château-Thierry **42,** 50–51,
    137
Chemical Agent Monitor
    110–111
chemical warfare. *See* nuclear-
    biological-chemical
    equipment
chicken plate **42**
chief of naval operations
    (CNO) **43**
China
    George Barnett 27
    Boxer Rebellion 35–36
    Smedley D. Butler 38
    Evans F. Carlson 41
    Clifton B. Cates 41
    Chosin Reservoir, Battle
        of 43, 44
    Daniel Daly 50
    James P. S. Devereux 52
    Hagaru-ri 66
    Han River Forts, Battle of
        67
    Thomas Holcomb 74
    Horse Marines 74
    Korean War 87
    Randolph McCall Pate
        119
    Lewis B. Puller 128, 129
    Lemuel C. Shepherd 138
    David M. Shoup 138
    Oliver P. Smith 139
    Jacob Zeilin 179

Choiseul Raid **43,** 88
Chosin Reservoir, Battle of *43,*
    43–44
    Hagaru-ri 66
    history of USMC 72
    Oliver P. Smith 139
CIA. *See* Central Intelligence
    Agency
Cincinnati, USS 93
Civil Air Patrol (CAP) 143
Civil War
    John Harris 68
    Charles Heywood 69
    history of USMC 71
    Charles G. McCawley
        104
    Jacob Zeilin 179
Cixi. *See* Tzu Hsi (Chinese
    dowage empress)
Clinton, Bill 141
close air support (CAS) 71
Close Quarters Battle/Direct
    Action Program **44**
CNO (chief of naval
    operations) **43**
Coard, Bernard 62
code 107–108
cold war
    Guantánamo Bay 64
    history of USMC 72
    Korean War 87
    Vietnam War 158–160
colonel (rank and grade) 131
color sergeant of the U.S.
    Marine Corps **44**
Columbia, USS 57
Combat Rubber Raiding Craft
    92
Combat Service Support
    Schools (MCCSS) **45–46**
    Combat Water Survival
        Swimming School 45
    Financial Management
        School 45
    Instructional Management
        School 45
    Logistics Operations
        School 45
    Personnel Administration
        School 45
    Supply School 45–46
Combat Water Survival
    Swimming School 45
combined arms team **46**
commandant of the Marine
    Corps **46**
    Act of July 11, 1798 1
    George Barnett 27
    William P. Biddle 34
    William Ward Burrows
        37

Clifton B. Cates 41
Leonard F. Chapman, Jr.
    42
Robert E. Cushman, Jr.
    48–49
George F. Elliott 54
Ben H. Fuller 57
Anthony Gale 59
Alfred M. Gray, Jr. 61–62
Wallace Greene 62
John Harris 68
Archibald Henderson 69
Charles Heywood 69
Thomas Holcomb 74
HQMC 68
James L. Jones 84–85
Paul X. Kelley 86
Charles C. Krulak 88
John A. Lejeune 93, 94
Marine Barracks 28
Charles G. McCawley
    104–105
Carl E. Mundy, Jr.
    105–106
Wendell C. Neville 108
Samuel Nicholas 110
Randolph McCall Pate
    119
John H. Russell 134
Lemuel C. Shepherd
    137–138
David M. Shoup
    138–139
Alexander Vandergrift
    157
Franklin Wharton 171
Louis H. Wilson, Jr. 173,
    174
Jacob Zeilin 179
commando force 40
commissioned officers (rank
    and grade) 131–132
communications equipment
    46–47
communism
    Dominican Republic 52
    Guantánamo Bay 64
    history of USMC 72
    Korean War 87
company 116
company clerk **47**
Constitution, USS (Old
    Ironsides) 69, 152, 161
containment (cold war) 87,
    158
Continental army 48
Continental Congress
    American Revolution 17
    Continental Marines 47,
        48

history of USMC 70
Samuel Nicholas 110
Continental Marines **47–48**
American Revolution 17
history of USMC 70
Samuel Nicholas 110
Penobscot Bay Fiasco
120
uniforms 150
Continental navy 93
Coral Sea 176
corporal (rank and grade)
133
corps 117
corpsman **48**
Corregidor 176
coup d'état 67, 81
court-martial 59, 172
Creek Indians 137
"The Crucible" 33
Cuba
George Barnett 27
Smedley D. Butler 38
Guantánamo Bay 64
history of USMC 71
Spanish-American War
142
Cuban missile crisis 139
Cuban Rebellion **48**
Cumberland, USS 69
Cunningham, Alfred A. 28
Curtiss Aircraft 4, 7
Cushman, Robert E., Jr. **48–49**
Cuzco Well 71, 142
Cyprus 73

D

Daly, Daniel *50,* **50–51**
Da Nang 62, 72, 158–160
Daniels, Josephus 27
Dauntless bombers 5
Decatur, Stephen 27
decorations and medals **51**
Marine Corps
Expeditionary Medal
51
Marine Corps Reserve
Ribbon 51
Medal of Honor 51
demilitarized zone (DMZ)
159
Devereux, James P. S. **52**
"Devil Dogs" 34, 174
Dewey, George 71, 142
Diem, Ngo Dinh 158
Dien Bien Phu 158
Discovery (space shuttle) 61
Distinguished Flying Cross 61
Diver Propulsion Device
(DPD) 121

division 117
DMZ (demilitarized zone)
159
Dominican Republic **52,** 62,
71, 72. *See also* Santo
Domingo
double trouble **52–53**
Douglas Aircraft 5, 6
DPD (Diver Propulsion
Device) 121
draft (conscription) 3
Dragon Weapon System *23,*
23–24
drill instructor 2, 32, *53,* **53**
drug trafficking 118
DUKM 20

E

EA-6B Prowler 5–6
Easter offensive 160
ECWCS (Second-Generation
Extended Cold Weather
Clothing System) 125
ECWT (Extreme Cold Weather
Tent) 122
Eighth U.S. Army (EUSA) 44
Eisenhower, Dwight David 64,
138, 158
Ellice Islands 3
Elliott, George F. **54**
embarked marines **54**
emblem, United States
Marine Corps *54,* **54–55,**
151
Emerson Electric 16
Endara, Guillermo 118
Engebi Island 55
Eniwetok Atoll, Battle of **55,**
104
enlisted marines (rank and
grade) 132–133
Enola Gay 145, 177
EUSA (Eighth U.S. Army) 44
Executive Order 9981 3
expeditionary force **55**
Extreme Cold Weather Tent
(ECWT) 122

F

F2A Buffalo 6, 105
F2H Banshee 6
F2T Black Widow 6
F4-B Phantom II 6
F4D Skyray 6
F4F Wildcat 6, 105, 161
F4U Corsair 7, 36, 87
F6F Hellcat 7
F8C-5 Helldiver 7
F8 Crusader 7
F8U-1 Crusader 61

F9F-8 Cougar 7
F9F Panther 7
F-117 Stealth Fighter 118
F/A-18A/C/CN Hornet 7–8
F/A-18D Hornet 8–9
Fallujah, Battle of 74
FFV Ordnance 23
Field Pack, Large, with Internal
Frame (FPLIF) 121–122
Fifth Fleet 135
FIM-92A Stinger 15
Financial Management School
45
fire support base **56**
fire team 115
first lieutenant (rank and
grade) 132
first sergeant (rank and grade)
132
First U.S. Army 176
FJ1–FJ4 Fury 9
flamethrower 164
Fleet Marine Corps Reserve
101
Fleet Marine Force **57**
Leonard F. Chapman, Jr.
42
EA-6B Prowler 5
The Functions Paper 58
Roy S. Geiger 60
Alfred M. Gray, Jr. 62
Paul X. Kelley 86
Charles C. Krulak 88
Victor H. Krulak 88, 89
Carl E. Mundy, Jr. 105
Randolph McCall Pate
119
John H. Russell 134
Lemuel C. Shepherd 138
David M. Shoup 138
Oliver P. Smith 139
Louis H. Wilson, Jr. 173,
174
flight (organization unit) 117
Ford, Gerald R. 104
forward observer **57**
FPLIF (Field Pack, Large, with
Internal Frame) 121–122
France
Belleau Wood 33–34
Smedley D. Butler 38
Clifton B. Cates 41
Château-Thierry 42
Roy S. Geiger 60
history of USMC 71–72
Thomas Holcomb 74
Quasi War 152
Saint-Mihiel 135
Lemuel C. Shepherd
137–138

Vietnam War 158
World War I 174–176
Francis Ferdinand (archduke
of Austria-Hungary) 174
fratricide 100
friendly fire 100
Frolic, HMS 161
fuel 144
Fuller, Ben H. *57,* 57
Functions Paper, The **57–58**

G

Gagnon, Rene A. *82,* 83
Gale, Anthony **59,** 69
Geiger, Roy S. *59,* **59–60,** 178
general (rank) 119
general (rank and grade) 131
General Dynamics 4
General Sherman, USS 67
Germany
Belleau Wood 34
Château-Thierry 42
Daniel Daly 51
Saint-Mihiel 135
World War I 174–176
World War II 176
Gerry, Elbridge 152
Ghent, Treaty of 109, 162
Gilbert Islands, USMC assaults
on **60,** 96, 144–145
Glenn, John H., Jr. **60–61,** *61*
Global Positioning System
(GPS) 121
GPS (Global Positioning
System) 121
grade. *See* ranks and grades
Gray, Alfred M., Jr. **61–62**
Great Britain
Bladensburg, Battle of
34
Wallace Greene 62
New Orleans, Battle of
109
Penobscot Bay Fiasco
119–120
World War II 176
Green Berets 92
Greene, Israel 67, 68
Greene, Wallace M., Jr. 42,
62
Grenada Invasion **62–63,** 73
Grumann Aerospace 4, 6, 7
grunt **63**
Guadalcanal *63,* **63–64**
John Basilone 33
"Pappy" Boyington 36
Evans F. Carlson 41
Clifton B. Cates 41
F4F Wildcat 6

Roy S. Geiger 60
Navajo code talkers 108
Randolph McCall Pate
    119
Lewis B. Puller 128
David M. Shoup 138
Solomon Islands
    campaign 140
Alexander Vandergrift
    157
Louis H. Wilson, Jr. 173
World War II 176
Guadalupe Hidalgo, Treaty of
    156
Guam **64**
    Robert E. Cushman, Jr.
        49
    John Glenn, Jr. 60
    Wallace Greene 62
    history of USMC 72
    Mariana Islands
        Campaign 97
    "Uncle Joe" Pendleton
        119
    John H. Russell 134
    Lemuel C. Shepherd
        138
    Oliver P. Smith 139
    Louis H. Wilson, Jr. 173
    World War II 176, 177
Guam (helicopter carrier) 62
Guantánamo Bay **64**
    Alfred M. Gray, Jr. 61
    Wallace Greene 62
    history of USMC 71
    Thomas Holcomb 74
    "Uncle Joe" Pendleton
        119
    David M. Shoup 139
    Spanish-American War
        142
Guerriére, HMS 161
guerrilla warfare 41
Gulf of Tonkin Incident 158
Gulf of Tonkin Resolution 158
gung-ho **64**
Gungi Marine **64**
gunnery sergeant (rank and
    grade) 132
gyrene **65**

H

Hagaru-ri, breakout from **66**
Haiti **66–67,** *67*
    Smedley D. Butler 38
    Daniel Daly 50
    Ben H. Fuller 57
    Roy S. Geiger 60
    history of USMC 71, 73
    Lewis B. Puller 128

John H. Russell 134
Lemuel C. Shepherd 138
Oliver P. Smith 139
Alexander Vandergrift
    157
Hamet, Yusuf (bey of Tripoli)
    114
Han River Forts, Battle of **67,**
    71
HARM (High-Speed
    Antiradiation Missile) 5
Harpers Ferry **67–68,** 68, 71
Harris, John *68,* **68**
Harrison, Benjamin 141
hash marks **68**
hasty defense **68**
Hawaii 35, 57. *See also* Pearl
    Harbor, Japanese attack on
HAWK 15
Hayes, Ira *82,* 83
Headquarters Marine Corps
    (HQMC) **68**
    Leonard F. Chapman, Jr.
        42
    Roy S. Geiger 60
    James L. Jones 85
    Paul X. Kelley 86
    Marine Barracks 28
    David M. Shoup 138
    USMC Women's Reserve
        155
    Alexander Vandergrift
        157
    Louis H. Wilson, Jr. 174
"hearts and minds" 159
helicopters 102–103. *See also*
    aircraft, rotary wing
helmets 151
Henderson, Archibald **69**
    Act of June 30, 1834 1–2
    Anthony Gale 59
    Second Seminole War
        137
Heywood, Charles *69,* **69**
HH-1H Iroquois *12,* 12–13
higher **69**
High Mobility Multipurpose
    Wheeled Vehicle (Humvee)
    171, *171*
High-Speed Antiradiation
    Missile (HARM) 5
Hirohito (emperor of Japan)
    178
Hiroshima/Nagasaki 145, 178
history, overview of USMC
    70–74
    after Vietnam 73
    American Revolution
        through War of 1812
        70
    Civil War 71

cold war conflicts 72
Grenada invasion and
    Operation Just Cause
    73
interwar period 72
Korean War 72
Persian Gulf War 73
post–Civil War Years 71
recent operations 73–74
Somalia, Bosnia and
    Rwanda 73
Spanish-American War
    and after 71
U.S.-Mexican War 71
Vietnam War 72–73
World War I 71–72
World War II 72
Hitler, Adolf 176
hit the deck! **74**
Holcomb, Thomas *74,* **74,** 143
Hoover, Herbert 110
Horse Marines **74**
hovercraft. *See* air-cushion
    vehicles
Howe, James D. 51
HQMC. *See* Headquarters
    Marine Corps
HRP Rescuer ("Flying
    Banana") 13
Hue, action in and around **75,**
    159
Huerta, Victoriano 157, 158
humanitarian relief 64, 141
Hussein, Saddam 74, 120

I

Improved ECWCS Fiberpile
    Shirt and Trousers 122
Inchon **76**
    history of USMC 72
    Korean War 87
    Lewis B. Puller 129
    Lemuel C. Shepherd 138
    Oliver P. Smith 139
Independence (aircraft carrier)
    62
Indian Removal Act of 1930
    137
Indian Territory 137
Indian Wars 136–137
indirect fire systems **76–80,**
    79
    Advanced Field Artillery
        Tactical Data System
        76
    AN/TPQ-36 Firefinder
        Radar 76–77
    AN/USQ-70 Position
        Azimuth Determining
        System 77

M-49 Telescope 77–78
M-90 Radar Chronograph
    78
M-94 MVS 78
M-101A1 105 mm Light
    Howitzer, Towed
    78–79
M-198 155 mm Medium
    Howitzer, Towed *79,*
    79–80
M-224 60 mm Light-
    weight Mortar 80
M-252 81 mm Medium
    Extended Range
    Mortar 80
Pack Howitzer 1923-E2
    80
Individual Ready Reserve 101
Individual Tactical Load
    Bearing Vest (ITLBV)
    122–123
Infantry Fighting Vehicle 171
Infantry Shelter 123
inspector-instructor **81**
Instructional Management
    School 45
integration 49
Iran Hostage Crisis **81**
Iraq 85. *See also* Operation
    Iraqi Freedom; Persian Gulf
    War
"island-hopping" 60, 97, 176
ITLBV (Individual Tactical
    Load Bearing Vest)
    122–123
Iwo Jima **81–83,** *82*
    John Basilone 33
    Clifton B. Cates 41
    Navajo code talkers 108
    Suribachi 143
    World War II 177
Iwo Jima Memorial **83,** 143

J

Jackson, Andrew
    Archibald Henderson
        69
    history of USMC 70
    New Orleans, Battle of
        109
    Second Seminole War
        137
    uniforms 150
    War of 1812 161, 162
Japan
    John Basilone 33
    Bougainville, Battle of
        35
    Evans F. Carlson 41
    Choiseul Raid 43
    Gilbert Islands 60

Guadalcanal 63–64
Guam 64
Iwo Jima 81, 83
Makin, Battle of 96–97
Mariana Islands
Campaign 97
Marshall Islands
Campaign 103–104
Midway, Battle of 105
New Britain, Battle of
108
New Georgia, Battle of
108–109
Okinawa 115
Peleliu 119
Roi-Namur, Battle of
133–134
Saipan 135
Solomon Islands
campaign 140
Tarawa 144–145
Wake Island 161
World War II 176–178
Jacob Zeilin 179
jarhead **84**
Java, HMS 161
Javelin 24
JCS (Joint Chiefs of Staff) 89
Jefferson, Thomas 28, 114
Johnson, Lyndon B. 158
Johnston, Philip 107
Joint Chiefs of Staff (JCS) 89
Joint Service Combat Shotgun
164
Jones, James L. *84,* **84–85**
Jones, John Paul 48

K

kamikaze 177
KC-130 Hercules 9, *9*
Kearny, Stephen Watts 179
Kelley, Paul X. **86**
Kennedy, John F. 158
Kevlar 151
Key West Agreement of
1948. *See Functions Paper,
The*
khaki 151
Khe Sanh 72, **86,** 159
King Air 90. *See* T-44 Pegasus
KLR 250-D8 Marine Corps
Motorcycle 172
Koh Tang 104
Korea 67, 71
Korean War *43,* **87**
Act of June 30, 1834 2
AD-1 through AD-7
Skyraider 5
Clifton B. Cates 41
Chosin Reservoir, Battle
of 43–44

FJ1-FJ4 Fury 9
John Glenn, Jr. 61
Alfred M. Gray, Jr. 61
Hagaru-ri 66
history of USMC 72
Inchon 76
Marine Corps Air
Station Cherry Point
28
MEB 116
Randolph McCall Pate
119
Lewis B. Puller 129
Defense of Pusan 129
Lemuel C. Shepherd 138
Oliver P. Smith 139
Louis H. Wilson, Jr. 174
Krag-Jorgenson rifle 164–165
Krulak, Charles C. **88**
Krulak, Victor H. 43, **88–89,**
89
Kuwait 73, 120
Kwajalein, Battle of **89,** 104,
177

L

LACV-30 91
lance corporal (rank and
grade) 133
landing craft 90, *90,* 90–92. *See
also specific landing craft*
Landing Craft, Air Cushion
(LCAC) *90,* 90–91
Landing Craft, Personnel
(LCP) 91
Landing Craft, Tank (LCT) 91
Landing Craft, Vehicle
Personnel (LCVP) 91–92
Landing Operations Doctrine
92–93
Laser Rangefinder AN/GVS-5
123
LAV-25 20
LAV-C2 Light Armored
Vehicle-Command and
Control 20
LAV-L Light Armored Vehicle-
Logistics 20–21
LAV-M Light Armored
Vehicle-Mortar 21
LAV-R Light Armored Vehicle-
Recovery 21–22
LCAC (Landing Craft, Air
Cushion) *90,* 90–91
LCP (Landing Craft,
Personnel) 91
LCT (Landing Craft, Tank) 91
LCVP (Landing Craft, Vehicle
Personnel) 91–92
League of Nations 103–104
leatherneck **93,** 150

Lebanon 72, 73, **93**
Lee, Robert Edward 67–68,
71
Legion of Merit 88
Lejeune, John A. **93–94,** *94*
Daniel Daly 50
history of USMC 72
Marine Corps Base
Camp Lejeune 30
World War I 175
Leyte Gulf, Battle of 177
lieutenant colonel (rank and
grade) 131
lieutenant general (rank and
grade) 131
Lockheed 9
Lockheed Martin 24
Logistics Operations School
45
Ludendorff, Erich 175
Lusitania 174
LVT and LVT(A) Landing
Vehicle, Tracked 22

M

M-1 .30-caliber carbine 165
M-1A1 Battle Tank 145–147
M-1 Mine Clearing Blade
System 147
M-2-HB Browning Machine
Gun 165
M-3A1 Antitank Gun 24
M-9 Armored Combat
Earthmover (ACE) 147
M-9 Personal Defense Weapon
165
M-14 7.62 mm rifle 165
M-16A2 rifle 32, 33, 165
M-17 Lightweight
Decontamination System
111
M-21 Remote Sensing
Chemical Agent Automatic
Alarm 111–112
M-40/42 Chemical/Biological
Protective Masks 112
M-40A1 sniper rifle 165
M-47 Dragon II 24
M-49 Telescope 77–78
M-60A1 Armored Vehicle
Launched Bridge (M-60A1
AVLB) 147–148
M-60 Machine Gun 165–166
M-82 special application scope
rifle 166
M-90 Radar Chronograph 78
M-94 Muzzle Velocity System
(MVS) 78
M-101A1 105 mm Light
Howitzer, Towed 78–79

M-113 Armored Personnel
Carrier 171–172
M-151 TOW 24–25
M-198 155 mm Medium
Howitzer, Towed *79,* 79–80
M-203 40 mm Grenade
Launcher 166
M-224 60 mm Lightweight
Mortar 80
M-240G machine gun 166
M-249 SAW 166
M-252 81 mm Medium
Extended Range Mortar 80
M-1911A1 .45-caliber pistol
166–167
M-1917A1 Browning Machine
Gun 167
M-1918A4 Browning Machine
Gun 167
M-1918 Browning Automatic
Rifle (BAR) 167
M-1919A6 Browning Machine
Gun 167
M-1921/M-1928A1 Thompson
Submachine Gun 167
M-1941 Johnson Light
Machine Gun 167
MacArthur, Douglas 87
Macedonia 85
Macedonian, HMS 161
Mackie, John F. 51
Madison, James 34, 172
MAGTF. *See* Marine Air
Ground Task Force
Maine, USS 71
major (rank and grade) 131
major general (rank and
grade) 131
Makin, Battle of 41, 60, **96–97**
Mameluke Sword *97,* **97**
Barbary pirates 27
Presley O'Bannon 114
uniforms 150
Manila 126
Manila Bay 142
marching music 141–142
Mariana Islands Campaign **97**
African Americans in the
USMC 3
John Glenn, Jr. 60
Guam 64
Kwajalein, Battle of 89
Marine Aircraft Group 36
97–98
Marine Air Ground Task Force
(MAGTF) 78, 79, 117
Marine Air Ground Task Force
Training Command *98,* **98**
Marine Assault Climbers Kit
123

Marine Aviation Weapons and
  Tactics Squadron One
  98–99
Marine Barracks 28, **99**
  William Ward Burrows
    37
  Charles Heywood 69
  James L. Jones 84
  Franklin Wharton 171
Marine Corps Air New River
  29
Marine Corps Air Station
  Beaufort 28
Marine Corps Air Station
  Cherry Point 28
Marine Corps Air Station
  Futenma 28
Marine Corps Air Station
  Iwakuni 28–29
Marine Corps Air Station
  Miramar 29
Marine Corps Air Station
  Yuma 29–30
Marine Corps aviation 117
Marine Corps Base Camp
  Johnson 2
Marine Corps Base Camp
  Lejeune 30
  Robert E. Cushman, Jr.
    49
  James L. Jones 85
  Lewis B. Puller 129
  School of Infantry 136
  USMC Women's Reserve
    155
Marine Corps Base Camp
  Pendleton 30, 42, 88,
  159–160
Marine Corps Base Camp
  Smedley D. Butler 30
Marine Corps Base Hawaii
  30–31
Marine Corps Base Quantico
  31
  Walter E. Boomer 35
  Clifton B. Cates 41
  Ben H. Fuller 57
  Thomas Holcomb 74
  Charles C. Krulak 88
  sniper 139
  Alexander Vandergrift
    157
Marine Corps Combat
  Development Command
  100
Marine Corps Combat
  Identification Program
  (MCCIP) **100**
Marine Corps Expeditionary
  Medal 51
Marine Corps Intelligence
  100–101

Marine Corps Logistics Base
  Albany 31
Marine Corps Logistics Base
  Barstow 31
Marine Corps Recruit Depot
  Parris Island 32
Marine Corps Recruit Depots
  31–32
Marine Corps Recruit Depot
  San Diego 32
Marine Corps Reserve **101**
  African Americans in the
    USMC 3
  Clifton B. Cates 41
  John Glenn, Jr. 60
  inspector-instructor 81
  Korean War 87
  Randolph McCall Pate
    119
  Persian Gulf War (1991)
    120
  Louis H. Wilson, Jr. 173
Marine Corps Reserve Ribbon
  51
Marine Corps Schools
  101–102
Marine Corps Supply **102**
Marine Expeditionary Brigade
  (MEB) 116–117
Marine Expeditionary Force
  (MEF) 117
Marine Expeditionary Unit
  (MEU) 117
Marine Forces **102**
Marine Helicopter Squadron
  One **102–103**, 103
Marine Hymn **103**
  Barbary pirates 27
  Chapultepec, Battle of
    42
  history of USMC 70, 71
  Presley O'Bannon 114
Marine One 102–103, *103*,
  103
Maritime Prepositioning
  Squadrons (MPSs) 73, **103**
Marshall, John 152
Marshall Islands Campaign
  103–104
  African Americans in the
    USMC 3
  Evans F. Carlson 41
  Eniwetok Atoll, Battle of
    55
  John Glenn, Jr. 60
  Wallace Greene 62
  Kwajalein, Battle of 89
  Roi-Namur, Battle of
    133–134
  World War II 177
Martin Marietta 16
Marxism-Leninism 62

mascot **104**
Massachusetts, USS 134
master sergeant (rank and
  grade) 132
Mayaguez incident **104**
Mazatlán, Mexico 179
MC-5 Static Line/Free-Fall
  Ram Air Parachute System
  (SL/FF RAPS) 123–124
McCawley, Charles G.
  104–105
MCCDC (U.S. Marine Corps
  Combat Development
  Command) **153**
MCCIP (Marine Corps
  Combat Identification
  Program) **100**
MCCSS. *See* Combat Service
  Support Schools
McDonnell Douglas
  A-4 Skyhawk 3
  A-12 Avenger 4
  F2H Banshee 6
  F4-B Phantom II 6
  F/A-18A/C/CN Hornet 8
  T-45A Goshawk 10
MCRC (U.S. Marine Corps
  Research Center) **154**
MCSF (U.S. Marine Corps
  Security Force) **154**
MEB (Marine Expeditionary
  Brigade) 116–117
Medal of Honor 51
  John Basilone 33
  "Pappy" Boyington 36
  Smedley D. Butler 37, 38
  Daniel Daly 50
  history of USMC 71, 72
  Louis H. Wilson, Jr. 173
Mediterranean Sea 114
MEF (Marine Expeditionary
  Force) 117
Mercury space program 61
Merritt, Wesley 142
MEU (Marine Expeditionary
  Unit) 117
MEU (SOC) Pistol 168
Meuse-Argonne 71, 175, 176
Mexico 68, 174. *See also* U.S.-
  Mexican War; Zimmerman
  telegram
Mexico City 42, 104, 155–156
Midway, Battle of **105**, 140,
  176
missiles. *See* air-launched
  weapons
Missouri, USS 178
Mitchell PBJ 9
Mk-19 40 mm machine gun,
  MOD 3 168
Mk-48 Power Unit and Mk-14
  Container Transporter Rear
  Body Unit 172

Mk-48 Power Unit and Mk-15
  Recover/Wrecker Rear Body
  Unit 172–173
Mk-48 Power Unit and Mk-16
  Fifth-Wheel Semi-trailer
  Adapter Rear Body Unit
  173
Mk-48 Power Unit and Mk-18
  Self-loading Container and
  Ribbon Bridge Transporter
  173
Mk-155 Mine Clearance
  Launcher 173
Mobile/Unit Conduct of Fire
  Trainer (M/U-COFT) 148
Modular Sleeping Bag 124
Mogadishu 141
Mohammed Reza Pahlavi
  (shah of Iran) 81
Monroe, James 59
Monroe Doctrine 136
Montague, Fort 17
Moros 126, 135–136
Morristown, New Jersey 48
MP-5N Heckler and Koch 9
  mm Submachine Gun
  168–169
MPSs. *See* Maritime
  Prepositioning Squadrons
MULE (AN/PAQ-3 Modular
  Universal Laser Equipment)
  162
Mullan, Robert 47
Mundy, Carl E., Jr. **105–106**
music 141–142, 152, 155
Muslims 27
MVS (M-94 Muzzle Velocity
  System) 78
MWTC (U.S. Marine Corps
  Mountain Warfare Training
  Center) **153**, *153*
Myers, John 36

N

Nagasaki. *See*
  Hiroshima/Nagasaki
Napoleon Bonaparte 152
National Defense Act of 1916
  174
National War College 85
Native Americans 107–108
NATO 73
Navajo code talkers *107*,
  107–108
naval relations **108**
Naval War College
  Walter E. Boomer 35
  Ben H. Fuller 57
  Thomas Holcomb 74
  Lemuel C. Shepherd
    138

Neville, Wendell C. **108**
New Britain, Battle of **108**
    Bougainville, Battle of
        35
    "Pappy" Boyington 36
    Oliver P. Smith 139
New Georgia, Battle of
    108–109
    "Pappy" Boyington 36
    David M. Shoup 138
    Solomon Islands
        campaign 140
New Guinea 176
new man rule **109**
new meat **109**
New Orleans 48
New Orleans, Battle of **109**
    Archibald Henderson 69
    history of USMC 70
    War of 1812 161–162
New Providence Island,
    Bahamas 17, 48, 110
Nicaragua **109–110**
    Smedley D. Butler 38
    Evans F. Carlson 40–41
    James P. S. Devereux 52
    Charles Heywood 69
    history of USMC 71
    M-1921/M-1928A1
        Thompson
        Submachine Gun
        167
    "Uncle Joe" Pendleton
        119
    Lewis B. Puller 128
    Alexander Vandergrift
        157
Nicholas, Samuel *110,* **110**
    American Revolution 17
    William Ward Burrows
        37
    Continental Marines
        47–48
Nixon, Richard M. 49, 159
NKPA (North Korean People's
    Army) 87
Noriega, Manuel 73, 118
North Africa 27
North American Aviation 6, 9
North Korean People's Army
    (NKPA) 87
nuclear-biological-chemical
    equipment **110–113**
NVG (AN/PVS-7B Night
    Vision Goggle) 163–164

O

O'Bannon, Presley 27, 97, *114,*
    114
OE-1 Bird Dog 9

OECS (Organization of
    Eastern Caribbean States)
    62
Offenbach, Jacques 103
oil 144
Okinawa **115**
    Leonard F. Chapman, Jr.
        42
    Robert E. Cushman, Jr.
        49
    Roy S. Geiger 60
    Alfred M. Gray, Jr. 61
    James L. Jones 85
    Charles C. Krulak 88
    Victor H. Krulak 88, 89
    Lemuel C. Shepherd
        138
    David M. Shoup 138
    Oliver P. Smith 139
    Vietnam War 159
    World War II 177–178
Operation Catchpole 55
Operation Cherry Blossom 35
Operation Deny Flight 73
Operation Desert Shield 120
Operation Desert Storm
    F/A-18A/C/CN Hornet 8
    F/A-18D Hornet 8
    M-1A1 Battle Tank 145
    Persian Gulf War (1991)
        120
    SLAP ammunition 25
    SMAW 170
Operation Dewey Canyon 159
Operation Eagle Pull 98
Operation Flintlock 133
Operation Forager 64, 135. *See
    also* Guam
Operation Iraqi Freedom 64,
    74, 120
Operation Just Cause 73,
    118–119
Operation Provide Comfort
    85
Operation Restore Hope 73
Operation Sea Signal 64
Operation Starlight **115,** 158
Operation Urgent Fury 62
organization, administrative
    and by major commands
    115
organization by units **115–117**
Organization of Eastern
    Caribbean States (OECS)
    62
OV-10 Bronco 9–10, *10*
Oxygen Transfer Pump System
    124

P

"pacification" (Vietnam War)
    49, 89, 158–159

Pack Howitzer 1923-E2 80
Pakenham, Edward 109,
    161–162
Panama **118–119**
    George Barnett 27
    William P. Biddle 34
    Smedley D. Butler 38
    Charles Heywood 69
    history of USMC 71, 73
    John A. Lejeune 93
Panama Canal 93
Parachutist Individual
    Equipment Kit (PIEK)
    124–125
paratroopers 43
Paris, Treaty of 70
Parris Island. *See* Marine Corps
    Recruit Depot Parris Island
Parry Island 55
Pate, Randolph McCall **119**
PBY-5A Catalina 10
Pearl Harbor, Japanese attack
    on
        African Americans in the
            USMC 2
        Robert E. Cushman, Jr.
            49
        history of USMC 72
        World War II 176
Peleliu **119**
    Leonard F. Chapman, Jr.
        42
    Roy S. Geiger 60
    Navajo code talkers 108
    Lewis B. Puller 128
    Oliver P. Smith 139
    World War II 177
Pendleton, Joseph H. "Uncle
    Joe" 30, **119,** 136
Pennsylvania, USS (BB-38) 49
Penobscot Bay Fiasco 18, 48,
    119–120
Pentagon 68
Peralte, Charlemagne 66
Perry, Matthew Calbraith 179
Perry, Oliver Hazard 161
Pershing, John Joseph 40, 71
Persian Gulf War (1991) **120**
    Walter E. Boomer 35
    history of USMC 73
    Marine Corps Air Station
        Cherry Point 28
    MEB 116
personal and miscellaneous
    equipment **120–126.** *See
    also specific equipment*
Personnel Administration
    School 45, **126**
Philadelphia, USS 27
Philippine Insurrection **126**
    Ben H. Fuller 57
    Charles Heywood 69

history of USMC 71
    Samar 135–136
    Spanish-American War
        142
Philippines
    George Barnett 27
    William P. Biddle 34
    George F. Elliott 54
    history of USMC 71
    Samar 135–136
    Spanish-American War
        142
    World War II 176, 177
PIEK (Parachutist
    Individual Equipment Kit)
    124–125
Pinckney, Charles Cotesworthy
    152
platoon 116
PLGR (AN/PSN-11 Precision
    Lightweight GPS Receiver)
    121
Poland 176
poolees *127,* **127**
Portable Collective
    Protection System
    112–113
Potsdam Declaration 178
prisoner of war 52
private (rank and grade) 133
private first class (rank and
    grade) 133
promotion system **127–128**
pugil stick 32, 33, **128**
Puller, Lewis B. "Chesty" *128,*
    128–129
Punitive Expedition (Mexico,
    1916) 40
Pusan, Defense of **129**
PW-9 5

Q

al-Qaeda 74
quad body **130**
Quasi-War with France. *See*
    U.S.-French Quasi-War

R

R4D Skytrain 10
Rabaul 36
RAC (Riverine Assault Craft)
    92
Ranger 48
Rangers 62, 118
ranks and grades **131–133**
    brigadier general 131
    captain 131–132
    colonel 131
    commissioned officers
        131–132
    corporal 132–133

enlisted marines
    132–133
first lieutenant 132
first sergeant 132
general 131
gunnery sergeant 132
lance corporal 133
lieutenant colonel 131
lieutenant general 131
major 131
major general 131
master sergeant 132
private 133
private first class 133
second lieutenant 132
sergeant 132
sergeant major 132
sergeant major of the
    Marine Corps 132
staff sergeant 132
Rapid Deployment Force 73
Raytheon 24
Raytheon Systems 16
Reagan, Ronald 62, 93, 118
recruiter **133**
regiment 116
Reising Gun 169
Reserve Officers Training
    Corps (ROTC). *See* ROTC
Reverse Osmosis Water
    Purification Unit 125
Revolutionary War. *See*
    American Revolution
revolver, .38-caliber 169
RH-53D 13
rifle grenade 169
Riverine Assault Craft (RAC)
    92
Rockwell International 16
Rodgers, John 67
Roi-Namur, Battle of
    133–134
        African Americans in the
            USMC 3
        Kwajalein, Battle of 89
        Marshall Islands
            Campaign 104
        World War II 177
Roosevelt, Franklin Delano 2,
    39, 176
Roosevelt, Theodore 54
Ross, Robert 34, 161
Rota 97
ROTC (Reserve Officers
    Training Corps) 42, 138
Royal Navy 119–120, 161
Russell, John H. **134**
Rwanda 73

S

Saboted Light Armor
    Penetrator (SLAP)
    Ammunition 25
Saigon 158

Saigon, evacuation of 73, 98,
    160
Saint-Mihiel **135**
    Daniel Daly 51
    history of USMC 71
    John A. Lejeune 93
    Lemuel C. Shepherd 137
    World War I 175
Saipan **135**
    Evans F. Carlson 41
    Wallace Greene 62
    Mariana Islands
        Campaign 97
    David M. Shoup 138
    World War II 177
Salee River pirates 67, 71
Samar, marine action in
    135–136
Samoa 62
Sampson, William T. 142
Sandinistas 110, 128
Sandino, Augusto 110, 128
Santa Anna, Antonio López de
    156
Santiago de Cuba 142
Santo Domingo **136**
    Dominican Republic 52
    Ben H. Fuller 57
    Randolph McCall Pate
        119
    "Uncle Joe" Pendleton
        119
    Quasi War 152
    John H. Russell 134
Sarajevo 174
Saratoga Chemical Protective
    Overgarment 113
SARPELS (Single Action
    Release Personal Equipment
    Lowering System) 125–126
SB-3865 Automatic Telephone
    Switchboard 46–47
School of Infantry 33, **136**
Scott, Winfield 42, 71, 155
SEALs 92, 150
Second-Generation Extended
    Cold Weather Clothing
    System (ECWCS) 125
second lieutenant (rank and
    grade) 132
Second Seminole War **137**
    John Harris 68
    Archibald Henderson 69
    history of USMC 71
secretary of the navy **137**
segregation 49
Selected Marine Corps Reserve
    101
Semper Fidelis 54, **137**
September 11, 2001, terrorist
    attacks 28, 64, 74
sergeant (rank and grade) 132

sergeant major (rank and
    grade) 132
sergeant major of the Marine
    Corps (rank and grade)
    132
17th parallel 158
Shafter, William R. 142
Shepherd, Lemuel C. **137–138**
Shoulder-Launched
    Multipurpose Assault
    Weapon (SMAW) 169–170
Shoup, David M. **138–139**
Sidewinder Missile. *See* AIM-9
    Sidewinder
Sigsbee, Charles D. 71
Sikorsky 11, 14
SINCGARS (Single Channel
    Ground and Airborne
    Radio Systems) 47
Single Action Release Personal
    Equipment Lowering
    System (SARPELS)
    125–126
Single Channel Ground and
    Airborne Radio Systems
    (SINCGARS) 47
Sino-Japanese War 41
SLAP (Saboted Light Armor
    Penetrator) Ammunition
    25
slaves and slavery 67
SL/FF RAPS (MC-5 Static
    Line/Free-Fall Ram Air
    Parachute System)
    123–124
SMAW (Shoulder-Launched
    Multipurpose Assault
    Weapon) 169–170
Smith, Holland "Howlin' Mad"
    88
Smith, Oliver P. **139**
sniper **139–140**
sniper team 140, *140*, *140*
Soldiers of the Sea **140**
Solomon Islands 35, 43
Solomon Islands campaign
    140
Somalia 73, *141*, **141**
Somoza, Anastasio 110
Sophie (archduchess of
    Austria-Hungary) 174
Sousa, John Philip **141–142**,
    142
        Charles G. McCawley
            105
        Semper Fidelis 137
        U.S. Marine Band 152
Sousley, Franklin R. *82*, 83
Soviet Union 87
space shuttle *Discovery* 61
Spain 109

Spanish-American War **142**
    George Barnett 27
    William P. Biddle 34
    Smedley D. Butler 38
    Daniel Daly 50
    George F. Elliott 54
    Ben H. Fuller 57
    Charles Heywood 69
    history of USMC 71
    John A. Lejeune 93
    Wendell C. Neville 108
    Philippine Insurrection
        126
    John H. Russell 134
    John Philip Sousa 141
    uniforms 151
Special Forces 150
Special Purpose Force (SPF)
    117
SPF (Special Purpose Force)
    117
squad 116
squadron 117
staff sergeant (rank and grade)
    132
Stilwell, Joseph Warren 60
Stinger Weapons System: RMP
    and Basic 15
Strank, Michael *82*, 83
Streeter, Ruth Cheney
    142–143, *143*, 155
Stuart, J. E. B. 68
Suez Crisis 72, 119
Sumter, Fort 104
supersonic flight 61
Supply School 45–46, **143**
Suribachi **143**
    Iwo Jima 81, *82*
    Iwo Jima Memorial **83**
    World War II 177

T

T-34C Turbo Mentor 10
T-44 Pegasus 10
T-45A Goshawk 10–11
TA-4J Skyhawk 11
Tachen Islands 72
Tactical Bulk Fuel Delivery
    System, CH-53E (TBFDS,
    CH-53E) 13
Tactical Petroleum
    Laboratory, Medium
    (TPLM) **144**
Taft, William Howard 48, **54**
Taliban 64, 74
Talleyrand-Périgord, Charles
    Maurice de 152
Tampico 155
Tandem Offset Resupply
    Delivery System (TORDS)
    126

Tarawa **144–145**, *145*
    Evans F. Carlson 41
    Navajo code talkers 108
    David M. Shoup 138
    World War II 177
TBFDS, CH-53E (Tactical Bulk
    Fuel Delivery System, CH-
    53E) 13
Tehran, Iran 81
"Tell It to the Marines!" **145**
terrorism defense 154
test pilots 61
Tet Offensive
    history of USMC 72
    Hue 75
    Khe Sanh 86
    Marine Aircraft Group
        36 98
    Vietnam War 159
Texas, Republic of 155
38th parallel 87, 129
Tilton, McLane 67
Tinian **145**
    Clifton B. Cates 41
    Wallace Greene 62
    Mariana Islands
        Campaign 97
    David M. Shoup 138
    World War II 177
Tonkin Gulf. *See* Gulf of
    Tonkin Incident
TORDS (Tandem Offset
    Resupply Delivery System)
    126
total immersion 32
TOW (Tube Launched,
    Optically Tracked, Wire
    Guided) Missile Weapon
    System 25, *26*
TPLM (Tactical Petroleum
    Laboratory, Medium) **144**
tracked vehicles **145–148**, *146*.
    See also specific vehicles
Training and Education
    Command 98–99, **148–149**
Trenton, Battle of 18, 48, 110
tribute 27
triple threat **149**
Tripolitan War 27, 70, 97
Trujillo, Leonidas 52
Truman, Harry S. 3, 87, 158
Tube Launched, Optically
    Tracked, Wire Guided
    (TOW) Missile Weapon
    System 25, *26*
Turkey 85
12-gauge shotgun 170
Tzu Hsi (Chinese dowager
    empress) 35

U

UAV (unmanned aerial
    vehicle) 151
UGV (unmanned ground
    vehicle) 151
UH-34/VH-34 Seashore 13–14
unconventional warfare (UW)
    150
uniforms 68, **150–151**
United Nations 87, 120, 141
United Nations forces 76, 87,
    129
United States, USS 161, 171
United States Military
    Academy (USMA) 54
United States Naval Academy
    (Annapolis)
        George Barnett 27
        Wallace Greene 62
        Charles C. Krulak 88
        Victor H. Krulak 88
        Wendell C. Neville 108
unmanned aerial vehicle
    (UAV) **151**
unmanned ground vehicle
    (UGV) **151**
urban warfare *151,* **151–152**
U.S. Air Force 104
U.S. Army 43, 118, 159
U.S. Army Air Forces 81
U.S. Army War College
    (USAWC) 60, 61, 74
USAWC. *See* U.S. Army War
    College
U.S.-French Quasi-War **152**
    William Ward Burrows
        37
    history of USMC 70
    Franklin Wharton 171
USMA (United States Military
    Academy) 54
U.S. Marine Band **152**
    William Ward Burrows
        37
    Charles G. McCawley
        105
    John Philip Sousa 141,
        142
U.S. Marine Corps Air-Ground
    Task Force Expeditionary
    Training Center **152**
U.S. Marine Corps Code **152**
U.S. Marine Corps Color
    Guard **153**
U.S. Marine Corps Combat
    Development Command
    (MCCDC) **153**
U.S. Marine Corps
    Development Center **153**

U.S. Marine Corps Mountain
    Warfare Training Center
    (MWTC) *153,* **153**
U.S. Marine Corps
    Reconnaissance Battalions
    150, **153–154**
U.S. Marine Corps Research
    Center (MCRC) **154**
U.S. Marine Corps Security
    Force (MCSF) **154**
U.S. Marine Corps Security
    Guard Battalion **154**
U.S. Marine Corps Women's
    Reserve 142–143, **154–155,**
    155
U.S. Marine Drum and Bugle
    Corps **155**
U.S.-Mexican War **155–156**
    Act of June 30, 1834 2
    Chapultepec, Battle of 42
    John Harris 68
    Archibald Henderson
        69
    history of USMC 71
    Charles G. McCawley
        104
    Veracruz 157
    Jacob Zeilin 179
U.S. Navy
    Dominican Republic 52
    Iwo Jima 81
    Kwajalein, Battle of 89
    Mayaguez incident 104
    World War II 176
UW (unconventional warfare)
    150

V

V-22 Osprey 14
Vandergrift, Alexander 60, 63,
    157
Van Tuong Peninsula 115
Vella Lavella 88
Veracruz **157–158**
    Smedley D. Butler 38
    history of USMC 71
    John A. Lejeune 93
    Charles G. McCawley
        104
    Wendell C. Neville 108
    John H. Russell 134
    U.S.-Mexican War 155
    Alexander Vandergrift
        157
VH-3D Sea King 14
VH-60A Black Hawk 14
VH-60N Seahawk 14, *16*
Vietcong
    Hue 75
    Operation Starlight 115
    Vietnam War 158, 159

Viet Minh 158
"Vietnamization" 73, 159
Vietnam War **158–160**
    AD-1 through AD-7
        Skyraider 5
    Walter E. Boomer 34,
        35
    Leonard F. Chapman, Jr.
        42
    Robert E. Cushman, Jr.
        49
    F4-B Phantom II 6
    Alfred M. Gray, Jr. 61
    Wallace Greene 62
    history of USMC 72–73
    Hue 75
    James L. Jones 84
    Paul X. Kelley 86
    Khe Sanh 86
    Charles C. Krulak 88
    Victor H. Krulak 89
    M-60 Machine Gun 165
    Marine Aircraft Group
        36 98
    Marine Corps Air Station
        Cherry Point 28
    MEB 116
    Carl E. Mundy, Jr. 105
    Operation Starlight 115
    OV-10 Bronco 10
    David M. Shoup 139
    uniforms 151
    USMC Reconnaissance
        Battalions 154
    Louis H. Wilson, Jr. 174
Villa, Pancho, expedition
    against. *See* Punitive
    Expedition
Virginia, CSS 69
Vogel, Clayton B. 107
Vought 7

W

Wake Island **161**
    James P. S. Devereux 52
    F4F Wildcat 6
    history of USMC 72
    World War II 176
Waller, Littleton 136
Walt, Lewis 159
War Is a Racket (Smedley D.
    Butler) 39
War of 1812 **161–162**
    Bladensburg, Battle of
        34
    Archibald Henderson 69
    history of USMC 70
    New Orleans, Battle of
        109
    Franklin Wharton
        171–172

War of Independence. *See*
    American Revolution
war on terrorism 64, 74
Washington, D.C.
        Bladensburg, Battle of
            34
        HQMC 68
        Marine Barracks 28
        War of 1812 161
        Franklin Wharton 172
Washington, George 18, 48,
    110
Wasp, USS 161
Wayne, Anthony 150
weapons, individual and
    crew-served **162–170.** *See
    also specific weapons*
Weldon, Felix de 83
West Indies 48, 57
Westmoreland, William Childs
    49
Wharton, Franklin **170–171**
wheeled vehicles *171,*
    171–173. *See also specific
    vehicles*
Wilson, Louis H., Jr. **173–174**
Wilson, Woodrow
        Santo Domingo 136
        Veracruz 157, 158
        World War I 174
women in the Marine Corps
    142–143
Wooly-pully 126
World War I **174–176,** *175*
        Act of June 30, 1834 2
        Belleau Wood 33–34
        Smedley D. Butler 38
        Evans F. Carlson 40
        Clifton B. Cates 41
        Château-Thierry 42
        Daniel Daly 50–51
        Roy S. Geiger 60

history of USMC 71–72
        Thomas Holcomb 74
        John A. Lejeune 93
        M-1917A1 Browning
            Machine Gun 167
        Marshall Islands
            Campaign 103
        Wendell C. Neville 108
        Randolph McCall Pate
            119
        Lewis B. Puller 128
        Saint-Mihiel 135
        Lemuel C. Shepherd 137
        Oliver P. Smith 139
        John Philip Sousa
            141–142
        uniforms 151
World War II **176–178**
        Act of June 30, 1834 2
        Evans F. Carlson 40
        DUKW 20
        gung-ho 64
        Thomas Holcomb 74
        M-1917A1 Browning
            Machine Gun 167
        Marine Corps Air Station
            Cherry Point 28
        Marine Corps Reserve
            101
        Mitchell PBJ 9
        Ruth Cheney Streeter
            143
        uniforms 151
        USMC Reconnaissance
            Battalions 154
        USMC Women's Reserve
            154–155
        Louis H. Wilson, Jr. 173
World War II: Pacific and
    Asian theaters
        African Americans in the
            USMC 3

John Basilone 33
Bougainville, Battle of
    35
"Pappy" Boyington 36
Evans F. Carlson 41
Clifton B. Cates 41
Leonard F. Chapman, Jr.
    42
Choiseul Raid 43
Robert E. Cushman, Jr.
    49
James P. S. Devereux 52
Eniwetok Atoll, Battle of
    55
F2A Buffalo 6
F6F Hellcat 7
flamethrower 164
Roy S. Geiger 59, 60
Gilbert Islands 60
John Glenn, Jr. 60
Wallace Greene 62
Guadalcanal 63–64
Guam 64
history of USMC 72
Iwo Jima 81–83
Victor H. Krulak 88
Kwajalein, Battle of 89
*Landing Operations
    Doctrine* 92–93
M-3A1 Antitank Gun 24
Makin Battle of 96–97
Mariana Islands
    Campaign 97
Marshall Islands
    Campaign 103–104
Midway, Battle of 105
Navajo code talkers
    107–108
New Britain, Battle of
    108
New Georgia, Battle of
    108–109

Okinawa 115
Randolph McCall Pate
    119
Peleliu 119
Lewis B. Puller 128
R4D Skytrain 10
Roi-Namur, Battle of
    133–134
Saipan 135
Lemuel C. Shepherd
    138
David M. Shoup 138
Oliver P. Smith 139
Solomon Islands
    campaign 140
Suribachi 143
Tarawa 144–145
Tinian 145
Alexander Vandergrift
    157
Wake Island 161
Louis H. Wilson, Jr. 173
World War II 176–178

X

XYZ Affair 152

Y

Yalu River 87

Z

Zeilin, Jacob 55, 156, **179**
Zelaya, José 109
Zero 6, 7, 105
Zimmerman telegram 174